D0320610

Thrown Away Children:
Max and Mia's Story

Also in the Thrown Away Children Series:

Thrown Away Children: Max and Mia's Story

By Louise Allen
with Theresa McEvoy

WELBECK

Published in 2023 by Welbeck
An imprint of Welbeck Non-Fiction Limited
Part of the Welbeck Publishing Group
Offices in: London – 20 Mortimer Street, London W1T 3JW &
Sydney – 205 Commonwealth Street, Surry Hills 2010
www.welbeckpublishing.com

Design and layout © 2023 Welbeck Non-Fiction Ltd
Text © 2023 Louise Allen

Louise Allen has asserted her moral rights to be identified as the author
of this Work in accordance with the Copyright Designs and Patents Act 1988.
All rights reserved. No part of this publication may be reproduced, stored in
a retrieval system, or transmitted in any form or by any means, electronically,
mechanical, photocopying, recording or otherwise, without the prior
permission of the copyright owners and the publishers.

A CIP catalogue record for this book is available from the British Library.

ISBN 978-1-80279-120-4

Typeset by Roger Walker

Printed in Great Britain by CPI Books, Chatham, Kent

10 9 8 7 6 5 4 3 2 1

Disclaimer: Any names, characters, trademarks, service marks and trade
names detailed in this book are the property of their respective owners and are
used solely for identification and reference purposes. This book is a publication
of Welbeck Non-Fiction, part of Welbeck Publishing Group and has not been
licensed, approved, sponsored or endorsed by any person or entity.

Every reasonable effort has been made to trace copyright holders of
material produced in this book, but if any have been inadvertently overlooked the
publishers would be glad to hear from them.

Foreword

The narrative which follows, like all my stories, is not just about the child, or in this case the two children, who I had the privilege of meeting when they came into my care. Just as with my own history, shared in *Thrown Away Child*, it's never as straightforward as writing just about the individual coming into care. To be honest, if I recorded events exactly as they happened, you would read pages and pages about nothing more than brushing teeth, combing hair, bedtimes, breakfast choices, and the myriad things that constitute the daily reality of caring for a child. No one person's story is a single act of drama. My aim is always to explore not just the complexity of emotions associated with abuse and neglect, but also their context and trajectory, their history, the catalysts, the how and the why of children ending up in care – as well as what happens to them while they are there, and the possibilities of what may happen beyond.

As my fostering career has developed (and I can count my experiences in decades rather than years), I have been involved with a great number of children, and have come to know their diverse families and situations.

That has taught me a great deal.

But the only conclusion I can really draw is that every single case is different. There are, of course, some common threads that show up repeatedly, overarching themes that contribute to children ending up in care: patterns like poverty, drug use and foetal alcohol damage, for example.

Yet Max and Mia's story is so different from all these well-worn tales, which is perhaps equally surprising as it is disturbing. It is, as always, as much about the parents as it is the children: how two people, with all the wealth, privilege, opportunity and influence that most of us could only ever dream of, can fall so foul of their own hopes and dreams. Moreover, it is about prejudice, and the way it can be found in unlikely and unexpected places.

In the end we are all just people, flawed and fallible, whose only power, for better or for worse, lies in the choices we make in our lives.

The cases I reveal in my books are all based on true experiences, but I have changed names and some details to protect their identities as they go on to build new lives and families of their own.

PART ONE:
Before

Angelina and Ben

I. Angelina

'And now we step through into the powerful goddess pose,' Ruchi says.

Ruchi is Angelina's yoga therapist.

It is a sunny June morning, already warm despite the early hour, filled with the promise of a beautiful day. The French windows are wide open, though the term 'French windows' doesn't quite do justice to the huge, grey-framed panels of glass that open to allow sunlight to flood across the expanse of oak floor in the West Brompton home that Angelina shares with Ben.

'Bend your knees slowly and tilt your tailbone downward. Very good. Feel that strengthening fire in your legs. Stay low, feel the pelvis open wide. Palms up to the sky. Now, seven cycles of breath.'

Angelina breathes deeply as Ruchi gives instructions, taking in the heavenly scent of the jasmine flower climbing up the side of the house.

'That's it, wonderful. Channel all the power and energy of the goddess as you sink lower into the pose, towards the earth.'

For a moment, Angelina does feel divine. This body of hers, which has done the tremendous job of carrying twins for nine months, is magnificent.

'That's it. Harness the maternal vibrations, not just yours, but of all women, everywhere. Now, and throughout the ages. Can you feel it?'

How glorious to be part of this divine sisterhood of birthing women. To know that women have given birth for thousands of years. For a moment, Angelina does feel it. All of it. Something beyond herself, something sublime.

'You can experiment with this as a birthing position, too,' Ruchi explains.

The session ends with Angelina completing *Shavasana* on her side.

'Truly relaxed,' Ruchi laughs. 'Now make sure you get plenty of rest today.'

'Same time tomorrow morning?' Angelina asks as she shows Ruchi out of the front door and down the wide Georgian steps to the street.

'Perhaps,' Ruchi smiles. 'But I think your time is very near. Soon you will be a mother. Perhaps even by this time tomorrow.' Her smile disappears, replaced by a frown. 'Take care.'

After taking a shower, Angelina calls Ben, as she has done every day since she began her maternity leave more than two months ago.

'Hey sweet, how's your day?' he answers.

She pictures him sitting back in his office at Azure, a successful recording studio in Camden, where he is a lead producer. She's proud of his achievements. Her husband has worked with some of the biggest names in the music industry over his 20-year-long career. Musicians come from all over the world to record in the building famed for its steel-beamed and silvered-glass façade. Much is made of its original architectural likeness to Sun Studio in Memphis, where Elvis made his first recordings; but the Camden studio, while on a similar corner-angled plot, was conceived on a much grander scale. It's a place Angelina knows well: it's where she and Ben first met, when Angelina landed her dream job as a receptionist in the iconic music mecca during her final year as a student, and where they fell in love. Ben still denies being captivated by her beauty at the interview, instead claiming that it was absolutely her secretarial credentials that got her the job. She, on the other hand, was very attracted to his stylish good looks, which transcended the 17-year-age gap between them – and meant that they were an item within a few months of her arrival at Azure. It was a dreamy romance, and they were a beautiful couple. Men had always commented on the unexpected fusion of her appearance and accent: pale skin and tumbling red corkscrew curls combined with the rolling Italian lilt of her mother tongue. The red came from her father. Her mother was grey these days, but had been raven-haired in her youth.

'Very good. I've just finished my yoga class, where I was a powerful goddess.'

'You're always a powerful goddess to me, babe.'

'And yet, you didn't say goodbye this morning,' she playfully accuses him, feigning hurt.

'That's because you were still sleeping, and if I've learnt anything from all those pregnancy books, it's that my baby-mama needs her sleep!'

He talks for a while about a project that he is working on with a Guatemalan marimba artist who has a 'fresh, exciting sound that Nile might be interested in,' and promises to take her to lunch the following day 'if the *cicogna* doesn't arrive.'

The ancient myth that white storks deliver babies is cross-cultural, and though Ben only knows a handful of

Italian words, somehow *cicogna*, for stork, is one of them. His terrible grasp of the language makes Angelina laugh, but she is always grateful when he tries.

'No sign of the *cicogna* with a bundle of babies so far today,' she assures him. 'But I'll let you know.'

'Ciao!' He signs off with one of his other 'fluent' Italian words.

Angelina sits for a while in the peace of the nursery, imagining what life will be like in the near future when it is full of new life. She and Ben have spent a small fortune on decorating the space, filling it with toys from Hamley's and paying Danny, a wonderful interior designer who has transformed many of their celebrity friends' homes, to paint a beautiful garden mural on the walls of the nursery. Angelina is thrilled with the results. The representations of nature make it soothing and tranquil. It has quickly become her favourite room in the house.

She folds and refolds the tiny vests and sleepsuits in the drawers, even though they are already perfectly arranged, and turns on one of the cot mobiles, enjoying the gentle music and hypnotic quality of the rotating rattles. It took some time to track down the baroque lullabies that she had loved as a child, and to avoid 'twinkle, twinkle, little star,' which every toy seemed to play here in England.

Her thoughts drift to the birth itself, replaying all the different possibilities in her head. She has watched a thousand episodes of *One Born Every Minute*. She knows all the permutations. She also knows that when the time comes, she will be in the best hands. Her preference would always have been for a calm, candlelit birth in a birthing pool, but that is unlikely. When the registrar discovered they were having twins, he said without hesitation or room for challenge that Angelina should expect to be on the surgery ward, 'just to be on the safe side.' It felt as if the choice had been taken away from her – but, under the circumstances, it can't be helped. Healthy babies are the priority.

Lunch is a quinoa, sweet potato and chickpea salad, though Angelina tosses in a few spinach leaves as an extra precaution to keep her iron levels up. She has monitored her diet carefully throughout the pregnancy, anxious to create the best environment for the lives growing inside her. She eats alone, outside on the raised porcelain patio, before deciding to take Ruchi's advice and get some rest.

She lies back on the sofa, cushions plumped behind her. The French doors are still wide open, a gentle breeze has taken the edge off the heat of the day and created a gentle susurration through the white muslin drapes, as if the house is breathing with her. She drifts off, dreaming of an army of white storks.

Suddenly, Angelina feels a sharp pain deep inside her. She knows, senses immediately, before she returns to full consciousness, that it is time. She takes a deep breath. She is calm. She has channelled the powers of the goddess. She has been carefully preparing for this moment and knows exactly what to expect. Her body is primed, ready.

She phones Ben again.

His current receptionist – her replacement, Saffron – answers the phone, and it is a few moments before she is put through to Ben.

'The *cicogna* is here,' she gasps, as a second wave of pain erupts over her.

II. Ben

For a second, Ben is unable to think straight. He looks at the receiver as if it's the head of a cobra that has somehow slithered into his hand. Even though they have been preparing for this day for months, now that it is actually here, he is paralysed. But he quickly pulls himself together and – happiest when he is in control and taking charge of something – sweeps back into action. The world will have to wait a little longer for the next big thing in Guatemalan folk music.

He presses a button and brings the cobra up to his face. 'Saffron, call me a taxi, please.'

'Consider it done, Mr Martell,' she says, importantly. Even in his dazed state he notes the reassuring efficiency of Angelina's replacement.

The marimba artist is more than understanding when Ben explains to him that his wife is expecting twins and has just gone into labour, waving him from the office with gushing good wishes. In the reception area, Saffron stands to say goodbye, and it turns into a kind of curtsey as she splutters her good luck message, such is her hero-worship of her boss. Ben exits the building on a strange high: buoyant with the goodness of the world, but also feeling as if he might be the first man in the world to experience fatherhood.

The taxi driver is as effusive as everyone else once he discovers Ben's news. The roads are clear at this time of day, and by the time they reach the West Brompton address, it is 'mate' this and 'mate' that, and Ben has heard all about the 'carnage at the business end' of the taxi-driver's wife's first delivery. He could have lived without some of the graphic detail, but it is someone else's story and provides a much-needed distraction. Angelina's birth tale won't be anything like that.

Supremely prepared, Ben has left the 4x4 in the drive facing the right way, with Angelina's suitcase already packed and in the boot of the vehicle. It has been there for the last three weeks, like all the textbooks tell you.

While the taxi is still pulling up outside, he can see Angelina through the vast bay window at the front of the house. She is silhouetted by the sunlight, pacing around the room. She has both hands pressed into her back and her elbows pushed out. Even though the taxi is on the company account, he stuffs a bundle of notes into the driver's hand as he exits.

'Thanks, mate.'

The taxi driver can't believe his luck. He's received the equivalent of a day's money in one short trip. Impending fatherhood does funny things to people.

Ben takes a deep breath. This is it. He is on the cusp of the happiest moment of his life. Of their lives. The day he finally gets to meet their children.

Though he is beside himself with excitement, he adopts as calm a demeanour as he can muster, for Angelina's sake, as he enters the house. She has to do the hard bit. He knows what his role is. The least he can do is to be the rock that she needs to get through the next few hours.

'Darling, I'm here.'

He flies towards his wife. Angelina is flushed, standing in a small pool of water. It is seeping through the oak floorboards into the empty space below, the area designated for Ben's new home studio. Or possibly a space for his wife to set up the organic beauty product business she has spoken about from time to time. If he's honest, in his mind, it is already the home studio. Tom, his architect friend responsible for the grand design of the house, has already put together some rough plans for how it could be developed. Ben and Tom both attended the same boarding school in Surrey and, like most of his fellow 'inmates', as they like to call each other, are still very close, living and working in London and all doing well for themselves. Ben likes clean lines and everything to be pristine, but today he doesn't mind the stain on the floorboards. It seems fitting, somehow: a christening stain. A symbol of new beginnings. The footprint of the stork.

He grabs the additional bag Angelina has prepared for them to take. As with everything else in relation to the pregnancy, they have read the textbook. The bag is filled with bottles of water, snacks, glucose tablets for energy, and some books and magazines for the slower moments of the labour. He helps her to the car, clipping her seatbelt in gently below her bump. He's still not sure he can believe that this is happening. He darts around the house, closing and locking the windows and doors.

Then, back out to the 4x4. It all takes mere seconds, but he feels as if he is in slow motion. He starts the engine but, before reaching for the handbrake, he first puts his hand over Angelina's.

'I love you, Signora Redilocks.'

10

Instead of the affirmation he was expecting in response to his favourite nickname, Angelina gives out an almighty shriek as the next contraction overtakes her.

Ben drives to the hospital. He takes what he designated weeks ago as 'route B', knowing that, even though it's slightly longer in distance, it will be fastest at this time of day. He has practised the journey several times, at different times of the day and through varying volumes of London traffic. His experiments mean that he is sure that he understands the timings. His navigation system agrees with Ben's calculations.

Nothing has been left to chance. Nothing can go wrong.

They make the trip in 22 minutes. Angelina has three more giant contractions in the car. Ben remembers all his reading, and calculates they must have been just over five minutes apart. There's still a way to go, but things are definitely moving at a good pace.

He reminds Angelina to rest between contractions. She seems distracted, not listening to his advice, as if she's retreated into a world of her own. He thinks this is normal, too.

He helps her through the doors to the hospital, and then rushes back to park the car properly.

He has paid, of course, for a private room. Between contractions, Ben helps Angelina into her robe. In the quiet moments, he stands and rubs her lower back, pressing down firmly as the midwife has shown him. He is the model of an attentive birthing partner.

In the violent moments, when Angelina throws herself onto various items of hospital furniture wailing and shrieking, he can only look on helplessly. He didn't realise that it would be so *animal*. He barely recognises his Signora Redilocks in those moments.

Hours pass. Professionals check things. Contractions keep coming, but they don't seem to speed up.

Nothing happens. He has a strange sensation of losing his footing, even though he is seated in a hospital chair, or pacing white floors.

'What's wrong?' he asks, anguished, once out of earshot of his wife.

'Nothing's wrong, Mr Martell. We're monitoring everything. It's all perfectly normal. She's six centimetres dilated, but things have slowed down a little. The babies will come in their own time, when they're good and ready. You can't hurry nature.'

'What can I do?' he asks, knowing that the question is futile.

'Let's put her in the bath,' suggests the midwife.

Ben pours water over Angelina's tummy, and sings songs to the unborn children, trying to encourage them out. He makes up words to the tune of 'Silent Night':

Birthday's here,
ou-t you come,
we're wait-ing,
for you now.
Hurry alo-ng,
we wish you were here.
Come out in heavenly pe-ace!
Come out for he-aven's sake.

Nonsense sentences, but some of it makes Angelina smile, at least. He tries desperately not to let his anxiety show as Angelina's pain increases.

'All is well,' the midwife tells him again and again, but the smile doesn't always reach her eyes and he detects a strain in her words.

He doesn't believe her.

Back out of the bath, Angelina is back on the gas and air, but at such a rate that the midwife takes it away. He's never seen his wife like this. She is no longer 'there' in the room with him. Her distance is accompanied by sounds that are deep and primitive and like nothing he has ever heard before. Listening with his musical production ears, he finds it fascinating. The level of concern for his wife that they provoke is alarming.

Finally, the midwife declares that Angelina is ready. 'Mrs Martell, it's time to push.'

'Thank god,' Ben murmurs, though he has never had cause to believe in a higher deity until now.

Angelina leans against the back of the bed, a bed on wheels that she has nearly pushed out of the room more than once over the last hour. The midwife has ensured that the brakes are now firmly on the wheels.

'Because you and the babies are not going for a tour around the hospital just yet,' she jokes.

Max comes out first. His delivery is straightforward, and after being whisked away for moments to conduct his Apgar score, the tiny creature is in Ben's arms. Max's safe arrival appears to give Angelina the extra bout of energy she needs to push for his sister.

Ben is busy cooing over Max, filled with wonder at the tiny miracle, and doesn't notice straight away how the mood in the hospital room is changing rapidly.

'His tiny fingers,' he croaks, and looks up at the midwife, who has her hands on Angelina's stomach, and is frowning.

'His sister has moved into breech position.'

Suddenly, everything seems to happen at once. There is rapid movement and intense activity all around him.

Professionals appear as if by magic. They call out things that he doesn't understand. The registrar, more nurses. It is all a blur. A sickening, numbing blur. He doesn't know what is going on. It is astonishing how many people are suddenly in this small room. Arms reach out for the child and Max is taken away from Ben. A baby is replaced by a folded surgical gown in his hands.

'Put this on,' a voice commands. Another nurse.

'Max will be fine,' the midwife says. 'We need to focus on Angelina and the second baby now.'

Angelina is helped onto the bed. Equipment comes flying through the doors. There is machinery everywhere and people in every corner of the room. Ben hears words that terrify him. 'Heartbeat dropping.' 'Is she—' he breaks off. 'Are they in danger?' he whispers.

Angelina screams, and his question is left unanswered. Ben is put in charge of the gas and air.

'Let her have as much as she wants.'

Ben feels impotent in the midst of all the activity. The urgency makes everything seem chaotic, but, at the same time, he understands that everyone knows exactly what they're doing. He tries to hold on to that thought. He holds Angelina's hand and finds that he has tears running down his cheeks.

He feels terrified. This is the most traumatic experience of his life. What on earth must Angelina be feeling? In all this haste there is no time to explain anything, but he gathers that Mia will be born by emergency caesarcan. The scene is so different from just a few minutes ago. It feels as though it must all be happening to someone else, some other couple, on one of the birthing programmes that they watched together. This wasn't how it was meant to be for them.

'More!' Angelina screams. He watches helplessly as she inhales the gas in deep, long breaths.

The registrar begins the C-section. Angelina no longer speaks in English. She screams and swears in Italian. The words degenerate into a sobbing wail.

'*Voglio il mio bambino*,' she cries, over and over again.

Hearing his beautiful wife screaming that she wants her baby almost breaks Ben.

Suddenly, at the point where he thinks he can't possibly take any more, out comes Mia. Wrinkled, much smaller than her brother and covered in blood, but after a second there is the miraculous sound of a cry.

The nurses and midwife all cheer. The umbilical cord is cut. The tiny baby is placed into a white towel and handed to Angelina, who seems to have lost all command of English and now seems only able to converse in Italian.

After all the drama and seriousness, the room is back to smiles. One of the nurses leaves to fetch Max back.

The ordeal is not over for Angelina, who now needs to be stitched back up, both from the cut of the caesarean and the tear from Max's birth. Ben is distracted by the business of meeting his children and concern for his brave wife, but he takes in a few odd details from the scene.

He sees a nurse gently wipe the registrar's face as he is busy with the needle, to stop sweat from dripping from it.

'Well done, Jacob. Well done,' the nurse whispers.

He realises then, with the nurse congratulating the registrar, how close they must have been to disaster. Jacob. Ben is usually good with names. It's important in his industry. But he realises that he barely knows the name of anyone in this room. And yet, he is so grateful to them all. That realisation causes him to cry once more, though he hardly knows why. A tap has been turned on inside him. He had no idea that it was possible to shed so many tears. It's ridiculous. He is so joyful that it is overwhelming: the happiness, the relief. He isn't a religious man, but he offers up a silent prayer of thanks.

He must let his mother know.

And then he is overwhelmed by sadness, and cries harder. Somehow, in the midst of the drama and the beauty, he momentarily forgot about the death of his mother, which took place in Angelina's second trimester.

He has barely had time to grieve for her properly, so caught up has he been in the excitement of the pregnancy and preparation for life with twins – but suddenly it hits him hard, compounded by the shock that he could possibly have forgotten, even for a moment, that it happened. What kind of son does that make him? What kind of father will he be? He aches for his own mother, feeling her absence deeply in this special moment. He is overwhelmed by the responsibility that burns so fiercely inside him, now that he has a whole family and not just Angelina to take care of.

He forces himself to focus on the present, snatching back the joyful feeling of fatherhood, so wonderful, so exciting. He picks up the phone to make the call to Italy. He can barely string the words together to let his in-laws know that they have become grandparents and that, although there were some complications, their daughter is doing well.

'It's a miracle. The *cicogna* came! Max and Mia are here!'

A cocktail of emotions is all mixed up inside him: relief that his new family are all okay, that the twins have arrived safely, shock at the traumatic nature of the birth, and gratitude that Angelina has survived the ordeal. And it's all mingled with the sorrow of not being able to share the joy with his own parents. Grief bubbles back to the surface. It's life. Sunshine and rain, day and night, good and bad. It's normal.

'Bravo, Ben!'

Of course Angelina's parents are on the first flight they can book themselves on. They have had their bags packed for weeks, on tenterhooks for this news. There are more tears of joy from the other end of the phone.

Little does Ben know how short-lived that joy will be.

III. Ben

Since Angelina has had such a traumatic experience with the birth, she is kept in hospital for slightly longer than usual. There are 72 hours of monitoring. Ben has paid for a private room with a second bed so that he can stay too. His beautiful wife still looks so pale and frail that part of him is glad to be staying at the hospital. It is also a blessing to have experienced midwives on call around the clock, to offer support with the constant rounds of feeding and nappy changing. Mia, in spite of her dramatic entrance into the world and lower birthweight, takes to breastfeeding, which Angelina is determined to do, much more easily than Max. Her brother is fretful, less settled, and doesn't seem to be able to latch on well.

It's amazing to see how different they are. Somehow, in all the reading about babies, he didn't actually expect them to have their own personalities, but already, only three days into the world, there is so much character in their faces. They are so sweet together, always seeking one another out, sleeping with their faces turned to one another, as though to continue the closeness of sharing a womb.

The journey back home from the hospital takes far longer than the journey there when Angelina was in early labour. Strapping the car seats in, with their precious cargo inside for the first time, is much more difficult than it was when he practised with them empty. Ben drives much more tentatively, agonising over every gear change and bump in the road, as if it is a personal attack on his family. The delay at the hospital has given Massimo and Emanuela plenty of time to be safely installed into the West Brompton home, so that they can be the welcome party.

Ben and Angelina can barely get through the door for all the flowers, soft toys, baskets of goodies and other gifts and cards that line the hallway. The staff at Azure have sent a framed pair of platinum discs, normally reserved to celebrate best-selling artists on sales of half a million singles, to congratulate the couple on the safe arrival of Max and Mia. Ben is delighted, and it's worth more than any of the music awards he's achieved.

'Look at these, babe,' he laughs as he shows Angelina. 'Life's winners before they've even got started! I'm going to hang them in the new studio when it's built.'

'You need feeding!' exclaims Emanuela when she sees her daughter. She has already been busy batch-cooking all of Angelina's favourite childhood dishes. There are several weeks' worth of meatballs, ragu sauces and gnocchi lining the freezer.

Ben pours the champagne, and they make a toast. 'To the luckiest children in the world, Max and Mia!'

Angelina's parents stay in the UK for a full month before reluctantly returning home. Ben takes an extended paternity leave, and so, for most of that time, there are four pairs of hands to take care of two babies. It's a good ratio that makes learning to care for the twins seem manageable. There are trips to the local park, a thousand photographs of the twins looking cute, long lunches with the usual good-natured arguments between Massimo and Ben about the relative merits of prosecco, champagne and English sparkling wines, shopping trips to central London, and sightseeing all over. By the time the twins are a month old, they've visited every major landmark and attraction in the capital and some further afield, though Ben has to admit that they've probably slept through much of it.

It all goes by in a blur of blissful moments as Ben navigates the process of adjusting to fatherhood and having to share his wife with demanding twins. Though, with Angelina's parents there, the reality is that he doesn't really need to do very much. For the first month, he exists in a bubble of love that even feels enough to make up for the loss of Ben's own parents. His father died a long time ago, but his mother's death is still recent and raw. Emanuela and Massimo, though, have enough love for two sets of grandparents.

Emanuela insists on printing out hundreds of photographs of the newborns to add to the wedding album.

'Nobody prints out photos anymore, Mama,' he hears Angelina groan. But it's lovely to flick through, to see how much they change day by day. Mia quickly catches up to Max's birthweight, and indeed, begins to overtake.

All too soon it is time to wave Angelina's parents away, and for Ben to think about returning to work. On previous visits, Ben has driven them to the airport for emotional, drawn-out goodbyes with Angelina by the security gates. On this occasion, however, with his paternity leave running out and time so precious, all agree that it would be better if they just call a car to take them to Heathrow.

'We'll be here again at Christmas!' Emanuela says, through gulping sobs.

'It will be here before you know it,' Angelina reassures her.

'And we can Facetime every day,' Ben explains. 'You will be able to see Max and Mia growing.'

'And you'll teach them Italian?' Emanuela asks.

'They'll have no chance, if they've got my linguistic genes,' jokes Ben. But once he closes the door on his in-laws, he becomes serious.

'Now we can be a proper family.'

IV. Angelina

Max is sitting in his bouncer. Angelina knows that he's really too young for it, but she wouldn't be using it yet if she didn't absolutely have to. She's also checked that newborns are fine in them for short periods, and she's adjusted all the straps so that he is safely secured. Angelina is lying across the nursery floor and has one foot balanced on the bottom wire of the bouncer's frame to keep him moving while she feeds Mia. She has to twist her body away from Max, so that he doesn't see what's happening and decide that he is hungry too, because feeding both at the same time is near impossible when she's on her own. She can only manage it when Ben is there. She can get herself into position, and he can hand her both babies. Max, although bigger and stronger at birth, doesn't latch on as well as Mia, so he's better on the bottle anyway, but she doesn't have one prepared and she doesn't have the Haakaa pump nearby. It's quite hard to keep gently jiggling him while keeping the top half of her body still so that Mia isn't disturbed. From here she has a strange view of the painted nursery walls. It doesn't look like a garden from this angle, just a jumble of clashing colours. It isn't soothing at all.

God knows what she must look like if anyone saw her. She wouldn't even want Ben to see her like this. It was so much easier when her parents were here and she only had to think about tending to one of the twins at a time.

It reminds her of doing a complicated yoga stretch, and it's not an entirely unpleasant feeling, because goodness knows her core is shot to bits and could do with a good workout. Catching sight of herself in the mirror, she realises that it's more downward drag than downward dog, what with the looser skin hanging over the top of her jeans. She knows she must be patient and allow her body to heal and recover. Beneath the denim, though she can't see them, she is acutely aware that the caesarean stitches are there. Healing well, but the scar will be permanent. A reminder for ever more of the nightmare of the hospital, the trauma of Mia's birth.

At least she could just about get back into her jeans a few days after the birth. That was something. She's heard of mothers who never regain their figure, and the nice doctors have warned her that twins do funny things to your insides, and it will take a while for her to feel like her old self. She has been told to look out for the baby blues. It's normal to feel a little down after birth. She's missing exercise, too. She will give Ruchi a call this afternoon and book in some one-to-one yoga sessions. Six weeks, she was told, is fine to start exercising, as long as she takes it easy and is sensible about what her body is capable of.

Ben took all of his paternity leave and more, but it went by so fast. He had to get back to his music clients, who all have tight production deadlines, and Ben is somehow irreplaceable in that process. This, being on her own, is much harder. In fact, each day seems harder than the last. She has been on her own for more than a month now. She doesn't seem to get any better at managing it all.

'Hire someone to help you,' Ben keeps insisting. 'Maybe one of those Norland nannies. They're the best. It doesn't matter what it costs.'

Angelina knows that the money doesn't matter, they can easily afford it, but she isn't concerned about the financial cost; it's the emotional cost. Ben doesn't understand that it is a matter of pride to her, to fulfil the role of mother. Italian families celebrate motherhood. She doesn't want paid help to parent. What would her own mother think? Large families are the norm back home. Looking after two children should be easily manageable. But it isn't. There is nothing that she can't do; she just can't do everything at once. And everything with the twins seems to happen at once, as if their body clocks are synchronised – which she supposes, after sharing a womb, they probably are. Both babies need feeding, or changing, or cuddling. The only thing that doesn't happen at once is sleeping. So there is never any time to get ahead with anything. No time to put a wash on or to sort out the clean clothes. There are piles of clothes everywhere, clean and dirty. All that lovely organisation from when they were planning the nursery has evaporated into a blur of milk, nappies, crying and mess.

The books say that she should get into a routine of going out and meeting friends with babies of a similar age. She had visions of baby massage classes and then sipping lattes in leafy cafes afterwards, but it isn't realistic. It doesn't work like that. The first baby massage class they did last week was good. Ben took the afternoon off so that they could all go as a family, and it was fine. A baby each. But the requirements stipulate that there must be one adult for each baby, and the following week there was an important meeting that Ben had to attend, so he couldn't make it.

'Pay someone to go with you,' he had urged. But Angelina has no intention of 'paying someone' to go out with her. That would be so humiliating – worse than paying someone to help at home. This week, even though Ben said he'd take the afternoon off, it seemed easier not to go. Instead, she has looked for things that she can do by herself with the twins. Not much, it seems. There is a baby rhyme-time class today. It will require enormous effort to get all three of them there, but she is determined. She is a powerful goddess. Women just like her have given birth for thousands of years. Twins aren't that rare. She should be able to cope. But why the hell is it so hard? Channel the bloody goddess.

However, Angelina has never felt less goddess-like as Max decides, at that moment, that he is now ready for his feed too. She rocks the bloody bouncing chair furiously with her foot to try and eke out a few more minutes for Mia to finish.

The class begins in just under two hours' time and is a ten-minute walk away, though Angelina will need to leave much earlier to be there on time. She is still not quite au fait with setting up the double pram. There are so many buttons and levers to contend with. It was definitely designed by a man who didn't practise opening it with at least one baby in his arms. Ben doesn't understand. And, even though their hallway is very wide, it isn't wide enough to keep the pram fully extended, so it has to be collapsed and put away each time it gets used. Ben wanted to keep it in the garage so that it was out of the way, but if it is there then Angelina can't easily access it anyway. She doesn't like to be in a different room from Max and Mia, let alone go outside without them, even for a moment. She'd never go outside to get it. So she wrestles with the partially collapsed beast. It's only a small issue in the grand scheme of things, but it's a frustration which causes her a great deal of anxiety.

The responsibility of trying to keep them alive is just overwhelming.

Mia doesn't like the bouncer. She's much happier lying on her back in the baby gym, although she doesn't always want to do that straight after a feed. It amazes Angelina how different they are, even though they are twins who shared a womb.

Today, though, Mia is compliant. While she stares at plastic things in the baby gym, Angelina manages to pump and feed Max. It is a very fussy, fretful feed and he barely manages to take anything at all. All that effort. It breaks her heart to have to throw milk away. They have an appointment later in the week to see whether his difficulties with feeding are being caused by tongue-tie. The health visitor is concerned that he isn't gaining weight as fast as his sister, even though he was the bigger one at birth.

She puts Max into the baby sling so that he is strapped across her stomach while she assembles the pram. For once, everything on the pram clicks easily into place. Perhaps she is getting the hang of this after all. She bumps the pram down the steps. Ben can carry it, but Angelina has been avoiding lifting anything other than the babies since the caesarean. Whoever designed these big houses didn't do it with prams and babies in mind.

When she goes back up to fetch Mia, she sees that Mia has been sick all down one side of the cute dress that Angelina had dressed her in ready for baby rhyme-time. Luckily, Max is still in the sling. He remains content in there while Mia is being changed. He goes into the pram last, and though he is still whinging, Angelina knows that the rolling pram wheels will keep him quiet for a while once they get going.

With eight minutes left till the class starts, they are out of the house.

It has been a marathon effort, but she's done it.

The class is good. Angelina is envious of some of the other mums with just one baby sitting on their lap. She finds herself talking to the woman next to her, who introduces herself as Glory, and her little girl as Gertie.

Angelina admires Gertie's cutesy ra-ra skirt and frilled top. Gertie is also sporting a matching bow to hold back her few wisps of hair. She looks gorgeous. Like the ensemble that Angelina had picked out for Mia, but had to change at the last minute.

'And you have two gorgeous boys!' Glory enthuses.

'Boys? Oh no, one of each, a boy and a girl.' Angelina looks down and realises that the sleepsuit she grabbed for Mia has tractors on it, and is in fact one of Max's. Not that it matters, she supposes.

'Excuse Mia's outfit. I had her in a gorgeous dress, but the inevitable happened just as we were leaving the house and I had to change her.'

'Oh my goodness, don't worry about that. I'm amazed you even get out of the house with twins.'

Angelina bridles a little at that, but she's not entirely sure why. It is, indeed, very hard to get out of the house, but she doesn't need that fact acknowledged by strangers.

'And what's your son called?'

Angelina must not have spoken very clearly when she first mentioned Mia, because Glory gushes, 'Max and Nina. Gorgeous!'

Angelina is so grateful to have a nearly-friend that she can't bring herself to make the correction, even when they are having a coffee afterwards and Glory rhapsodises about how Angelina must be a marvel coping with two when she herself struggles with only one. They exchange numbers, agree to meet for the class again the following week, and Angelina feels a little glimmer of hope.

V. Angelina

Angelina can't make the class the following week. Max's feeding is all over the place and she isn't able to get anything down him at all, so she is forced to text Glory and cancel.

Ah, such a shame, but I completely understand. Gertie will miss Max and Nina!

Gertie is about two months old and doesn't have the faintest idea who Max and Mia are, but never mind. She wonders how people can be so vacuous.

Glory invites Angelina swimming. She's hired a private, heated pool locally, and booked an instructor for the babies, but it falls on a day of recording for Ben, who can't come with her. There's no way she can take both twins by herself, even with an instructor. Though exactly what an instructor can be instructing eight- and nine-week old babies to do in the water is anyone's guess. Angelina cancels again.

Week by week as the twins grow, they seem to spend even more time awake, and demand more and more and more of Angelina. The longer she doesn't leave the house, the harder it becomes to even consider doing it at all. She knows it can't go on like this, so today she has invited Glory and Gertie to her house. At least that way she has half a chance of coping.

Max and Mia are still having their morning nap when Glory arrives.

'Come in, come in! So good to see you and Gertie again!'

Angelina can't help but admire the way that Glory is able to dismantle Gertie's pram with one hand, holding Gertie in the other. 'You make that look so easy,' she says enviously. 'My pram's a nightmare to collapse.'

'I found it tricky at first, but I seem to do it multiple times a day. I can do it in my sleep now.'

Despite being another wealthy West Brompton yummy mummy, Glory is suitably impressed by the house when Angelina takes her on the tour, talks through the renovations they've already completed, and outlines Tom the architect's plans for the rest of the house. She also shares Danny's contact details at Glory's request. They're thinking of decorating soon and need a good interior designer. Danny is one of the best, and his work compliments everything structural that Tom created. Angelina realises how much she has missed female company. Because Glory gushes about everything, she's easy to talk to and the conversation flows.

Glory admires a large black-and-white photo of Ben that hangs on the wall in the open-plan living area, a professional shot taken by a well-known photographer not long after Ben and Angelina met.

'Is that your husband? He's a dish! Bet you have to keep your wits about you to hold on to him!'

Angelina had never thought about this before. They were so infatuated with each other when they first met that it had never occurred to her that she might need to 'hold on' to him. She thinks about the fact that she hasn't let Ben come anywhere near her since the birth. At first, she could blame the caesarean recovery as a legitimate reason for keeping him at arm's length – but the truth is, she hasn't felt attracted to him since the birth. It was all so traumatic. There were two sets of stitches to heal; she had torn underneath when Max was being born, as well as being cut open for Mia's delivery. The thought of ever being sexually intimate with Ben, or with anyone, ever again seemed impossible. She realises that it's not just the shock of what she's been through – though why did no one tell her that the aftermath of giving birth would feel like she'd been hit by a train? – but it's also the fear. The fear of becoming pregnant and having to go through anything like that again. The safest way to avoid it is to keep Ben distant. It isn't worth the risk.

She thinks of Saffron, Ben's attractive new receptionist, her replacement at Azure. She remembers, too, that as yet still un-booked yoga appointment. Despite her saggy, scarred body, Ben would never be unfaithful. Surely. He loves her too much. He's been his usual, tender, patient self. For now, anyway.

'Still, I don't think you've got anything to worry about. You're absolutely gorgeous, too. I'd kill for those curls!' Glory gushes on, smoothing down her own sleek bob that doesn't look as if it is in need of smoothing down at all.

It's been so long since she's had a friend that Angelina has forgotten how to do some of this. She realises after Glory pauses that a compliment is expected of her in return. 'Oh, thanks. I love your cut, though, so classic. You'll have to let me know the name of your stylist.' Angelina has also half-forgotten that there are even such things as hairdressers, so little time has she had for herself since the births. She just about managed to get a comb through her hair before Glory arrived. She suddenly feels self-conscious, and is relieved when the baby monitor leaps back to life and reveals that at least one of the twins has woken.

'Excuse me while I pop to the nursery. Make yourself at home. Feel free to introduce Gertie to some of the twins' toys.' She was about to say 'Max and Mia's toys' but doesn't want to make Glory uncomfortable by pointing out that she keeps getting Mia's name wrong. 'I'll be back in a moment.'

It is Max who has woken. As ever, he is fretful, looking for food, but his feeds are so unsettled. The tongue-tie diagnosis has been confirmed, and he'll have the operation to cut it in the next few days. Things should get easier after that. God knows they couldn't get any harder. She leaves Mia sleeping on, and takes Max downstairs.

'Aw, is he playing up again? Poor little mite.'

Something about Glory's manner begins to grate. What can she know about how much Max plays up? It sounds to Angelina as though it is somehow an implicit criticism of her parenting. What right does Glory have to the casual 'again', as though it happens all the time? She knows that Glory is only trying to be friendly, that it is her who is being irrational, but she can't help herself.

'And how's little Nina? Is she still sleeping?'

There is nothing rude or untoward about Glory's question, apart from getting the name of her child wrong, and that is partially Angelina's fault for not correcting her sooner. Perhaps it's her comments about Ben, or perhaps it's her manners more generally, but something just snaps inside, and a fury Angelina can't explain rises up suddenly inside her. 'Look. It's Mia, okay? Max and Mia! Not Max and fucking Nina!'

'Sorry, I didn't mean to get it wrong! There's no need to swear at me. Cover your ears, little Gertie, we don't want you hearing those nasty words, do we?'

But Angelina isn't finished. 'And what kind of a name is Gertie anyway? Get out of my house.'

Glory fumbles a bit more with her pram in her haste to get out.

Christ. She feels better for letting off some steam. Glory is pointless anyway. An airhead. They have nothing in common beyond being new mothers. They would never have been real friends.

But the bravado doesn't last long. It had been nice to talk to somebody, to feel a little bit less lonely.

Angelina realises that she is shaking. Suddenly, she bursts into tears. She has no idea who she's become. She's never shouted at anyone like that before. She doesn't know what came over her. Is it too early for a glass of wine to settle her nerves, she wonders?

VI. Angelina

Angelina turns on the taps to fill the bath, taking care to mix the temperature of the water carefully so that it won't scald Max and Mia. She used to enjoy spending time in the bath herself, but now the architectural plants around the clawfoot bathtub have been replaced by alphabet letters in netting and plastic water squirters shaped like puffer fish in garish colours. It has been taken over by the twins.

She knows she should feel more grateful. On paper she has a wonderful life. She wants nothing more. Or at least nothing material. Some women can't have children at all, and here she is with two at once. She is one of the lucky ones. But that knowledge brings guilt. Especially since on a day-to-day basis it feels anything but lucky. Goodness, it is hard. Angelina wasn't in any way prepared for the sheer tedium of it all. The idea of setting up a small organic beauty product business has faded fast, especially given that Ben keeps talking about converting the whole of the sprawling basement, which she once, naively, thought might have been earmarked for her, into a studio with accommodation for visiting musicians.

Everything feels so different from the heady days at the start of their relationship. After a whirlwind romance, they had married in Angelina's village. It was exactly what she'd always dreamed of. The perfect wedding in a picturesque setting that she loved dearly. They couldn't have been happier. Angelina's parents were delighted with her choice and they had taken to Ben straight away. Her father liked him. He had taken Ben to one side for 'the chat', and expressed his absolute conviction that Ben would do everything in his power to take care of his daughter and that she would have a good life.

And, in a way, he's right. About the first part, anyway. Ben assures Angelina repeatedly that she doesn't need to return to work, that they have plenty of money. She should want for nothing.

But money has nothing to do with it.

Their stunning home, which came at an enormous financial cost but with such emotional investment in the choosing of fixtures and fittings, feels like the house of a stranger. Never mind the fact that Ben spent over a million pounds renovating the five-storey townhouse – it could be anyone's home. The enviable life that she once shared with Ben has become as grey and unyielding as the frames of the folding doors. Their gorgeous garden view is now filled with plastic playthings, and Angelina no longer really knows who she is. If someone were to ask her what her interests are, she'd no longer remember. It makes her wonder if she ever really knew.

She looks around at the 'beautiful' house. It is light and designed to be tranquil. The 'space' as Tom, their architect, calls it, flows from one area to another. The light pours into the kitchen and living area even on the blandest and greyest of days. But it is nothing like the light that Angelina grew up with in the little village outside Florence. It feels as if it must have been a different person entirely who ran wild and free with her sister and all their cousins.

Angelina thinks back over the different choices she has made. The twists and turns that have led her to this point. Aged 18, she applied for a gap year in London. It had seemed like such a glamorous and desirable location. Inspiration came from the music scene and the fashion she had seen in magazines like *Vogue* and in videos on YouTube. She had to work hard to reassure her doubting parents, who were worried about her coming to live and work in London. Supportive of her decisions but reluctant to let her go, they did everything they could to keep her safe from afar without stopping her from living her life. At the start, her father had travelled to England with her, and stayed for the first week to help settle her into a shared house in Putney. Fondly, she remembers how he created a line of communication with the landlord and his wife to 'keep an eye on Angelina'. He had thought he was being discreet, and Angelina never let on that she knew, aware that the arrangement offered some reassurance to her anxious parents. It worked in her favour too, because it meant that they were not on her case all the time. Life had seemed so exciting then. There was so much promise, so much to discover and enjoy.

It is as if she has lost all interest in life itself. She no longer has the energy or enthusiasm to meet up with anyone, even old friends for lunch. And the new mummy friends from various baby and toddler clubs have never really materialised. Angelina can't make it back to rhyme-time for the second class because it coincides with Max's frenotomy, the procedure to correct the tongue-tie. He is still fretful afterwards, and she is reluctant to go to the next one. Then, when she does make it back a few classes later, everyone has moved on without her, and they are all arranging meetups and excursions. They offer to put her in the WhatsApp group, but all their plans make her feel exhausted and she soon deletes it.

She thinks back to Glory and Gertie. The one time she momentarily had a chance to make a friend, it didn't last long. Shouting and swearing at somebody isn't conducive to building friendships. Angelina doesn't quite understand what happened there, or why she reacted the way she did to somebody who was just trying to be nice.

Even things that Angelina can do at home, like yoga, become too much effort. When Ruchi comes, it is never a good time. One of the twins will be playing up, and any kind of calm will be unattainable. Since her short-lived friendship with Glory, she hasn't tried bringing anyone back to the house. The twins have had no play dates, only each other for company. Angelina pours herself a glass of wine. She has been doing this earlier and earlier in the day. It makes the afternoons easier to bear.

It has been a very isolating time. She feels so out of the loop, distanced from the world beyond her front door.

The woman who chose every tiny detail of the nursery, who so longed to meet her babies just a few months ago, has disappeared. To Angelina, she seems unrecognisable, as if she was another person entirely.

Too late, she remembers the running bath. She runs into the room to find it overflowing, suds seeping over the sides and slopping onto the floorboards. When Ben comes home, he finds Angelina huddled in a ball on the wet floor, sobbing.

PART TWO
Louise

Max and Mia are four years old

Chapter One

We're at the airport in Kefalonia, waiting in the departure lounge for our flight home. It's been a few years since we've all been abroad. Financial constraints and the sometimes inflexible nature of foster care can mean that holidays are more likely to be camping in Pembrokeshire than coasting around the Costa del Sol. But I was recently paid more money than anticipated for one of my paintings. Not a life-changing sum, but unexpected, and enough to take us to Greece during the half term for some sun and sea. It was all very last minute, but worth it. We had a great time. Lloyd, Jackson, Vincent and Lily all look relaxed and as tanned as I've seen them in a long while. Jackson is the eldest, and he looks up from his mobile to spot our gate as it comes up on the departures board, just before the announcement is made over the echoing tannoy.

'Would passengers for flight EZY5134 to Bristol please make their way to Gate 3A ready to board.'

My phone rings as we're in the midst of that chaotic business of gathering up bags and checking that everyone has got their jackets and water bottles.

'It's the placements team,' I say. 'I'd better take it.' They all know what's coming. I repeat what's being said to me so that Lloyd can hear.

'Twins. Four years old, a boy and a girl, from London.'

He shrugs, non-committal.

'I'll call you back. Send through the details. I need to talk to the family before we make a decision.'

By the time we complete the short walk to our gate, Lloyd has hatched a plan to drive to IKEA with Jackson in the morning and get bunk beds.

I take that as a yes.

'We've never had twins before,' observes Vincent.

'True.'

'Are they identical?'

'You heard the conversation. You know just as much as me. But I don't think, if it's a boy and a girl, that they can be identical. We'll find out, I guess.'

By the next morning, Lily and Vincent have decided that they're tagging along on the IKEA trip too. 'In case we need something for our rooms.' Funny how they can suddenly be united in an enterprise such as this. Vincent is the youngest of my birth children, and Lily is our long-term foster child. She's been with us for years now.

On one level, all of them being out of the house this morning is all the better for me, clearing several hours of the need for any childcare and bringing the rare opportunity of time at home alone. On another level, however, I feel certain that there will be financial repercussions.

'Just be strong as you walk through the marketplace at the end,' I caution. 'And do your best to resist buying any more cheese graters and watering cans. We have more than enough.'

I know, even as I say these things, that I'm probably wasting my breath. I can already picture their return: they will be clutching picture frames, potted plants, and funky-coloured wastepaper bins. No doubt something will need assembling. I'm not sure I can cope. I finish my advice on a different tack. 'You've just been on holiday. You don't need anything else.'

'Yep,' says Lily, doing nothing to alleviate my concern.

'And the holiday cost a fortune,' I remind them. I feel better for saying it, even though I know my words are falling on deaf ears. Home is where you put the stuff while you are out getting other stuff. I once saw that motto on a fridge magnet that I just about resisted buying.

'Better take some bags,' I concede.

At the very least, Lloyd is going to have to fork out for marzipan slices and meatballs. Impossible to get out of an IKEA store without those. I have a momentary desire to get hold of some more of the long-stemmed wine glasses they do, and it occurs to me that I could go with them and make a day of it. Then I realise that I must have taken leave of my senses, and anyway, the mountain of washing parked outside the washing machine is calling to me. I swear it crawled further into the centre of the room when my back was turned. If this were a parking bay, it would have been clamped, so far 'over the line' is the pile as it spreads further and further across the kitchen. The epic proportions are the result of indiscriminately spilled-out suitcases, a manoeuvre that the family have classed as 'unpacking'. Oh, the bonus extras that a holiday generates.

'Enjoy,' I call as the front door slams behind them. 'But be strong!'

Douglas and Dotty, my two jackawawas, have their own plans for the washing pile. They appear to be setting up new sleeping arrangements there, having been away on their own little holiday. They spent the week being looked after by Millie and Mitchell, my newly married step-daughter and her husband, and they will have been thoroughly spoilt there, I have no doubt. I need to stage an intervention with this washing. I tip the dogs off the pile and ignore their disgruntled expressions. The beach towels I take out to the garden to shake off. They appear to have arrived back at the house complete with half the sand from the beach.

It occurs to me that the timing of the IKEA trip may have something to do with the work-shy characteristics of the rest of my family. How convenient to leave me behind on the first day back to do, well, everything. I shall be in need of one of those long-stemmed wine glasses by the time I get through this lot. Ah, well. They can keep their Swedish utopia. I can get more done without them anyway.

Washing load number one is soon in, the coffee machine is on, and the sun is shining. It's only 8.30 am and I'm feeling good, ahead of the game. Twins sound like a handful on paper, but I'm hoping that, being twins, they may actually make fostering life easier by being able to comfort and entertain one another in the early days of being in a strange house. I go up to the room that the twins will be in to start cleaning and moving furniture. With a bit of effort, I flip the single bed on its side and drag the mattress and the frame into the spare room to make room for the bunk beds. It takes a good deal of pushing and pulling on my own, and I'm not as cool, calm and collected as I was half an hour ago. Nevertheless, I press on. I get the toolbox from the cupboard in the conservatory so that I can dismantle it and put it away. It seems like a bigger job than I first thought, and I experience a little internal struggle which goes something along the lines of, 'Why don't I just wait and let Lloyd do this when he gets back?'

The little duologue playing out in my head then argues, 'But I'm a modern woman. I can put up bookshelves with ease. This should be a doddle, and why should I wait for a man to do it?'

I grapple with nuts and bolts for a bit, then emit a sigh as the first voice wins. It is not a doddle. My skills lie elsewhere. Lloyd can do it later.

I get my Hattie vacuum cleaner, press 'turbo' and find myself enjoying the satisfaction of capturing cobwebs that appear to have decorated the room in our absence. It becomes slightly addictive, and I end up doing the whole of upstairs. I make a mental note to tell Vincent not to eat Pringles in his room, or at least not to get them on the floor if he docs. A check of the clock tells me that it's only 9.15am. I must go on holiday more often. It is another note to myself that I know will fade as the reality of how much money we save by being at home asserts itself. It has been an expensive time away. The treats mount up. As do the chores.

As I head downstairs, I pick up my phone and see a couple of missed calls. I evidently haven't heard the rings above the dulcet tones of Hattie sucking debris from the carpets. One is from Moira, our current supervising social worker, who, because I can't spell and was in a hurry when I saved her number, is listed as 'Mowra'. I decided not to amend it. It has an exotic ring to it and, anyway, I tell myself that she'll never see it so she'll never know. Also, we seem to have been through a string of supervising social workers lately, so perhaps she won't last that long anyway. The other is 'number withheld', but I know that it will be the placements team checking if we are still available for Max and Mia.

Time for that coffee. I make a beeline for the machine, eyeing up the three remaining Jaffa cakes, snacks left over from the drive from the airport last night. This time I hear my phone ring. It's a mobile number that comes up, and I know by its timing that this will be the children's social worker. Sure enough, I'm right.

She sounds okay, friendly enough. Younger than me, maybe mid-thirties – I love playing 'guess the profile of the social worker'. It provides hours of entertainment. I have encountered so many over the years. I don't mean to sound unfeeling. Foster carers must find joy whenever they can. Her name is Beatrice, but I can call her 'Bea'. Well, that's all nice, but I don't reciprocate. There's no way she's calling me Lou.

She is collecting the twins from London and will meet them in a hotel where they are staying with social workers. All being well, they will be with us by mid-afternoon. My interest is piqued a little. I'm curious as to why they are in a hotel. In my experience, when children and mothers are placed in a Travelodge or Premier Inn, it's a measure that's been put in by the police or children's social care in order to keep them safe. It's my first little niggling worry. Perhaps these children have been in some sort of danger in the familial home.

When I get off the phone with Beatrice-but-call-me-Bea, I ring Moira straight back. I need more background information: a picture of their story, what's been happening for them, would be really helpful. So much guesswork takes place in the early days of a foster placement. Sometimes a little help is required.

Moira gives me a good half an hour of time, which these days, for a busy social worker, is an unexpected bonus.

I'm appreciative because I receive increasingly quick text messages in response to my questions and requests. The old Egress system that we used to use for communication was replaced a while ago by some new all-bells-and-whistles system, which I'm afraid that I've never had the time or headspace to learn.

I'm not alone. Many of my fellow foster carers have also found it overwhelming. The new system requires that we have a local authority email in addition to a private email. It's another layer of bureaucracy, another password to remember, another thing to log in to. I also don't think it's necessary, and on my less forgiving days, I consider it actually a bit of a cheek. I'm not employed by the local authority, and I don't have a contract with them. Perhaps it would be easier if I did.

It's not just with social services. I've reached a stage where I think I'm experiencing some kind of digital information overload. Online banking, for example, I hate. If I want to buy something that has just been advertised to me, I have to fill out a form. I'm not a fan of a form, generally. As an artist, I'm a kinaesthetic person, who likes to 'do'. People like me are increasingly forced to live in a world designed and created by visual learners. It's not the kinaesthetic people like me who design websites or technology or IKEA instructions – which is why Lloyd can sort the bed out. Life coaches will tell us that we need to protect ourselves from abuse and stress. If a person in our lives generally makes us feel bad or anxious, then the advice is to have as little to do with them as possible. Block them on your phone, unfriend them on social media. I take the same approach with technology and online forms. They make me feel anxious, so I block them out of my mind. It's not a technique I can apply across the board; sometimes there's no getting away from it. I don't think the tax man would be particularly sympathetic to my perspective. But if it doesn't seem absolutely necessary then I'll do everything I can to avoid it.

'I don't know much, Louise, but I'll give you everything I've got. The twins were in a hotel with their mum because a fight had broken out in the women's refuge, where they were staying after being removed with the mother from the familial home.'

'It sounds as if they've been through quite a bit of drama,' I say diplomatically, though my first thought, rather judgementally I'm afraid, is that the twins' mum might be a bit violent if she's been fighting in a refuge centre. Having spent a formative part of my youth in less salubrious parts of the South coast, a picture arises in my mind and an accompanying phrase, 'rough as guts'. I don't know what the etymology is, but I'm imagining alcoholism, and potentially challenging children. I've looked after children from some of the toughest and roughest families imaginable, although so far none of them have called their children 'Max' and 'Mia'. Those names don't quite fit the vision I'm creating. Nothing much is adding up. I feel a bit lost at sea. I think deep down I probably still want to be on holiday, and wonder what I've let myself into by agreeing to take them.

'The reason they're being moved so far from London is that there's a drastic shortage of foster carers in London right now, and keeping the twins together was paramount, though it made it much more difficult for them to be fostered in their local area.'

That certainly rings true. It's what I keep hearing about in relation to practically every county or city in the land. We're a long way from London, though, so they're being removed from everything they know. I realise that we're in a privileged position to be able to take in two rather than one more child.

Moira carries on, doing her bit to butter me up. 'So it goes without saying that we're just so grateful to you for taking in twins. And I'm sorry I don't have more details for you at the moment. I'll let you know when I do.'

I try to focus on the positives. It's exciting to have twins. We've never looked after twins before. But they're going to generate an awful lot of washing, I suspect. I put another load of holiday washing on while I'm still talking to Moira. It barely makes a dent in the pile.

I don't dwell on that, and instead jump on to my laptop and begin researching twins. I soon realise that there are so many more questions I should have asked. I've heard of identical twins, but a quick Google gets me into the realm of fraternal twins, and conjoined twins. Blimey, there's a world of twindom out there that I wasn't aware of. I need another coffee as I try to process the science. Fraternal twins are the result of the fertilisation of two separate eggs with two different sperm during the same pregnancy. Fraternal twins may not have the same sex or appearance. They share half their genomes, just like any other siblings. Conjoined twins are twins that are born with their bodies physically connected.

I realise how little I know, and have my first tiny doubt that I might not be the right person for this job. I push it aside. The bunk beds, probably already on their way back from IKEA, won't be the solution if that's the case. That reminds me, I didn't check with Moira or Bea if we can get our money back for the bunk beds. I'll follow that up later. I already know it's going to be an expensive trip.

I read on. Conjoined twins occur once in every 50,000 to 60,000 births. Approximately 70 per cent of conjoined twins are female, and most are stillborn. Okay, very unlikely. So, my money is on fraternal or identical twins.

Sometimes I wish that they'd provide us with photographs of the children coming to our homes. The rationale for not doing this is that foster carers, who start each placement as temporary, may pick and choose the children according to what they look like. It's another of children's social cares' unfathomable 'great' ideas. Like the one that was in *Vogue*, when I was a child in care myself, that reminded foster carers not to hug a looked-after child. There was specific advice: if you do wish to initiate physical contact, 'stand behind them and put your hands on their shoulders.' How bloody weird and threatening is that? It was when I was on the receiving end of it, anyway. Some of these sociologists were, in my humble opinion, a little out of touch.

Bizarrely, it's only people who *potentially* want to adopt a child that can have a look at a photograph. I wonder if potential adopters, who could be any of us foster carers, see the photograph and process that image with no bias at all. It seems unlikely. I wrote a book called *How to Adopt a Child* and, sometimes, I felt like I was writing about *Alice in Wonderland* when it came to some of the rationale for adoptions. One gem, for example, was that until recently, the authorities used to say adopted children were not allowed to stay in contact with their foster carers. The idea was that a 'clean break' was the healthiest approach. This seems to me to be a philosophy from the Dark Ages.

The reality is that I'd love to see a picture of the children coming into my care. I wouldn't be put off by their picture at all. If anything, I suspect I'd be even more excited. I know

I have been on the very rare occasions when a photograph has been available. It's not like dating sites where people put pictures up of themselves from ten years ago, filtered and flattering. But, as an artist, I'm used to observing faces. I like doing it. I'm interested in people. Of course I am, or I wouldn't be fostering.

I extricate myself from the black hole that is twins on the internet and make sure I keep an eye on the time. I know that the Allen crew will be tucking into the Swedish meatballs and marzipan slices right about now, and my tummy is beginning to feel jealous. I look in the post-holiday (and sadly quite bare) cupboards, and wonder if I have the right kinds of things to feed four-year-olds. I think back to what the boys ate at that age. As far as I can recall, they ate just about everything. I remember Vincent's nursery school reporting their shock when he had Szechuan egg curry in his lunch box. Both boys were weaned on Farley's Rusks and olives. Actually, I quite fancy a Farley's Rusk for lunch. It might be quite dangerous to have those back in the house again. But some children, like Lily, arrive at our home and find something as innocuous as non-frozen chicken nuggets from the cold counter too exotic for their taste buds. I decide I'll whip to the supermarket after lunch and cover all bases: fruit, cereals, beans, chips, maybe some microwave meals, pasta and, of course, pizza. At that age, they tend to like cheese and tomato, I'm sure. I make a list, then check my phone to see if Bea has sent an update. Nothing.

I'm pacing the kitchen like a cat on a hot tin roof. I always feel like this before the arrival of a new placement, and it's all doubled this time with it being twins.

I look at the phone once more and see a picture message from Jackson on WhatsApp. He's holding a new floor cushion and some sort of lamp for himself. Then one arrives of Vincent. He has a flat pack desk. Of course he does. And, uh oh, Lily looks like she has the whole store. Lloyd looks frazzled next to her, in spite of the wondrousness of a suntan.

I zip straight out to the shops. This used to be a relatively straightforward enterprise, but after our town's new regeneration scheme, the reality is that there's nowhere to park and businesses are folding as a result: 'regeneration' has had the opposite effect in practice. I manage to park as close as possible to the shops without still being in my own driveway. I also have to play the game of avoiding the traffic warden, so I keep my eyes peeled as I throw things into the boot. She's actually very nice until she gives me a ticket, which she has done a few times. Once was because the wind blew my paid parking ticket off the window area as I shut the boot. To add insult to injury, she'd chatted away to me as I was buying the ticket that day, but still wouldn't accept that I shouldn't have a fine. Today, I escape unscathed, mission complete. As I slam the boot shut, the phone goes off. It's Bea, with the twins onboard, and they're an hour away.

Quick, action stations.

Chapter Two

Everything is ready.

Lloyd and the children have phoned to say that they're also about an hour away, travelling from the opposite direction to Bea. I hope one of the parties hits some roadworks so that there isn't a simultaneous arrival at the house. I live in dread of frantic arrivals for new children. It's important to keep those first few moments as calm as possible. I walk the dogs to release some of their energy too. I sit and wait to hear from Mowra-Moira. I can't believe it. She tells me she's about an hour away too. Terrific.

I walk around the garden deadheading anything I can. I sweep the barbecue area and tidy the children's outdoor toy box. I'm not good with these kind of pockets of time that aren't long enough to do anything worthwhile. It feels like a waste of precious moments. I find myself rearranging my hair, gathering it back into a claw clip while I stare at myself in the hall mirror. I remember, when I was younger, older women would say, 'Oh, I never look in mirrors these days.' I understand it, but I make a conscious effort to make sure that I do. I'm not used to seeing my face tanned, but I give it a good check over for signs of ageing. I'm not afraid of ageing, as long as I can keep an eye on it and do it my way. I notice that there is a hair sprouting from underneath my chin. How delightful. I'll get rid of that when I'm near my tweezers. The hair on my body seems to be receding backwards. Lily is at that stage where her hair is pushing forwards. I haven't mentioned it to her, but she's developed a lovely monobrow. It's wonderful. I remember mine at her age. Now the hair has faded away.

I hear the sound of a car engine. I turn quickly. I've no idea in what order all the arrivals are going to cross the finish line that is our house. It's a white car, so I'm hoping that it's Lloyd and the crew. It is. The wheels have barely finished turning and I've already got the doors open, like we're in the aftermath of some dangerous heist.

The boot is bungeed-shut and looks as if half the shop is bulging out. Big boxes are strapped to the roof. That's the bunks.

'Hello darlings,' I say, but that's the niceties over and done with. 'You need to quickly get out and do what you need to do at speed. Max and Mia are on their way. They should be here any minute.'

The children know the drill. If we're honest, we quite like the drama. It's a good kind of drama, at least. The IKEA bounty is shoved quickly through the front door. The boys manoeuvre the bigger pieces of furniture and take them upstairs to the twins' room. Lily follows with various bits and pieces that were definitely not on the list, and the bulging blue IKEA bags tell me that those WhatsApp photos didn't tell the whole story. The allure of the marketplace has definitely beaten them on this occasion. Weak. Lloyd pulls out a pale blue watering can and offers it to me like it's the holy grail. I shake my head and try to avoid sneering. I would never have been suckered into such frivolous purchases. (I definitely would.)

I encourage Lloyd back outside to move the car so that Bea can park.

Next up is Moira, in her rather flashy Audi. As she makes an ordeal of clambering out, I realise she is rather short.

'Well, that is a super shiny car of fabulousness, isn't it?' I comment.

She looks straight back at me and says, 'I hate it.'

Life is nothing if not interesting. We'll get to the bottom of that little conundrum later.

I usher her inside and put the kettle on, explaining that we have just had an IKEA delivery and that Lloyd will put the beds up in a bit. I don't explain that the 'delivery' has been courtesy of my family.

'Lloyd, do you have the receipt?' I call out.

I've learnt to be ruthless about receipts in the era of pitiful teeny-weeny allowances that wouldn't cover basic living expenses in the 1970s, let alone half a century later. There is nothing clever or noble about not claiming what you are entitled to. I thrust the receipt into Moira's hand and smile, daring her to challenge.

She glances down at it and says, 'Yes, of course,' which she should, because the price of the bunk beds is a bargain £250. Lloyd's done well, until Lily comes in with another receipt, laughing. 'Oh dear, we nearly forgot the mattresses. We had to go back in. That's why you got the watering can.'

The mattresses were £165 each, so the total just on beds for the twins is £580. That's a bit steep but, if we didn't claim the money, we'd be working for free for nearly a month, and everyone's been at pains to tell me how brilliant it is that we are able to take in twins. In the grand scheme of things, the authorities are still getting a bargain.

'We'll see what we can do,' she says to the additional expenditure, which isn't exactly in the affirmative, but also isn't a 'no'.

I fix a coffee for Moira and we're sitting at the large pine kitchen table drinking it when there is a knock at the door.

Here we go. My tummy does a little flutter. Moira stands and pats down her hair. To date, I've not met a social worker who doesn't also get a flutter of excitement as the new children arrive at the door. Allen household children know exactly what to do. The boys hang back until much later, so as not to overwhelm. Lily also waits, but comes in first, usually after half an hour or so, because she is a foster child herself and knows how to welcome newcomers to that role.

Lloyd puts the dogs in the garden and shuts the backdoor. Dotty is most put out.

I head to the front. Bea stands tall, imposingly close to my front door, blocking its frame so that there's a slightly awkward, too-intense moment as we encounter each other for the first time, and I find myself taking a step backwards. Nobody likes being wrong-footed, but it's particularly disconcerting in your own home. I take an instant dislike to her, but also, bizarrely, discover myself holding out my hand to shake hers – not something I usually do.

Then I hear myself say, 'Hello there,' in the politest manifestation of my voice, at a pitch that barely sounds like me, and just about manage to resist the impulse to curtsey. I'm not quite sure why she's having this effect on me. I'm not easily intimidated these days, especially not by social workers. I take a closer look. She has long, dark hair that hangs wildly around her shoulders, as if she's just returned from a bracing walk across the moors rather than stepped out of her car. Her waist is cinched in by, wait, are those actually riding jodhpurs? And shiny boots right up to her knees. Well, it's certainly a look. And not one that I've ever encountered in children's social care. Her appearance suggests that she'd be more at home completing the Badminton Horse Trials than supporting in the neediest homes. My resolve to dislike her intensifies when she frowns dismissively at my proffered hand. In the space of about five seconds, she's managed to make me feel very foolish indeed. She strikes me as being full of herself.

Two young children stand slightly behind her. They are clearly terrified as she nudges them through the front door. Poor little things. Their heads are down and their bodies are stiff.

Bea is evidently a hearty, ruddy, outdoorsy type, and these little cherubs don't seem to have a trace of that in them; they are pale city kids who are probably used to a local park at best. It's a total clash of worlds, and makes me wish that Bea would just buzz off and let me get on with it. But of course there are all sorts of formalities to deal with before that can happen.

I nudge boisterous Bea towards the kitchen so that I can hang back to speak to the children. Lloyd plays his part impeccably, gesturing to Bea to follow him. He has her measure after decoding my eye chat. That's what years of marriage can do. Strip down the need for any verbal communication. I make my eyes wide, then narrow them to squints and back again, blinking rapidly. It acts like a kind of Morse code, though I wouldn't be able to explain the cipher to anyone else.

She clippity-clops down the hallway, like the horse I imagine she wishes she'd ridden to get here, leaving me to get a proper look at Max and Mia.

I bend down so that I'm at the children's level and not towering above them. They are standing tightly together.

'Hello,' I say. 'I'm Louise and I expect you've had a long, confusing day already. You're going to come and stay with me for a little while, and we are going to do our best to make that as easy as possible for you. Now, you've had a long journey. I expect you need the loo first, don't you?'

They shake their heads in unison. They are surprisingly well dressed. That might even be a Moschino jacket that Max is wearing, and they don't come cheap. This is unlike the majority of foster children who arrive here, but I can still smell sweat emanating from them as a result of the stress they've been under. They each have thick, reddish hair, which emphasises their pale skin, and they both look drawn and tired. My heart aches for them.

In the kitchen, Bea has thrown her somewhat scuffed bag onto the kitchen table. It does little to improve my first impression of her. If this had been one of the children I would have said, 'Bag off please, that's been on the floor, this is where we eat!' Perhaps I should.

As I walk behind Bea to get to the kettle, I notice a little piece of straw poking out of her thick, unruly hair. Novelists sometimes describe characters as having a 'mane' of hair. I've never understood that until now. She has a centre parting. I remember, as a child, thinking I wanted hair that did that. I used to envy the singer Crystal Gayle and actress Ali MacGraw from the 1970 film *Love Story*. But Bea's hair is far wilder and could probably do with some conditioner. Meow! I need to rein myself in. On the other hand, it's kind of insulting. A visit to a new foster carer doesn't seem worthy of a change of clothes or brush through the hair, as far as this woman is concerned.

I encourage the children to have a drink and, using more Allen silent communication, I eye Lloyd, then nod upwards, to have him text Lily to come down. I think we need her services far sooner than we expected.

Lily absolutely thrives on being the ambassador of the foster family. She excels at being the family meet-and-greeter. It takes no time at all for Lily to appear in the kitchen.

'Hello,' she says, in the jolly children's television presenter voice she reserves specifically for occasions such as this one, and that we never seem to hear at any other time. She has in her possession the iPad. It's an old trick of hers to break the ice with TikTok videos of kittens doing daft things and similar fluffy nonsense. She can already tell that I'm on a mission. Before I have the chance to turn round, she has the twins in her spell. She ushers them out of the back door to meet Dotty and Douglas.

Dotty first deploys her 'Halt! Who goes there?' bark, then very quickly switches to her high pitched 'woowooo' that she only does for children. I lean across the sink to catch a glimpse out of the window, and see two hesitant but curious children standing on the garden path while Lily re-enacts her best impersonation of a Butlins Redcoat. I notice that Bea is tucking into her coffee and biscuits and hasn't spotted that the children are outside. Will this woman do nothing to redeem herself? So far, she hasn't stopped talking about herself. There is a close to zero chance that we're going to get on.

I stand by the sink to keep an eye on the children. They are still standing as if they're stuck together. Lily is trying to get them to throw a ball for the dogs. I'm not sure why, because this is a fruitless exercise. Dotty and Doug come at the end of a long line of dogs in my life, and I made a conscious decision not to teach these two to fetch a ball or stick. Been there, done that, and I don't need my life to be even more demanding than it already is. The twins, though, stare down at the ball on the ground as if it has just fallen out of the sky.

I tune back into the meeting in my kitchen. Boring but necessary conversations about paperwork. I zone out until I hear 'West Brompton'. I know this area because when I was a fashion stylist, a life that seems a century or so ago now, my editor lived with her husband in an enormous house there. It was beautiful. She had two children who I was fascinated by, because I had never, until then, known people with 'staff', let alone children with staff. The children had a Spanish nanny, who was very quiet. The makeup artists and I naturally assumed the husband was having an affair, because that's what nannies were for back then, wasn't it? I remember the children were very rude and spoilt, but knowing what I know now, I might be tempted to reframe that and suggest that the children were neglected and consequently living without healthy boundaries.

'West Brompton?' I say. 'That's a pretty well-heeled part of the world.' It strikes me now that 'Max and Mia' sounds like a fashion label. I turn my head to look out at the children once more, and Lily is doing brilliantly. I can see lots of enthusiastic pointing and gesticulating, though I can't hear what she's saying. The dogs have wandered off. The twins still haven't moved an inch apart from one another. My curiosity is really piqued as to what has happened to these children, if they belong to the West Brompton world that I know. This is going to be interesting.

Back to the meeting. Bea is still talking. She has ignored my interjection entirely and is giving her thoughts about the twins. I take it all with a pinch of salt. She met them five hours ago and, for most of that time, they have been in the back of her car. Now she's the world's authority on them. 'They're lovely children,' she says, 'polite and happy.' I'd substitute 'scared' and 'bewildered' and probably add 'missing their mum.'

'I don't expect they'll cause you any problems.'

No, you wouldn't, I think. *Because they're not living in your house.*

Perhaps my thoughts aren't very well disguised, because Moira gives me a look which warns me not to speak. She's already tuning in to the Allen household communication methods, it seems.

'Right, well then, if that's everything covered then I guess we'd better let the Allens get on,' I hear her say.

Oh goody, and now we can begin our work. 'Bye, Bea,' I call out and, for some reason, it sounds funny and I have to stop myself from laughing out loud. I think Moira clocks on to this too, because she takes charge of ushering her out into the hallway.

'Enjoy the rest of your day,' Moira calls.

'Oh, no chance of that, I've missed what I should have been doing,' Bea says, cheerfully. 'It was supposed to be my day off,' she adds. Perhaps I should cut her some slack. She certainly didn't look dressed for work. Perhaps she has been busy doing a good thing instead of what she really wanted to be doing today. I'm quick to judge people sometimes. But it's easy to do when young lives are at stake.

After showing Bea out, Moira makes her own departing noises. 'I hope you all have a lovely evening; call me if you need me.' It sounds reassuring, but I know that it's an empty offer. The mobile number I have is a work phone which she won't answer past 5pm, and who can blame her? Setting boundaries is all about looking after your mental health, and social workers, like foster carers, have more and more pressure put on them. So, a cup of tea and some of those rather interesting biscuit cake things in a large bag that Lloyd bought from IKEA can go a long way. By now, the boys are lurking at the top of the stairs. I can see them in one of the hallway mirrors. They'd never make good spies. I think they want the biscuit cakes too.

I close the door behind Moira and hear a commotion from the garden. Lily has run in from the garden.

'Louise, Louise, they hit me.' Uh oh, that is an astonishingly quick disintegration from the scenes I beheld a few moments ago. I hold Lily by the shoulders and look into her face. She is genuinely upset. I head towards the window to see where they are.

'Okay, Lily. Tell me exactly what happened.'

'I was being nice to the children. I got the teepee and beach tent out of the shed because all children like playing in them. I thought it would be fun. But the boy, Max, started hitting me, and then the other one joined in. What did I do?'

I look at her arms. Both are red where she has been struck and there is another mark on her right leg.

I give her a hug. 'I'm sure you didn't do anything.' I think she's in shock, because the tears begin to flow now.

My boys come flying into the kitchen, not to help their poor distressed foster sibling but instead to see what is going on, what the drama is. The boys stick their heads around the corner of the conservatory. The twins are throwing the teepee across the lawn. I watch Jackson's expression darken. Even though he is far too old to want to go in a teepee, it was once his pride and joy. He had it in his bedroom when he was little and kept his teddies in there.

'Don't worry,' I say. 'We'll sort this out. Stand back.'

I open the back door, ignore what they're actually doing, or at least avoid directly drawing attention to it, and defuse the situation by calling out, 'Max, Mia! Time for a wee and a biscuit!' The magical power of the word 'biscuit' rarely fails. They stop enacting what seems like a petty act of violence against the teepee. I don't get the sense that they are actually violent. They clamp themselves back together and the whole scene seems quite heart-wrenching.

'Welcome, my little friends,' I beam, and invite them into the kitchen. Lily wisely stands to one side as the boys grab the new IKEA biscuits and put them on a plate. The rule is 'AFSB' or 'Allen Family Stand Back' whenever we have guests. Let others go first. I'm a stickler for manners.

Max and Mia come in and Vincent offers them a place at the kitchen table. My children have seen this before, and whenever there is an incident involving a foster child, my mantra is to 'see it from their point of view'. I don't quite know what's going on here yet. Perhaps they aren't used to sharing if they've come from a wealthy family background. Perhaps they're used to having a teepee each; I don't know.

I switch the radio on, and jolly music fills the room. Max and Mia gulp down a big glass of squash each and happily tuck into the biscuits.

Jackson heads out to the garden and begins brushing off his teepee. I see his mouth moving. He's talking to the dogs. They have evidently decided to stand well back from Max and Mia. Like the children, they are very used to unusual behaviour. I watch as Jackson carries the teepee and beach tent back to the shed, and carefully stores them. A young man now. It's funny how you only see that in little snatched moments. I turn back to Max and Mia, who look as if butter wouldn't melt in their mouths. But something caused the bizarre teepee furore. What is it that lurks darkly in their past?

Chapter Three

While Lloyd, Jackson and Lily put up the bunk beds, and Max and Mia are settled with some drawing at the kitchen table, Vincent decides that he wants to do some baking. I am an avid viewer of the *Great British Bake Off*, but it's fair to say that I enjoy the stage set far more than the baking. I celebrate his desire to bake by sitting at the kitchen table scrolling through Facebook posts and raising my head occasionally to check on his measuring and mess-making. It therefore takes me a few precious moments to notice that he is holding the packet of flour a good two feet higher than the bowl as he tips it in.

'Vincent!'

But it's too late. Clouds of white powder now coat the kitchen utensils, food mixer, toaster and most of the hob. The floor looks like an establishing shot from *March of the Penguins*. My fault for not paying more attention. I openly chide myself for my own teenage behaviour, being lost in social media.

'Oh, but you're so not!' Vincent says, his tone incredulous.

'Not what?'

'Not being like a teenager. Only old people use Facebook.'

And that tells me.

I clean up and remind myself that this is what having children in your life is really like. Vincent puts the cakes in the oven and we set the timer.

In the hall are two suitcases, smart ones. There are also two Trunkis. They look different to the ones the boys used to ride around airports on; these must be the most up-to-date versions. I lug them up to the bedroom where the bunk beds are coming along nicely. Lily has chosen some rather fantastic children's bedding on their behalf and is busy wrestling a duvet into a green cover with bicycles on. A pale blue set with a cake pattern lies folded on a chair, awaiting its turn. I nod approvingly. 'Good choice! Maybe let them choose which one they each want. And which bed they'd each prefer to sleep in.'

'I *know*,' she says. I forget sometimes that she is just as adept, if not more so, as I am at this.

I turn my attention back to the suitcases. It takes me two trips to collect all four, as the larger cases are quite heavy. It's a pleasant surprise to have children arrive with a decent amount of stuff. All too often, we've had placements begin with a sorry half-filled bin liner of odds and sods. We've had some children turn up with nothing at all. I flick open the big cases. Both are well packed, with neatly folded piles of clean, good-quality clothing. There will be no need for me to raid my emergency supplies for these two. They have an entire wardrobe of beautiful clothes. Just then I smell burning.

'Vincent!'

I am expert at walking off and forgetting about things in the oven. Just because I am female and a mother doesn't automatically make me good at, or even vaguely interested in, baking. Vincent doesn't seem to have heard the timer either. I hear his feet skittering along the corridor as he hurtles towards the kitchen.

The twins are sitting quietly on the sofa, still engrossed in *Paddington 2*, which I put on for them. The film seems familiar to them, or perhaps it is the shots of London that they recognise, I'm not sure.

'Would you like to go and see your new beds?' I ask, my voice trying to suggest that this is an exciting development in the day.

They look so sweet together, but their enthusiasm doesn't match mine. They look tired. I naturally hold out my hand as I would for any child, and little Max takes my hand and Mia holds his. Our little human train travels through the hall and up the stairs towards their bedroom.

The duvets are laid out across a chair and half on the floor as if we're at the start of a sales pitch in a Turkish rug seller's shop. Max and Mia hold hands, hesitate, point, look at each other, change their minds, then confer for a moment. Mia chooses the cake duvet and bicycle pillow while Max picks up the cake pillow. Lily and I share an expression that acknowledges how sweet that little exchange is. We then set about installing the bedding, which is actually quite a trick, as both of them want the top bunk.

'Well, perhaps you can take turns.'

I say this knowing full well that it will probably not happen in practice, but it's another trick of the parenting trade: to let them feel that they have some control. At four years old and in their sorry circumstances, they may not have had control of much for some time.

We all have a lovely time sorting out the room and helping the twins to find new homes for all their things. Their cases really seem to have been lovingly packed. They have designer everything. Their little slippers are in Hamley's carrier bags. I become more and more curious as to where these two have really come from. Just what is their story? Lily squeals delightedly at their cute little outfits.

Drawers are quickly filled. Two-thirds of the way down Mia's suitcase, I spot an envelope. I go to the same spot in Max's, where a corresponding one nestles for him. Their names are written in nice ink on the front, almost like professional calligraphy. Sometimes, social workers want us to run everything by them; a letter or card such as this would have to be 'approved'. Not today. After being Bea'd, I have no desire to get back in touch with her until I absolutely have to.

I sit the children down on the bottom bunk and hand them the cards. Perhaps it's unprofessional, but sometimes our instincts are our best tools in this world. I don't think a poison pen letter or a lump of Semtex will be in either of these envelopes. The twins open their envelopes and their faces light up at the sight of the pictures. Mia has a pink fox on her card winking, and Max has a green frog croaking 'I love you' in a little speech bubble. They are clearly not accomplished readers.

'Would you like me to read you the messages?' I ask.

They smile and nod, settling further back into the bottom bunk, Max reaching for Mia's hand once more. I read out Max's first.

Darling Max, when you read this, you will be settling into your foster home. I am sorry that you are not with me and sorry that you feel sad, but I want you to know that things will get better and Mummy loves you to the moon and back. I will do everything I can to see you soon. Remember to eat all your vegetables. Love you, Mamma xxx

God, I'm a mess. I don't know if I have it in me to read Mia's. I straighten myself out and secretly try to wipe my tears away.

Dearest Mia, you will be settling into your foster home when you read this. I hope you are happy and that the people are kind.

I break off. It's no good. I'm crying again. Pull yourself together, Louise. *Mummy and Daddy are so sorry that this has happened, but I want you to know that I am doing everything I can to see you soon. Eat up all your vegetables. Look after each other. Love you, Mamma xxx*

The tears are really falling now. This is a reminder to all of us that, quite frankly, 'shit happens'. No matter what children's social care or judges say, many parents, whose behaviour is not good enough to look after their children, still love their children. Oh, these poor little dears. Their little faces look slightly happier after reading the messages. I suspect they have no idea why I'm crying.

'Shall I put your lovely cards on the windowsill, so you can look at them whenever you want?' I manage to say, which gives me a few valuable seconds to turn away and pull myself together. Thankfully, Vincent chooses that moment to interrupt, barging in proudly with a plate held aloft.

'Would you like to try out my cakes?'

Max and Mia's hands reach up towards the proffered delights enthusiastically, but I look at the clean duvet covers and pristine new beds and suggest that perhaps we'd better enjoy them downstairs in the kitchen.

I finish tidying away the last few things in each case, and then relocate my bright, enthusiastic voice to say, 'Let's go and try out these cakes then, shall we?'

Max reaches out to hold my hand. I can feel those pesky tears coming back again.

Vincent's cakes are surprisingly yummy, and provide the perfect distraction. We all enjoy them, and I have looked after enough children to know that if they make the food themselves, they will eat it and it will be amazing. The twins sit rocking in their chairs, eating and smiling as Jackson does his best to entertain them. I love this moment. I know it's very early days, but dare I say this looks like it could work?

Vincent seems to have used every dish and utensil that we possess, and I find myself clearing up the kitchen for a second time within an hour. Flour is plastered into nooks and crannies and, oh wait, is that flour on the *ceiling*?

Cleaning provides some time to think about what we might have for dinner. I pick up the children's referral and notice that they like pasta. I suspect that my macaroni isn't quite going to cut it. I wonder if they have their own table at Locanda Locatelli in London.

Who are these children? I think of all the celebrities they could possibly resemble, and my imagination goes into overdrive. There are enough high-profile individuals in the media who are embroiled in messy court cases – marriage breakdowns or drink and drug scandals – that fill the gossip columns. I wonder. Since I am yet to acquire a Michelin star, I select a couple of jars of pasta bake sauce from the cupboard. The red one, I think. I parboil the pasta, chuck it in a big dish with the sauce, and give it a generous sprinkling of cheese on top. I've remembered to preheat the oven. In it goes. I close the oven door with a flourish and convince myself that I am a domestic goddess.

I can hear Lily chatting away to the twins. She's earned her stripes today, that girl. The earlier teepee incident has clearly passed by now. She introduces Max and Mia to the 'soft toy' toy box. It's interesting to me that, even though teenage Lily is still a child herself in so many ways, she embraces the idea of looking after younger children so well. I remember a colleague from back when I taught at the university (or as we disparagingly called it then, 'da college knowledge') once talking about his rather large family. He had seven children and was firmly of the view that, if you only had one child, you had it tough because you had to do lots of work. If, on the other hand, you had multiple children like him, then they simply ended up looking after themselves. I suspect that he had a rather put-upon partner lurking in the background, and that she may very well have presented a different view but, as I watch Lily, I think there might be something in what he says.

Because there is so much pasta to bake, it takes a while and I have the best part of an hour to lay the table. That gives me plenty of time to locate the smaller glasses and toddler-sized cutlery for Max and Mia's little hands. They're the boys' old cutlery sets, which they were once very fond of. One set has fish at the end of the handles; the other has boats. I cut some fresh flowers for the table, stand back, a tea towel clutched to my chest, and inhale the atmosphere of a perfect family home, counting my blessings. The house feels lovely. Cosy, welcoming and full of love. Oh, I'm the full Ma Larkin this evening.

I walk to the door and begin calling out all the names: 'Jackson, Vincent, Max, Mia, Lily, Lloyd!' Quite the roll call. They tumble to assemble, apart from Lloyd, who has a habit of disappearing just before dinner and requires calling for a second time. Like most households, we've all settled on our favourite places at the table over time. It's not just the position at the table; each chair is a different style and colour. Nothing matches, each one is quite distinctive. This can lead to some awkward moments. It can sound petty when a new child comes to the table and I hear myself say, 'Sorry, love, Vincent sits there in the green chair' or 'Sorry, darling, that's Jackson's spot and his red chair' but these two choose to sit together on the two unused seats. Hooray! One less thing to deal with. They look at the cutlery sets, carefully arranged – and, just as with the duvet sets, they mix up the boats and fish so that they are sharing again. I make a mental note to make sure I set it up that way next time. Lily gives me the 'that's adorable' look again.

Max and Mia don't say much beyond 'please' and 'thank you', but they sit and eat nicely at the table, which is a good few steps ahead of some other children we have fostered. They are shy in their unfamiliar surroundings, but that's totally understandable. I'm happy that they are eating and seem relatively settled. Everyone eats their dinner – even Lloyd, who, on any other day, would likely moan about having to eat children's tomato pasta. Generally, he would rather have our dinner later with food that requires a drizzle of something delicately flavoured, rather than something that needs to be coated in a thick cheesy sauce to taste of anything. But the first night of a placement is crucial in establishing the right tone. The first night 'togetherness' is traditional and important. After that, life kicks back in and the children can be here and there: clubs, friends and so on.

I have to confess that, as time has gone on, Lloyd and I have veered towards a preference for different food a bit later in the evening so that we can have a glass of wine and a chat by ourselves. Otherwise, we probably wouldn't talk about anything other than this lot. But most conversations find their way back to the children anyway, even if we start out talking about something completely different. Lloyd regularly complains about it. 'Oh, there must be more to life. Remember when we used to talk about blah blah blah.'

I, on the other hand, see myself as a total realist, and tell him off for being miserable whenever he heads down this well-worn path of seeing the grass as having been greener in the past. I don't see the point in pining after another life while living this one. It's a waste of time as far as I am concerned. We are here in the now, so we might as well get on and live it.

It occurs to me as we finish eating that I have paid absolutely no attention to the care plan, and I'm not sure if the twins are going to school or nursery. When they all leave the table and the children go into the sitting room to play, I take a closer look at the paperwork. The care plan doesn't seem to know either. *Inquiries to be made by Louise regarding local school*, I read. Actually, no. Technically, that's Bea's job. I also notice on the care plan that Bea works for an independent fostering agency, rather than the local authority. It doesn't surprise me, but it isn't ideal – as I have a view on these organisations, and it's not one that would come with a five-star review on TripAdvisor. I look this particular organisation up and yes, it's one of the ones I don't like, because they are owned by venture capitalists. I'm not convinced (and that is putting it diplomatically) that venture capitalists, shareholders and offshore accounts provide the best way to look after our most vulnerable children and young people.

I read the care plan again, and it dawns on me that Bea has basically stitched me up to do her job. Hmm. She might have to do a little less mucking out stables and a little more mucking in with the logistics of what will happen to Max and Mia, as far as I'm concerned.

A commotion erupts from the sitting room, interrupting my train of thought.

By the time I reach the door of the sitting room, Jackson is holding a dog under each arm. 'Woah there, little ones,' I hear him say.

It looks as if a fight has broken out between the twins. They kick and shove each other across the floor. I bend down to be at their level, and just as I'm about to speak I get a whack across the back of my head.

Max and Mia stand in front of each other, red-faced and breathing heavily. They stare each other down, and then Mia says, with real venom, 'I hate you, you fucking arsehole.' To be fair, her pronunciation is excellent; Ts and Gs enunciated perfectly with no glottal stops. I'm not sure I've ever heard such beautifully executed swearing.

'Well, that's nice,' I say to try and distract the children, guessing that they must have picked this up from their parents. I'll ignore it, and assume that they're overtired. I notice the time. Nine o'clock is late enough for little people, especially after such a day of massive upheaval. I suspect that they may be about to pass from the safe zone into the 'oh nooo' zone.

I look at Jackson. 'It's okay. I'm sure Max and Mia are tired and need their beds. What a big day it has been for them with so many new people to meet and things to get used to.' I carry on in this vein as I encourage them upstairs to pick up their wash bags, which are pristine like everything else. I'm curious again. If their mother packed these, they have not been touched while the twins were in emergency foster care these past couple of days, so what were they wearing and using? They each have a wash bag, packed as if they were going on a little holiday. I get the toothbrushes out and take them to the bathroom. They are calm, and clean their teeth in a good mood, all hatred and 'fucking arseholes' apparently forgotten.

We're on our way back towards their bedroom to get their pyjamas on when Vincent appears in the hallway with his old copy of *The Very Hungry Caterpillar*.

'Ah, thank you, Vincent, that's lovely,' I say, smiling at his thoughtfulness.

Max and Mia climb into their respective beds, with Mia in the top bunk, for tonight at least. I pull over the comfy chair and settle myself in to read the book. 'In the light of the moon a little egg lay on a leaf,' I begin. By the time that the hungry caterpillar has popped out of the egg on Sunday morning and eaten through one apple on Monday, Max's eyes are glazing over and Mia is already asleep. I carry on reading anyway. I like the final part where he builds a small house that he calls a cocoon around himself before pushing his way out and emerging as a beautiful butterfly. It strikes me that poor little Max and Mia have some serious cocoon building to do over the next few days, weeks and months.

Chapter Four

Moira calls.

'How are you all? How did the first night go?'

I look out of the window with dread. Yesterday's sunshine is gone. The sky is a patchy collage of different greys. Some patches are heavy with rain. Rain which, to me, feels as if it has come from hell rather than the heavens. That's because our house sits on a floodplain in a village, where some poor decisions have been made to alleviate flooding, and ended up making things worse. I belong to a 'flood resilience' group on WhatsApp, made up of similarly affected households in the local area, and it is already busy this morning with messages piling in, pinging through Moira's words. The tension in the atmosphere, and the mood of the group, is palpable when the clouds hang this way. Things are very bad here. One day I know that the floods will cost someone their life.

I focus back on Moira. 'Yes, we're all good. Thanks for checking in. The twins seem to be settling in well, all things considered, but they have these strange flashpoints that result in sudden, erratic outbursts of anger. And it's peculiar. It verges on violence. Way beyond an ordinary tantrum. I don't know what the triggers are. I guess only time will tell.'

'I see. That doesn't sound good. What happens?'

'I'm not really sure. They seem to be calm and happy one minute, then they can turn on a sixpence to being aggressive and angry. I suppose they are only acting out what they saw at home, mimicking what they know. And they are so well spoken, but they have an extensive knowledge of swear words. I don't think they have the faintest idea what they mean, or that they're bad words. But it is strange. Do you know anything more about the parents and their situation?'

'I do. And you're probably not going to like this, but you need to take the children to a contact visit to see their mum, pretty much straight away.'

My first reaction, years ago, to an announcement like this would have been simple acceptance. I wouldn't have questioned it at all. I would simply do as I was told, having been brainwashed into a 'yes, sir' mentality, borne of the wish to be the best foster carer in the world. These days I am less accommodating. I don't want to jump at someone else's whim. I'm more like that old fart at the back of the workplace who mutters and grumbles at every initiative. Experience tells me that the very moment that the twins are settling into my house is not the same moment to see their mother. On the other hand, they are clearly missing her, and I don't know what's in their history. She may not have been the problem, or even part of the problem. I remind myself that I have no idea what has been going on for them.

I sigh. 'You're right, I don't like it. Have you seen or heard from Bea?'

In my head I make buzz sounds as I think about it. It's childish, but it makes me feel better. I notice, out of the corner of the view through the kitchen window, a tiny slash of blue in the sky. This is good news indeed. Suddenly my negativity lifts. I can put worries about the house and our safety to one side for the time being.

'Yes, the communication about the contact visit with their mother, Mrs Angelina Martell, came through her.'

I'll bet it did. But feeling less vulnerable and anxious about the floods makes me immediately more upbeat.

'Where, and what time?' I ask.

'I don't have all the details. Bea will be in touch sometime this morning. The idea is to travel to a location halfway between here and London. They will have contact for one hour.'

'You're joking.' My mood plummets again. 'So, what you're telling me is that I will have to drive for four hours just so they get an hour together? What the hell is the point in that? If we're going to do this, it should be done properly. The children are missing their mother badly, and that means that an hour isn't enough. It will do more harm than good.'

My voice seems to be rising in pitch. I feel very emotional on behalf of Max and Mia. For so many contact arrangements in the past, I've advocated for them to be reduced in frequency or shortened in length but, with Max and Mia, something is yelling at me that they need more time. They need to see their mum.

'I've just received an email from Bea as we've been talking, actually. It says that she will be out to see you on Thursday at 10am.'

I smile to myself and think cruelly, *oh yes, when she's finished at the stable perhaps*. I wonder if she will be wearing jodhpurs and riding boots again. I'm almost looking forward to seeing her to find out if I am right about the horse-riding – or perhaps she just fancied a roll in a haystack that day.

'You're copied into that email, but I know you won't have seen it.'

She's right. She knows that I haven't yet signed up to the new email system that comes with our county email address. I've got three email addresses already, including Google Mail. I hate the assumption that everyone is happy to keep learning new systems at the drop of a hat. I'm not. I have so much else to do, and most of it is more interesting than learning a new email system. I'll resist for as long as possible. Particularly since I've also heard that the county councils are giving the new email addresses to external organisations that they have commissioned to support foster carers. I think this is a way round the data protection regulations, GDPR. I'm critical of how and what kind of information is shared around in the system. Often, in the case of a new placement, I want to know more, but equally, I'm concerned about who knows what. A foster carer I know well received an allegation. It was unsubstantiated, but by the end of the day an external company, who she didn't even know she was signed up to, had called her, already knowing all about the allegation. They are definitely not having my email address if I can help it. Moira asks me every now and then, because foster carers who have not signed up for the new address get chased. We have the same conversation each time. I know from her responses that she isn't unsupportive, and would probably be doing exactly the same thing if she was in my position. She asks the question, ticks the box to say it's been asked, and we carry on being human.

We change the subject. I tell Moira that I will contact the local schools and see if the twins can get into a reception class. They can begin from the September after their fourth birthday, so they're of school age. I also remind her that I'm not prepared to go further than my area as I will be expected to drive, and the last time I looked, the petrol allowance was the same as when I worked at the university. That is a long time ago now.

'It should be Bea's job, but—'

Moira cuts me off. She is starting to know me well. 'Okay. Let me know how you get on.'

Even though it's the weekend, and I don't expect to hear back straight away, I email the heads of four local primary schools, let them know my news about Max and Mia and explain that they could probably benefit from reception or nursery places as soon as possible. I know I could. In my other working world, I've just had my first children's book accepted by a publisher. The illustrations take a long time to produce, and I can't run around after these little angels all day, every day. I need some uninterrupted time during the day to be able to meet my deadlines.

Hats off to the parents of twins. Any more than that, triplets even, and I think I'd have to seek medical help. I think that Max and Mia are gorgeous but, blimey, they are already intense work. They have a simmering kind of anger that isn't far from surfacing at any moment, though so far no further major outbursts. Both of them also wet the bed last night, which hasn't done much for my washing pile woes. I didn't mention it to Moira because it wasn't anywhere in the paperwork that it was a problem. I'm assuming that they were overtired, overstimulated and overwhelmed by being in a new environment. It doesn't matter much, because they have smart new mattress covers on the bunk beds.

None of those things are particularly problematic on their own. I've had plenty worse to deal with over the years. It's just the constant feeling of 'double trouble', the way they both seem to need things at exactly the same moment, so

I always feel as if I'm being torn in two. Or that life would certainly be far easier if I could clone myself.

Both were up early this morning, so that precious pocket of the day is no longer mine, and that also makes a difference, adding to the feeling of relentlessness.

I let the older kids enjoy a lie-in. They'll be back at school tomorrow and normal life will resume after the excitement of a holiday abroad and new foster siblings. I decide to brave it and take the dogs up to the top fields for a walk, along with Max and Mia. Dotty and Douglas are still wary of the twins, but they all need to get used to each other. I bought Lily a wildflower pocket book a little while ago, but it hasn't moved from the kitchen table. I decide that I'll take it with us, along with some water and a few little snacks. The hill up to the big fields and woods is quite steep and they only have little legs.

We set off at quite a pace and they don't seem to mind. We reach the top in good time, after lots of encouragement from me to keep going at the steeper bits. The dogs are thrilled to be back here. They've probably missed this walk while we've been away. Having been looked after by Millie and Mitch, my step-daughter and her partner, they seem to be very happy to return to old routines. I let them off the leads as soon as we get to the track. They're desperate to explore and leave all their little doggy messages up there.

The children seem to love it too, and I have another Ma Larkin moment as they charge into the field, arms outstretched, like something from *Swallows and Amazons*. I always smile when I see children and dogs run in fields. Witnessing others act out the sense of freedom that they are experiencing makes me warm inside. Every living thing –

animals and humans – has a right to that feeling. It's better than money or anything materialistic.

They run and run and I can't stop smiling. As we walk through the woods, I show them a picture of a flower in Lily's book and ask them to find it. The dogs seem better with them after we get into the woods, less wary. Perhaps it was their outbursts of anger that worried them.

Mia is successful and finds a flower. She picks the head off the stem before I can remind her not to pick the flowers, but no one is here to see, so I don't say a word. She holds the flower to the picture in the book.

'Look, Louise!'

I know it is no match at all, but Mia's so excited about her find that it's not what she needs to hear.

'Wow, Mia, good spot!'

This makes Max more ambitious to find his own flower. He comes back from pacing out three square metres, looking down intently at the forest floor, clutching a piece of long grass. I quickly flick through the book to find anything that looks green and say, 'Wow Max, you have sharp eyes, too. Good work!' Perhaps this is terrible parenting, given that they've found nothing much at all, but I prefer to think of it as kindness and confidence-building. They are so happy with their horticultural prowess. The dogs pick up on it too, with their wagging tails and weird sneezing that they seem to do when they're happy.

As we get towards the bottom of the hill, my rural idyll rapidly evaporates when Max tries to take Doug's lead from me.

Thwack. Mia wallops Max. 'Take that!'

I don't quite see what happens, but it's some kind of retaliation, and not without force. Before I can intervene, the two of them have an almighty scrap, and the effing and jeffing begins again. One of my fellow dog walkers, who I regularly see on this route, looks at me with a raised eyebrow as I try to break them up.

'Looks like you've got your hands full there, Louise,' she says, cheerfully, as she walks by with Barnie, her beautifully ageing black Labrador.

When we get in, I notice that Mia's lovely pinafore has a tear right up one side. I take her upstairs to change while Max goes into the sitting room to play. He is already confident and comfortable in the house, it seems. Mia though, seems sad.

'Cuddle?' I say, tentatively. She leans in to me, and this is the first cuddle we have. The poor child is most definitely in need of a huge cuddle in my opinion, and has been for some time, so I pick her up and point her towards the bedroom window, where we can see Doug and Dotty chasing each other around the garden. Suddenly, it turns a bit nasty, and Dotty starts on Douglas with a bit of a snarl. Uh oh, what dreadful timing. But Mia points at the dogs, then looks back at me and says, 'Like Max and Mia,' with a little resigned shrug.

What a perceptive girl. Thank the lord for two daft dogs. At least she has a sense that sometimes siblings can fight. Still, the way Max and Mia go at it is certainly not normal.

The rest of the afternoon is quiet. We have a lovely easy lunch of fruit and sandwiches. Because of the age of the twins, I made a prudent purchase of some Dairylea spread when I did my whip round the shops yesterday. You might think I'd brought in the crown jewels to see the way the other children react. One tub has almost been demolished. I'll have to add double that to the shopping list. Perhaps the older ones are nostalgic for a taste from their own childhoods. The novelty will probably wear off soon.

Max and Mia snooze on the floor cushions in the sitting room, worn out from their walk and fight. I take full advantage of the few moments of freedom this offers and nip to my studio to check my emails. There is an email from Bea with the contact arrangements. Next Thursday, from 1–3pm in Salisbury. I smile to myself and think, *well done, Moira.* She's managed to wangle two hours and pushed the visit back a few days, giving them a little bit longer to settle in. Good on her.

Over the years I've learnt not to say anything about a contact visit like this until the day itself, when I know it will definitely happen, and not be prevented by a bureaucratic intervention or a simple change of heart. I am fairly convinced that if Max and Mia see their mum and it is a positive experience, it will help them so much. While they definitely have anger issues, nothing about these children makes me think that they are unloved. I'm keen to meet their mother myself and, if I'm honest, get to the bottom of what's going on. I think carefully about the logistics, wondering if it would be better to drive or get the train. I look at the price of train tickets. I'm keen to turn it into a bit of an adventure, and to differentiate it from the hours that the children spent stuck in the back of Bea's car getting all the way to us from London. I email Bea back, copying in Moira.

While I'm washing my hands, I notice that my tan has faded far too quickly. That little Greek break that we only returned from last week feels like a lifetime ago, and looking after these two cherubs is exhausting.

Chapter Five

The first night it happened, I thought it was because the twins were really tired, but Max and Mia wet their beds on the second night, too. I wash the bedclothes again, putting it down to them feeling anxious and everything still being so new. On the third day, I go out and buy night-time pull-ups. It's a tricky one because, generally, I'd rather stick with it and wake them up when I go to bed to get them to use the loo, rather than treat them as babies. I hold on to the idea that this is simply a temporary measure and maybe, if they see their mum, it will help with the anger and bedwetting issues. It's not their fault and I make no fuss whatsoever about it. We just keep bobbing along in the mornings. I've known parents and foster carers that shout at their children about bed-wetting, and even, in some cases, punish their children for something they aren't able to control. I remember attending a training session at the start of my fostering career, where the speaker was talking about soiling. A male delegate, who I'd already pegged as being a bit of a twit, piped up.

'If they do that in my house, they'll have to strip the bed themselves and learn how to use the washing machine.' I hope he wasn't approved to be a foster carer. I guess it depends how desperate they are.

The bigger children are settling back into the routine of school life once more, and the next morning, as soon as the older children have left for school, I set Max and Mia up on the floor in my studio with a roll of wallpaper lining paper and a large pack of crayons. I put on Vincent's old and much-loved *Winnie the Pooh* CD, narrated by Stephen Fry. It seems that the twins find his voice as soothing and reassuring as I do. Still in their pyjamas, they are happily engrossed in their task, which gives me a few minutes to jump on to my email and chase the schools to see if there are any spaces available for the twins. I didn't expect to hear over the weekend, but we're a few days into the new half term now, and I know that by law, looked-after children are given priority for placements, and rightly so. I believe that children of parents in the forces and traveller children have a similar priority, ahead of children who already have siblings in a particular school. Sadly, many of our local schools come under the banner of 'pay or pray', in other words: private or faith schools. We're certainly not paying, and children in these priority groups usually don't have the opportunity to pretend to go to church and demonstrate an appropriate level of faith in the run up to admissions. I don't want to pull any kind of legal card. I hate enforcing what I know on good people, unless I have to. So, I'm thrilled when Debbie, the head of Hawfinch Primary, messages me to say that she will have spaces for both children, one in each of their two reception classes, since it is the school's policy to separate twins if they can.

I'm impressed. I hadn't even thought about that side of things. She explains that the idea behind putting them in separate groups is to help them thrive independently and understand their own identity. I can see why this might be important. In the short time they've been with us, I've noticed that Max generally seems like the more dominant one, and they are clearly competitive. I can also see, just from the drawings they are doing now in front of me, that they may well have different learning needs. Mia seems to have stronger fine motor skills and is much more delicate and measured in her approach, compared to her brother. They distract each other too, which doesn't bode well, but I also see the way that they operate as a team when they need to. I think the school's policy might be useful in this particular situation, to help break the less helpful patterns of behaviour that we've witnessed so far.

The problem is one of timing. Debbie has space for one of the twins in two weeks' time, and then we would have to wait a little longer, approximately two more weeks – so a month in total – for the other one to start. This is less than ideal, and is going to be hard in all sorts of ways. I see paintings and illustrations, already imagined for my children's book, evaporate, and the publisher's deadlines sail away. Still, it's better to have those dates in the calendar than to remain on tenterhooks, waiting to hear.

'Great,' I say, even though it isn't quite.

We've made it to Friday night at the end of a long week. The older children have survived their return to school. Our new arrivals have survived their first week in the Allen household, with relatively little upset. We've started the process of getting the twins into school. We have made some kind of order from all the chaos, though it still feels chaotic. For a moment, though, the children are all settled together in the television room. This is no mean feat. We had to overcome the initial moans and groans at having to return to a U-certificate film to accommodate Max and Mia. *Toy Story* is a perennial favourite, a crowd-pleaser that offers something for everyone. Even Jackson and Vincent have been persuaded to forgo something darker, moodier and gun-laden in favour of seeing Woody and Buzz Lightyear go head-to-head. It's not quite *Alien versus Predator*, but it will do for all of us. There's a nostalgic value that cuts across the age range in the room.

Ordinarily, I'd probably wait until the little ones are in bed to have a drink, but Lloyd has already poured me an enticing glass of red and it would be churlish to refuse.

I wander back into the sitting room with my glass to enjoy Woody and Buzz team up to escape the clutches of mean kid Sid, and perch on the end of the sofa surveying the scene, both on screen and off.

Max and Mia are curled up and turned slightly towards each other, mirroring each other's movements subconsciously. Max has his right thumb in his mouth, Mia her left. I know that dentists will discourage thumb-sucking at this age, but my goodness they look cute.

I don't really notice Mia move.

I think I'm side-tracked by Buzz zooming around the screen in super-speedy loop-the-loops, when all of a sudden she's by my side.

'I think you've had enough of that fucking wine, Louise,' she says.

Before I can stop her, she has hurled the wine glass and its contents at the sitting-room wall with enough force to break the glass as it catches the bottom frame of a painting hanging there.

None of us can do anything other than look on in shock as the red liquid trickles down the wall into the pile of smashed shards on the carpet, like pooling blood.

'Not much of a U certificate in here after all,' Vincent quips after a moment, which at least serves to break the horrible tension in the room.

'I think, perhaps, we're a little overtired at the end of the week,' I say, ushering Mia towards the hallway. 'So, let's get you ready for bed, shall we?'

Mia nods meekly, as if those words couldn't possibly have come out of her mouth. Her hands hang limply by her sides, so incapable of that kind of anger that it would be possible to believe we all imagined it if it weren't for the evidence on the wall and floor.

I have no idea what caused the outburst. But Mia meant it when she threw that glass, that's for sure. It has to have been the glass itself rather than the film that triggered the reaction, I'm sure of it. I'm reminded of the bizarre moment with the teepee on the day they first arrived, and the 'quaint' swearing exchange. This was much less quaint but no less strange.

The rest of the weekend flies by and suddenly we're in to the second week of the placement. I'm wishing the days forward, because it's clear to me that Max and Mia need to see their mother. I think about those beautiful little cards, still sitting on the windowsill in their bedroom. Bea confirms all the details for my meeting with Mrs Angelina Martell. I bet she is thinking about nothing else but seeing her children. I try to build up an image of her with the scant information I have. The only other Angelina I know of was once married to Brad Pitt. So I'm imagining a beautiful American, but perhaps she is of Spanish or Italian origin. The children have reddish hair, so I wonder about which side of the family that comes from. I know very little about their dad, not even a name. This is not a mainstream foster situation, whatever a mainstream foster situation might be. But I detect something else going on.

After dinner on Tuesday, I sit down with Lloyd to talk through my idea of taking Max and Mia on the train. He agrees that it's a good one, and offers to take us to the station. I plan a trip to the supermarket to get plenty of snacks, since experience tells me that nothing will be provided when we arrive.

On Wednesday, I spontaneously decide to take Max and Mia to the beach. There are many to choose from that aren't too far away. I have the south-west coastline at my fingertips; well, via the car, at least. The weather is quite fresh and autumnal, but nonetheless I feel that a change of scenery will be good, and time on a beach is great for children. All that lovely fresh air makes even the most resistant of sleepers drop off.

I keep seeing the different ways that Max appears to be the dominant one out of the two. I notice that he tends to choose their games and takes the lead in their dynamic. Mia usually reacts to his behaviour. I wonder if he was first or second out. He is physically strong but, having said that, Mia can definitely hold her own despite being generally placid. And she doesn't hold back from defending herself. I hate to say it, but sometimes Max feels like a little bit of a bully. I have to come to a decision soon about which one starts school first, and I'm drawn to the idea that it should be Max, for that reason. As soon as I think I'm committed to that decision, I change my mind again. If Max is already at school, he will have the upper hand over Mia even more than he already does. I keep reversing my decision. Mia should go first and establish herself. She'll also get a chance to make friends and have something new to talk about when she comes home. It will be more important for her than for Max, allowing her to have the limelight for a change. I think it will do Max a world of good to have to get used to even just a month of not being the top dog. I think I'm getting closer to the right choice. I don't want to get this wrong and, ideally, they should start on the same day – but life just isn't ideal, or people like me would not be foster carers.

Our impromptu beach day is a success and, as I'd hoped, both children are exhausted by the outing and almost fall asleep at the table in the evening. I take them upstairs to get ready for bed slightly early, determined to get through the bedtime routine fast this evening. So much is going on and I haven't had a chance to sit down with the others about their homework yet – or, in Vincent's and Jackson's case, their lack of homework. The school have emailed a 'polite notice to parents' reminding us of the requirements, which instantly makes me feel guilty and as if I'm a failure, no matter how polite it is. It is also a timely reminder that, even in the early stages of a new placement, I must focus on the balance in the house and make sure that my birth children, as well as my foster children, get the attention they need. As far as Max and Mia are concerned, there has been no reference to, and certainly no repeat of the wine glass incident or the swearing, but Lloyd and I have made sure that we're not drinking anything. If and when we do, it'll take place after Max and Mia are in bed.

I'm a woman, wife and mother, so pretty much even the act of moaning has the effect of making me feel like I'm failing.

Speaking of failure, I have no answer for why the other children have decided to forget all their learnt behaviour about keeping the bathroom tidy. Damp towels are strewn across the floor. Toilet roll is unravelled across the towels. Toothpaste is stuck to the sink and – my biggest bugbear – wee on the floor. Seriously, the boys are old enough to get this. It's not difficult. I know that in the mornings they are still dozy, and taking aim might be less easy, but this level of carelessness is not necessary. I turn Max and Mia away from the bathroom and get out clean pyjamas.

'Now, I would like you to get changed into your pyjamas and put on your own pull-ups while I go and clean up the bathroom. Can you manage that? Those big children aren't setting a very good example to you two, are they?'

I don't want them in there with that mess. Once it's cleared enough, I let them in to clean their teeth and have a wee. I check the pull-ups, and then it's quickly into beds. I sit in the chair and select a slightly worn, bent-over-the-edges copy of *Peace at Last* by Jill Murphy. This was Jackson's favourite bedtime story years ago. Max and Mia snuggle under their duvets and both have their heads facing me to listen. I begin the story and by the time I have reached 'Mr Bear was tired, Mrs Bear was tired and Baby Bear was tired', they are already fast asleep. 'And it seems that Max and Mia were tired, too,' I finish, and tiptoe out of the room.

Back downstairs, I ask the older children to keep the bathroom tidy. 'I shouldn't need to say this, but I'm particularly unimpressed with the pee on the floor, toothpaste squeezed out into the sink and the mess of unravelled toilet paper that looks as if the Andrex puppies have paid a visit. I've lost count of the number of times I've asked you to hang up your towels. Seriously!'

Before I have even finished the last sentence, Lily is interrupting. 'It wasn't me!' Vincent and Jackson similarly deny responsibility, but with the outrage that comes from having been wrongly accused. I really believe that they haven't done it. I'm slightly at a loss, so go on to call Lloyd, as the only other person who could possibly have been responsible. 'Was it you who left the bathroom in such a state?' I thunder.

He looks at me with a raised eyebrow, as if I am going slightly mad.

'No.'

I know it isn't the twins. It just can't be. I look at the bigger children with the accusatory stare of an angry head-teacher searching for the culprit who set off the fire alarm, but can manage nothing more than a rather impotent, 'Well, it was *one* of you!'

I decide to leave it there and check with them on the other high-profile subject in the house.

'Now, the other thing I need to discuss is homework, which has also been less than perfect.'

Vincent mumbles something which I decipher along the lines of him thinking that he'd got away with it.

'Vincent,' I say. 'Answer me honestly. Am I going to get a phone call or an email from Mr Brown when you go into school tomorrow?'

He looks a little shifty, but then has the decency to admit, 'Er, yeah, maybe.'

'And what are you still doing down here?'

'On it,' he says, dashing upstairs.

Jackson has mysteriously disappeared by this point.

The conversation continues in the morning. I ask this same question. 'Did you get it done? Am I going to get a call from Mr Brown today?'

'Yeah, I got most of it finished.'

'*Most* of it?'

'I'll do the rest at lunchtime.'

'I'm not quite sure that's the idea of *home*-work.'

Well, we shall see. Meanwhile, Jackson, the sneaky wotnot, has already gone. I hear the front door click as he makes his escape.

Lily begins to hum as she loads up her school bag. She's just about to dump it on the kitchen table while there is still food out: spread, a cereal box, marmalade jars. I see her realise her mistake without me having to intervene, and she places the bag on the chair. There are so many keyrings and trinkets attached to her black Adidas bag, I suspect they make it far heavier than the contents. She's happy because her halo is intact – she knows she's off the hook with the homework. She's quite studious and organised and, most of the time at least, she does it as soon she gets in from school. This is in marked contrast to the boys, whose first instinct is to head up to their rooms to game. After they've taken an armful of crisps and drinks with them, that is.

I decide to have a much quieter day today after yesterday's beach adventure, so that Max and Mia are in fine fettle to see their mum. It's a big journey and will be a significant day emotionally, so they need to be well rested. I have already decided that I won't tell them exactly what's happening until we're just a couple of stops away from Salisbury. Consequently, this morning, they sit and watch a couple of episodes of *Pingu*, a very good friend of mine, and a regular life saver. This enables me to catch up on a bit of work. Firstly, I compose an email to explain to my editor that I am running a bit late. I know I could get up at 5am every morning to enable me to write in peace and quiet before the children all wake up, but, equally, this placement is taking its toll. Not in the way that some of my previous placements have, where behaviour is constantly challenging or I have to try and avoid certain triggers, but just in terms of time on me. Two four-year-olds are hard work. One four-year-old would be plenty. Two is double trouble. Trouble is the wrong word. Just double work. Two people to get ready. Two beds to make. Two more mouths to feed. Two sets of teeth to brush. Important minutes escape from my working day, and I can't seem to get them back. I do sit in bed sometimes and tap away first thing, but Lloyd complains, which I suppose is fair enough. I tend to sit in my studio until the early hours of the morning some nights, working on my books or illustrations. The downside is that, sometimes, by 7am, my eyes are firmly stuck together. This is not an ideal situation in a busy household where everyone needs to get out of the door, but a quick coffee and shower usually does the trick. There just aren't enough hours in the day.

My editor is also super busy and probably won't read my email until tomorrow, but I feel better for having written it. I scan through my other emails and wonder when I will get time to unsubscribe from most of them. I read the latest posts in the Foster Carers Forum on Facebook. I love it, and I love contributing. Sometimes I worry that my comments are a bit too forthright. Then I think, what the hell? Foster carers have been treated appallingly for years, and this is a platform where a few home truths won't go amiss. Foster care sits on a strange fulcrum whereby a problematic weight of hard-core Christian values from another time are balanced with the demands of greedy profit-driven privatisation. It's a very strange culture and one that isn't particularly healthy. The system is also flooded with recent graduates, fresh-faced but in influential positions, often living at home, drawing from the bank of mum and dad, with no real-life experience but bucket-loads of bias and judgement. That's why I like going on this group. It's a bit of a release from all of that, and these kind of spaces are important.

By force of habit, I also check the weather forecast. So far, no horrible weather warnings are out there on the horizon. No rain from hell today. Out of my studio window, I see a lovely day. A few clouds, but nothing threatening. I hope it continues like this when we go on our jaunt to see their mum tomorrow.

After lunch, but before we start the craft project that I've planned with shaving foam and rice – an old favourite that I'm sure will go down well – we go to the big supermarket. I pull out one of the huge trolleys and load both children into it. I used to do this when the boys were very little, and I genuinely haven't seen the health and safety warnings that I only notice on the way out of the store. Max and Mia love it. Of course they do: all children love it. I also find it's a quicker trip if they are contained in the giant basket on wheels. We choose grapes, crisps, nice bread for sandwiches, two tubs of Dairylea and some other weird sandwich filler thing that's recently come onto the shelf, but I know won't last because the packaging looks like poison. I grab a bag of doughnuts for the others and some sweets for the train. They are being quite good today, though I still see the imbalance of power. Max likes to be the one to point things out, to reach for things first, to physically dominate Mia. I also notice how Mia accepts this as the status quo, almost a bit too compliant in her demeanour. I will have to think of some games that will address this.

When we get back, we play the memory game with the shopping. Max and Mia take it in turns to complete the sentence, 'Today I went to the shops and I bought...' adding one more thing to the list each time.

As with everything else, Max does better with the game but, as I watch them, I wonder if that is because Mia lets him. Does she do that out of habit, fear, fatigue, or does she have another motive? I learnt a long time ago never to underestimate children, and never to think they are stupid. Children see, hear and understand so much more than some adults give them credit for. This, I think, is where adults sometimes go wrong and then reap what they have sown.

When the other children get back in from school, they hoover up the doughnuts as I knew they would, and throw their bags and shoes everywhere. It's a daily ritual. They dump stuff down. I twitter around like a hyperactive parrot, saying, 'Pick up your bag, pick up your shoes, pick up your brain.' Then there are the eyes raised to heaven, followed by the huffing and puffing, until finally each item is begrudgingly removed to its rightful place. All that needless energy spent on re-enacting the same scene over and over again.

At bedtime, Max and Mia fancy a swap, so we have to change over bunks and bedding, though still maintaining the mix-and-match approach. The little lights attached to the bed are left on for a while as they thumb through some books. Mia switches hers off first and turns over. Max falls asleep with his book on dinosaurs still in his hands. It's been a relatively uneventful day, which counts as a win as far as I'm concerned. I turn off the light and feel nothing but care for these two troopers who have no idea what lies ahead. I hope tomorrow is a success.

In the morning, another Allen ritual. During the ten minutes prior to departure for school, I call out, at regular intervals, things like 'homework', 'PE kit', 'water bottle' and 'snacks'. Eventually the door clicks closed three separate times, even though they all go the same way. Heaven forbid that they should be seen in public with a sibling. Peace reigns. The twins are playing in their room. That is an advantage of two: they play together and keep each other entertained, especially first thing in the morning.

I tidy up and prepare for the train picnic. We can choose some extra treats at the station on the way back. They will like that, I'm sure.

I hurry them along, realising that a bit of an atmosphere is brewing, and I'm creating it. We can't afford any fights today. We haven't got time. Lloyd is in his office on a call to one of his European colleagues. I do enjoy all the different accents that float out of his studio. I quickly make one last check of the emails to see if a cancellation has come through. No, we are all good to go.

Good to go apart from the last-minute toilet trips, and a change of clothes for Max, who decides he isn't happy with his top.

'I want a different one, Louise.'

'Yes, of course you do, my little poppet.'

Then there's a scrabble around for the particular teddy that Mia wants to bring, a lost shoe, a shoe taken off after I have already helped them on once. It really is not easy getting out of the house with two under-fives in tow, but finally we're ready. The twins still don't really know what's up, but this is one of my tried-and-tested strategies for managing a contact visit when I haven't met the parent before. I gather up Max and Mia and explain to Douglas and Dotty that we're going out for a while and will see them later.

'So, be good while we're out!'

They understand plenty, I'm sure. And if I'm not home, they just sleep all day anyway. Lloyd finishes his call and we clamber into the car so that he can drop us at the station. It's interrupting his work day, but will save me finding a parking spot and paying for parking for hours and hours. We wave goodbye to Lloyd and head into the station.

Ours is a very small station, towards the end of a rural line, but it looks very sweet. Hanging baskets are bursting with autumn displays, and filled troughs of foliage line the platform. The only thing spoiling the scene is that the gorgeous fields that used to surround this tiny little station are full of lorries and bulldozers. Our village has fallen victim to the housing shortage. There are hundreds of cookie-cutter houses being built, supposedly to address this. Given that not many people I know could afford one, especially younger people starting out in life, I don't really understand how this helps anyone, nor why these should be the only type of home available. Millie, my grown-up step-daughter, wants to build a house in a tree. I love the idea, but it has little chance of happening. It makes me feel sad, and not least because I know that these massive developments are making the flooding in areas like this much worse. I know there is a need for this housing, or at least the media tells me that is so, but the planning of infrastructure around such a sizeable development doesn't seem to be there.

I stand in the middle of the platform while we wait for our train. The rush-hour commuters are already on their way to London. Left behind are the day-trippers, the shoppers, the away-day returns. I hold the children's hands and wonder just what the future holds. For me, for them, for all of our children. Life is generally harsher, one way or another, towards children who have been through the care system. I so hope these little poppets will be alright.

As the train makes its way around the bend and into the station towards us, both children are ecstatic. It's an absolute joy to witness their delight in something so simple. Max counts the train carriages as it pulls into the station. We carefully climb onto the train and find four seats with a table. I take their coats and travel rucksacks to hang up. The coats they arrived with, but the travel rucksacks are new. I found them in an online sale, and they were even more of a bargain if you bought two. We settle down to watch the country display out of the window. I imagine it is a world apart from the urban sights that these two are used to. I point out cows, trees, a tractor ploughing a field, sheep, horses, hills and all sorts of things. Max and Mia are sponges, soaking it all up.

Often when I'm out and about in public with newly arrived foster children and we are feeling our way with the rules, I want a neon flashing disclaimer sign to wave around. He isn't mine. I'm not responsible for the fact that he's banging his head repeatedly against that wall, or it's not my fault that she's making a scene in the middle of the supermarket.

Not with this pair.

They are immaculately behaved. They sit so upright, prim and proper in their train seats. I see their little legs swinging beneath them when they momentarily forget themselves, but otherwise they are conscious of the behaviour they are presenting to the world. They stay nice and clean in their clothes, not wrestling and wriggling and scrunching them up like some children might.

I'd like to be seen as responsible for these children, but someone else has put all the groundwork in, taught them good manners, encouraged them to be well turned out, to speak politely. And somehow, even though they've had a couple of moments where they've lost control at home, I can't help but feel that they know enough not to behave that way outside the home. They are a little enigma, these two.

Thus far, I have made today about the train journey itself, without a specific destination. But I decide that I will deviate a little from my original plan to put off revealing where we are going until we are almost there. Instead, I give them time to settle into the rhythm of the journey, but not long. I wait only a few stops out of the station before I say to the children, 'I have a surprise for you.'

They turn to me with eager anticipation, wide-eyed.

I lean towards them across the train table and whisper, 'We're not just going on a train journey. We're going to see your mummy.'

My heart does a little cartwheel inside my chest as I watch their faces light up like torches. If there was a way I could bottle their expressions and pay to see their reaction again and again, I would. It is fantastic!

The children look first at each other, backwards and forwards, and wriggle and clench their hands with excitement. As they sparkle and fizz, I pull out some card and coloured pencils.

'Would you like to make a card each to give to your mummy?'

'Yes, yes!'

'Yes, please!'

Of course they would, and their efforts occupy the rest of the journey with purpose.

I smile, as I hear the polite exchanges that take place between them.

'Would you pass me the rubber?'

'Have you finished with the red pencil?'

So grown-up.

It feels like no time at all before I have to start tidying away the activities and go to put the snack wrappers in the bin. The latter is actually easier said than done. I stand up and look around helplessly, clutching the rubbish for a few seconds until a very kind man points to the wastepaper basket which is hidden under some seats.

Max and Mia are suddenly very quiet.

I only read into this that they are collectively over-whelmed. Sometimes I have been with children who are terrified of seeing their family, who have finally been released from a terrifying situation and are being plunged back into a meeting with the perpetrators, or the facilitators. Judges, who may well have never met the children but are positioned to think they know best, force them to have contact anyway. It may well be the very last thing they need. With these two, however, I am convinced that it is absolutely the right thing to do. I'm basing it on their behaviour generally, the way they talk about their parents, their mum in particular; the cards that she has sent, the care with which their suitcases were packed. I'm judging too, but at least I have met and spent time with these children.

As we walk through the station, one child holding each hand, I catch sight of the picture we make in a mirrored shop window. Both their little faces burn with concentration. I haven't a clue what they are thinking, but it will, inevitably, revolve around their mother and the meeting that we're about to have.

Once we're out of the station, I notice a little gift shop next to a large newsagents and convenience store opposite.

'Would you like to choose your mummy a gift?' I ask.

'Yes, yes, yes!' they shout. Of course they would.

We wander around among ornaments and scented bath things for a few moments, but nothing grabs them. What do you choose as a present when you are four years old? Probably the thing you want most for yourself: sweets. We head into the newsagents where they choose some sweets, and then traipse back to the first shop for a nice gift box.

Outside once more, I wave at a taxi. I pull a piece of paper with the address of the centre we are visiting from my pocket and sit between Max and Mia in the back. They are still very quiet.

'How are we feeling?' I hear myself say. 'Are you excited?'

They nod. Of course they're excited, it's a ridiculous thing to ask.

It takes 15 minutes for us to pull up outside the building. Then a few minutes to sort out payment and the necessary receipt. I'll definitely be putting my claim in later. That little journey cost another £15 on top of the train tickets.

We go inside and I follow the arrows to 'reception'. I hold their hands and walk round to the desk, where I point out to the children all the lovely pictures painted onto the walls. Someone remembered that children come here; it's a colourful, friendly place. I have been to a few that are awful and feel more like undergoing a punishment of some kind. We are met by Jill, the contact worker, who I had been told would be here. She is perfectly friendly and I judge her to be a bit older than me, or perhaps she just looks like she is.

'Do you think that the children might use the loo before we go in?' I ask. They are bursting on two counts, but empty bladders will mean a better quality 'hello' with their mum. I take the children to the bathroom and wash their hands. I brush their hair and make sure they have clean faces. I want

Angelina not to worry that her children aren't receiving the care they need and deserve.

Once that's all done, we meet Jill back in the lobby and she asks me how I want to play it. 'Do you want to stay while the contact takes place, or come back at the end?'

'What do you think would be best?'

When she shrugs, I say, 'Perhaps, if I just say hello to her at the start, maybe that will help the children?'

I daren't add, '…and their mum'. I also don't mention that in our training we are told categorically that the parents and birth family are not our problem. In reality, the parents are the reason why children come into care, whatever the detail of that reason might be. Jill disappears for a moment, and then returns to say that Angelina would indeed like to meet me.

I suddenly feel nervous.

Jill pulls open the heavy double doors into the room. I let go of the children's hands as they run to the arms of their mum.

'Mummy, Mummy!' they squeal, each vying to be the loudest. Oh dear, I think my eyes are starting to leak a little. I see a mass of red curls dangle over Max and Mia as she gathers them in to her, and the gasp as Angelina is overwhelmed by the enormity of the moment.

'Oh, *miei bei bambini*,' she coos, or something that sounds like that.

I watch her as she clasps her babies. She hasn't raised her head. From here it looks as if she is inhaling her children. I know I would be if I'd been apart from my children for, I work it out, over a fortnight now since they came into care, and 12 days since they arrived with me.

'*Vi amo tanto*.'

She repeats the words over and over, breathes them over Max and Mia. I don't speak Italian, but they sound to me like tender words of love. I was wrong to think that they didn't need this contact visit while they were settling into my house. They absolutely did. My fears were unfounded.

All their shades of red hair are mingled into one. Together they look like an autumnal leaf display. After long moments of cuddles, Angelina finally lifts her head. My god, she's beautiful. She is absolutely gorgeous. Stunning. She belongs in a magazine, or on a catwalk. She is nothing like the countless worn-down women I have met over the years in rooms like this one. She doesn't belong here. I am more curious than ever. What on earth has got them all to this point?

Chapter Six

I keep a respectful distance, standing a good three metres or so away, not wishing to intrude on this touching family reunion. Though I'm on the other side of the room, I lock eyes with Angelina. We don't speak, but much is said. Her eyes seem to be saying, 'thank you'. Mine, I hope, communicate that she is most welcome, and that I'm going to do my absolute best for these children. I want her to hear this loud and clear in the whispering quiet. She gives me a quick nod. It feels as if we have an understanding.

She is younger than I expected: I would say not much older than my step-daughters, who are in their mid-twenties. She is willowy, but not fragile. Her movements are elegant, but she looks tired. Her skin is delicately pale, a beautiful ivory colour, as if she has been carved from alabaster, imperfections polished away. The loose, peachy-hued shirt she wears works amazingly with her skin and hair. She certainly knows how to dress. Her jeans are expensive; the stitching is uniform, the cut and quality of the denim is good and the fit is flattering. As someone who tends to buy her annual two pairs of jeans from Sainsbury's, thrown in the trolley with as much hope as judgement, I can safely say that Angelina's jeans must have cost a fortune. She is also wearing, if I'm not mistaken, a pair of Jimmy Choo's: suede, mink-coloured trainers. Her appearance is effortlessly stylish, and yet it is the overwhelming tiredness that I notice above all else. I wonder about her. Who is she? Is she a model, an actress, a singer? She has a kind of aura that the rich and famous exude. A presence, a way of being, that I can't quite put my finger on. One that says, 'I am someone'. I've noticed it on the odd occasion when I see sports personalities close up, or celebrities in real life. I suppose it is what constitutes the 'X factor'.

I stand back and watch Max and Mia delight in their mother's company. Other contact visits I've attended in the past have been awkward, stilted exchanges that are far too uncomfortable to watch. Not this one. It is easy to see that she loves her children, has missed them desperately. It's also easy to see that Max and Mia feel the same way. They most certainly love her in a very open and genuine way. Sometimes, when I have been in the company of birth mothers whose children have been taken away from them by the authorities, I feel that they try to create a pretence that all is well and that they love their children. It is almost as if they try too hard to compensate for whatever has gone wrong.

I heard a mother once say to her child, 'You will always be my baby, and even when you're thirty you will still sit on my lap, like this.' I remember it sounding like the oddest thing.

For a start, how could they even know that they'd still be alive when their child is 30? Moreover, why on earth would a 30-year-old wish to sit on their mother's lap? Watching Angelina, there is no pretence, none of that kind of posturing; no playing to an audience of any kind. Hers is not a showy demonstration of love towards the children. She somehow manages to keep it private, even though Jill and I are looking at her. It is almost as if, after that moment of locking eyes, she has mentally removed us from the room. She whispers to the children words that I can't hear, but somehow not in a secretive way. I suddenly and quite painfully feel that I'm surplus to requirements in this moment.

I remove my gaze and step over to Jill to start a conversation, so that we are both distracted from being casual onlookers to this personal time. But Mia runs up to me and interrupts, grabbing my hand to drag me over to Angelina.

'Come to Mamma!' Mia is excited about us meeting and talking. I have thought several times that this little girl has a quality of kindness and maturity about her that runs deep, and isn't yet shared by Max. Perhaps he will grow into it.

Mia tugs at my big straw shopping bag for the cards and sweetie gifts. Angelina is delighted by the offering and reads out their messages, which make her very emotional. Then she opens her eyes wide at the sweets. 'My favourites. Aren't you clever and thoughtful? What very kind children. I don't know if I will be able to eat them all by myself, though. Do you think we should share them out and you can help me?'

Max and Mia nod solemnly.

Angelina hugs them again and mouths a 'thank you' to me over the top of their heads. I nod back, but with my eyes closed. I'm not sure why, but it's how it comes out. I feel slightly as if I'm in a film, and Angelina is the lead, the superstar. At the same time, everything about Angelina is also authentic. She is, I think, the real deal. I think I have developed an instinct for these things. It's very hard to witness the exchanges between mothers and children when you know some of the background, perhaps that the adults have hurt their children or sexually abused them or allowed others to. I know so little about what has happened, but

Angelina doesn't have the looks or any of the hallmarks of an addict or a drunk. She definitely doesn't have the demeanour of a victim. I am more confused than ever about what has gone on for her beautiful children for them to have ended up in care.

I move back away again, as I'm well aware of how precious these moments are, how limited their time is, and how little privacy this setup offers. I try to engage Jill in more conversation to enable this little group to spend good time together. There are storybooks and games at the centre. Angelina settles Max and Mia on the beanbags so that they can read and play together. She seems to want to make the most of every second.

Jill seems like a nice woman and, like me, loves dogs, so I encourage her to waffle on about her dog, Charles. I hear about all his little habits and what he gets up to on their walks, and how only this morning he had a right old set-to with a cockapoo. Though I nod, smile, raise my eyebrows at the right moments and make all the right noises, inside I'm dying of boredom. I play the role of an enthusiastic air hostess while she speaks, but really I want to observe the lovely scenes playing out on the other side of the room.

The vacuous talk doesn't take much headspace, and gives me time to think. I have a little idea, but have to reconcile it in my head before I act on it. I know what all our training says about birth parents and our level of interaction with them (i.e. none), but I decide that particular training session was a very long time ago. Perhaps I have forgotten all the details, and anyway, times change. I know what the rules are, but I also know why they are there, and generally it's for protection. I've been on the receiving end of some pretty unpleasant interactions with birth parents on a couple of occasions when they've got hold of my contact details when they shouldn't have, so I know the reality of why those rules are in place. But, but, but rules are for the governance of fools and the guidance of wise men (and women), as someone more knowledgeable than me once said. I look at my idea from all angles and yes, I'm almost at the point of being able to fully justify to myself what I'm about to do. I just need the opportunity to present itself, which it does after a second cup of tea.

Jill says, 'Are you alright here for a moment while I nip to the loo?'

I feel a flash of guilt before I've even acted on what I've decided I am going to do. That's because Jill is nice and evidently trusts me, and I feel like I'm exploiting her kindness, which isn't a pleasant feeling. Nevertheless, as Jill leaves, I delve into my straw bag and find my purse, which houses a few of my business cards.

I check that the coast is clear. The door of the room has a glass panel, so I'll see if Jill returns unexpectedly. I approach the little group of redheads and lean towards Angelina. I hand over my business card.

'It would be nice to stay in touch,' I whisper. 'If you wanted to. My mobile number is on there.' She absolutely understands what I mean, what I've just done, and slides my card deftly into her jeans back pocket, with a gentle nod and another glance of gratitude. Oh, I could get into so much trouble, but what the hell? I put myself in her shoes as one mother to another and imagine how I would feel in her position. I'm convinced I've done the right thing, and I'm as certain as I can be that she'll respect my effort to reach out and not use it against me.

I move back to where I was sitting, and when Jill returns,

it's as if I haven't moved from the spot. We change the subject from dogs, and I ask about somewhere nice locally to take the children for a bite to eat. She has a good suggestion for somewhere child-friendly that will do pizza and pasta, and I make a note of the address. The clock approaches the end of the session. I wait as Jill gently brings it to a close. She does so with kindness and plenty of warning so that it isn't abrupt.

Angelina explains to Max and Mia that she isn't disappearing, and that she will be in contact with them very soon.

'Absolutely, children,' Jill beams. 'I'm sure the next visit will be set up in no time at all. The time will fly by!'

'No time at all,' I repeat, pointedly, knowing that the conversation is operating on different levels for the different people in the room.

I still slightly dread the actual moment of goodbyes, but the children handle it well and seem okay. Again, this is facilitated masterfully by Angelina as we gather ourselves together. She keeps it very casual and avoids the big, theatrical farewell. It's another confirmation to me that Angelina is a good mother, who loves her children without question, because she makes this easy for them. The dramatic, emotional scenes I've seen play out too often in rooms like these, I have come to understand, are actually all about the parents. Either they are making a show for the social workers or contact workers, or trying to convince their children that they are actually good parents.

Angelina gently kisses them first on their cheeks, then on their foreheads. She tells them first that she loves them, and then, 'You must be very good for Louise.'

No one has ever said that before.

I've been in this game a long time, and this is one of the few occasions where the departure feels as though we are working together to do what's best for Max and Mia, rather than for the adults around them. We do not need them to be upset.

I head for the restaurant that Jill recommended. I know that I won't be allowed to claim this back, but decide that today they need a treat and a kind distraction from the sadness and confused emotions they must, inevitably, be feeling. As we get into the taxi after they have eaten their fill, my phone pings. It's a text from an unknown number.

Thank you so much for letting me have your number, Louise. I can't thank you enough. Now you have mine. X

It has taken her the best part of an hour to text. I wonder if she has been holding off or deliberating about whether to get in contact with me or not. But I know that this is the right thing to do. The next thing I need to do is to explain my action to Lloyd and convince him that we keep this between ourselves. He's a by-the-book person with our foster children. Unlike me, he didn't grow up in the care system and doesn't always get the nuances of certain situations.

I think about my reasons. I'm sure it will help the twins to feel better and improve their behaviour. I've also made a judgement about Angelina's character. He will argue that I don't have all the information, and he's right. But my intuition has taken over in its absence. I have to make sure he doesn't tell Moira. He'll want to, because he likes to keep everything above board. We've also been affected by accusations and untoward behaviour from birth parents of children we've looked after previously, so part of his rule-following is to cover himself, to protect us. It won't be the easiest job in the world.

I text Lloyd a good half an hour before we arrive at the station to give him time to pick us up. Max and Mia do not stop chatting the entire way home. They don't only talk about their mum, they discuss the cows in the fields, the funny stone buildings and the electricity pylons. They really are like little sponges soaking up everything around them. Angelina has bought them some lovely presents that help the journey whizz by too. Max enjoys looking at the pictures in his new book about vegetables having a party, and makes a start on his box of early-years Lego. Mia is thrilled with her string bag of plastic fruit and another string bag of a tea set. They both have new cuddly toys which they don't let out of their clutches, let alone out of sight. I wonder if we can make little beds for them later when we get home. I'm sure the bear and the owl will fit into tissue boxes with some fabric from my rag bag. They'll enjoy that.

Lloyd and I strap them into their car seats and they begin to show the first signs of tiredness. Max starts to rub his eyes and Mia becomes very quiet, kind of retreating into herself. I decide that a snack and bed is the way to go, even though it's a little bit before their usual bedtime. They've had a big day.

By the time we get back to the house, the others have already had their tea, filling themselves up with toasties. A while back, Lloyd bought a toasted sandwich maker the insides of which you can take out to wash. It was expensive, but it's actually a sensibly designed kitchen gadget. Finally. It's also popular with the children. In fact, the children love it so much that this evening, I discover, they have made four rounds of toasties each. There won't be any bread left for breakfast, but they've enjoyed themselves.

I put the twins in the sitting room to watch something easy while I sort out the kitchen. I say the word 'homework', and Vincent shoots upstairs. I understand this to mean that he has not yet done it. I can tell by Jackson's poor poker face in response to the word that he also has not done it, but thinks that he can play it cool and style it out, giving the impression that it's all under control.

'Can I see yours, Jackson?' I ask, innocently.

He disappears too, for a good hour.

Next I call out to Max and Mia. 'Right then, you two, time to go up and do our teeth.'

Too late. They are already both sound asleep. I pick up Mia first to carry her up, as she is currently on the top bunk. I wake her up to have a wee and put on the pull-up nappy and her nightclothes. I have, in my pocket, her owl, who would like to sleep now as well. I steady Mia into her bunk and pull over her duvet. She is out again in a second, a contented little light.

I go back down to get Max, but Lloyd is already walking up the stairs with him cradled in his arms. I go through the same routine with Max, and he takes his new bear and snuggles it tight, no doubt thinking of his mother. What brave children they've been today. But they somehow seem to be taking it all in their stride.

Lloyd stands out on the landing and signals 'glass of wine'. I return with a tilted nod that translates as, 'Are you kidding? Of course.' I take one lingering look at these two little darlings, tufts of red hair sticking up against the pillows, before turning out the light. After meeting Angelina today, I really hope this works out for them. It's so hard not to have an opinion about what should happen in each case, especially when you're so close to the children, and my opinion this time is that they should end up back together again. This family is markedly different from the majority that I have seen wind up in the care system. And that's quite a large sample. It is an ever more curious case.

Lloyd pours the promised glass of wine and gets the Bombay mix out from the cupboard, while I sink down into a chair at the kitchen table. How very '90s Bombay mix seems. I take him through our day. I tell him about Angelina and how I couldn't believe how beautiful she was or how gracious. I also explain about me giving her my number.

'Honestly, I think, if you could have witnessed that scene then you'd have done the same thing.'

He probably wouldn't, but he doesn't judge me. Both of us are tired of being bossed about by a broken system that often doesn't make sense.

'And just don't say anything – yet – to Bea or Moira, will you? For now, anyway.'

He agrees to keep my 'secret.'

Jackson comes down into the kitchen.

'How's the homework going?' I ask.

'Cool.' He pauses for a moment. 'But that's not why I've come down. I was going to have a shower but the bathroom is a mess.'

I make a face. 'Okay, I'll go up and have a look and sort it out.'

'More wine?' Lloyd asks, already lifting the bottle.

'Is the Pope Catholic?' I say, by way of an answer as I head up to the bathroom.

I'm cross from the moment I look in. Jackson wasn't wrong. There are towels on the floor, splatters of wee around the toilet, toilet rolls across the floor once more, and the hand towel has been chucked over the plant in the corner, breaking some of the stems. Inside the shower, the lids of the hanging shower gel bottles have been left open, and shampoo is on its side, also open. Three different rivulets of colour puddle to the shower floor. Jackson follows me in. I open my mouth, but he beats me to it.

'No, it wasn't me.'

'Was it Vincent?'

He shrugs. 'I don't know, Mum.'

'Well, it can't have been the twins, can it?'

I quickly tidy up enough so that Jackson can get in the shower. I then walk up to Vincent's attic room, feeling cross enough to stomp, and knock on the door.

'Vince, can I come in?'

'Yeah, I've done my homework.'

When I open the door and look in, I find him gaming, but he does stick his thumbs up and repeat, 'Ma, I've *done* it.'

'Excellent. Now, what about the bathroom?'

'Nothing to do with me. I didn't do it.'

'Do you know who did?'

A shake of the head and he's back engrossed in his game.

Well, one of them did it, so it's only a matter of time until I find out which one.

I go back downstairs and tell Lloyd.

He rolls his eyes, echoing my own thoughts. 'Well, it's one of them.'

While he moves about the kitchen topping up the glasses again (mine has mysteriously emptied once more), I text Angelina.

Max and Mia are fast asleep. They've had a lovely day.

She texts straight back. *Thank you so much, Louise, for*

letting me know. I am grateful for all that you are doing for Max and Mia, and they seem happy. x

Now, again, that's never said by birth parents.

In the morning, Max and Mia don't stir during all the getting-out-of-the-door-to-school chaos that reigns in that first hour of the day. It's not like them at all, they're usually early risers, but they had a lot to deal with yesterday, so I leave them to it. It may also signify that they feel more relaxed and safer since seeing their mother.

I pop my head around the bathroom door and see, once again, fresh mess. This cannot go on. I find myself gripping the side of the sink in rage. How dare they? I'll have to sit both boys down together later.

Eventually Max and Mia wake up and, after breakfast, I take the children and the dogs for a walk up the hill. I can tell by their sluggish steps that they are still tired, so I plan, ruthlessly, to tire them out even more so that they settle down into a gentle lazy day and I can catch up with some work. They are both well behaved and calm. I have the wildflower book with me again, so I send them hunting for more flowers and leaves. They love this game and though they never seem to find the right flowers, they don't seem to mind, and the enjoyment is in the looking.

When we get home, I make them a second breakfast: a very civilised state of affairs, as all hobbits would no doubt agree. Pippin from *Lord of the Rings* would certainly approve. I cook some chocolate croissants from the freezer. The smell is delightful and quickly fills the house, enough to bring Lloyd in from his study, sniffing the air.

I remind him that he is on a diet after a recent health check at the doctors. I won't share what the doctor said, precisely, but Lloyd was most indignant. I call the twins in, offering them beakers of hot chocolate. I try and gauge how they are after yesterday without asking the question directly. They seem fine. Not fazed or knocked out of kilter, as far as I can tell.

'Shall we have some cartoons when we're finished?'

'Yesss peeese Louiiiseee,' they squeal in unison with beaming smiles. They really are such a sweet pair. And my plan works. They watch for a while and then both nod off obligingly for a couple of hours, enabling me to work on one of my illustrations.

The rest of the day continues in a gentle fashion. It's fine enough after lunch for Max and Mia to play outside while I cut back some of the foliage in the garden. I drive them around the garden in the wheelbarrow, to squeals of delight, as if it's the most exciting mode of transport ever invented. I take a photo of them sitting in the wheelbarrow enjoying an ice cream and send it to Angelina, who replies quickly.

Thank you so much, Louise, that is a beautiful picture and they look like they are having great fun x

The children begin to arrive home, always recognisable from the tell-tale sounds of the kitchen cupboards and drawers opening. I can hear David Attenborough's accompanying voiceover in my head: *It's at this time of day that the creatures forage urgently for snacks that will sustain them until their main meal. See how they rummage, and can tell with just a quick scan whether anything new has appeared in the cupboards and drawers since the previous day. They make short work of a packet of biscuits and some crisps, tossing packets away with practised ease. It's desirable for their choices to contain high quantities of sugar…*

I carry on tidying the garden tools safely away and lock the shed. I'm always careful to do that, just in case these little cherubs decide to do some gardening of their own. It's still a lovely afternoon, a fair bit of heat left in the sun, and I watch it light up their red hair. I keep thinking about Angelina and what on earth could have happened to this family to warrant the care system becoming involved.

In the kitchen, all three of the older children are mucking about, seeing if they can throw Wotsits into each other's mouths. I wonder, briefly, what Mr Attenborough would make of that in the imaginary documentary, but the mess from the misses reminds me of our current bathroom issue.

'So, who's the culprit?' I say. 'Now that I've got all three of you together, I want to get to the bottom of who is messing up the bathroom. It's not good enough, and it's got to stop. You're all old enough to know better.'

There are various predictable mutterings and protestations.

'Look, this isn't a joke anymore. It's got to be someone, hasn't it?' I begin to feel quite cross. I don't like the idea of any of my children lying, especially to me. 'I'm afraid I'm not buying the "it's not me" line. We're beyond that now. Someone here is playing up.'

Vincent is quite rude, not his normal self, raising his voice a notch higher than I'm used to. 'For god's sake, Mum, why do you think it's me?'

Then Jackson pipes up, 'Yeah, Mum, why do you keep on blaming us?'

The conversation begins to feel a little more heated than I'd like. I find myself raising my voice to match theirs. Then, I notice Lily standing by the fridge looking at her phone. For some reason, in the midst of this already angry moment, I find her nonchalance supremely irritating, and I cross the boundary from a little bit cross into furious. They all disappear up to their rooms.

'Aren't you overreacting a bit to a couple of towels?' as a parting shot doesn't help my mood. I'm left downstairs feeling frustrated because one of my sons is lying, and I don't like it one little bit. I feel totally wound up and I don't know what to do about it.

Dotty and Douglas come racing in from the garden, usually a signal that it's time for their tea. But Dotty isn't her usual yappy self. Instead, she is standing by the back door looking at me, her head tilted to one side. I wonder what's going on.

I go out into the garden and, to my absolute horror, the back gate latch is up and the gate is banging back on itself.

There is no sign of Max and Mia.

Chapter Seven

I call out 'Max, Mia,' instinctively, but I know they aren't there. Something plummets inside me, probably a vital organ, and the panic rises to take its place in sickening lurches. I run around the gate and into the back lane, but I can't see a thing. I run back into the house calling for Lloyd.

He comes into the kitchen, but not as fast as I think he should in response to the urgency of my call, which also winds me up.

'Max and Mia have gone out the back gate!' I shout. There is no time for recriminations, no time to have a conversation about why the catch wasn't down, or whose fault that might have been. I just panic more. I call the children. They must be able to tell by the tone of my voice that this is not about the state of the bathroom. They come running down and I explain what has happened.

Jackson switches into adult mode. 'Right, Vincent and I will go and look down all the lanes.'

Vincent, remembering my panic when I thought he had vanished when he was about five years old, reminds me that he was asleep under the bed in the guest room the whole time. 'I hadn't left the house at all.'

'Yep, good thinking. Let's make sure that all bases are covered.' We charge Lily with checking every bedroom and cupboard in the house. But I feel sick. I know they aren't here. The image of that swinging gate haunts me.

Dotty is by the front door where we keep their leads. While she's not quite in the *Lassie* category, her tilted head and insistent look reminds me that it was her who first alerted me to the fact that Max and Mia were missing. Perhaps she 'knows' something and is trying to tell me. I call Doug and put their leads on, grab the keys and follow Dotty's nose. I'm aware, even as I'm doing it, that I'm clutching at straws.

Lloyd is already outside, running up and down the road calling out 'Max' and 'Mia' at regular intervals. There is a bit of me that is so ashamed that we, the foster family, have lost the foster children. I mean, I'm meant to know what I'm doing with all this.

What made them run off?

A couple of my neighbours jump in to join us in our search. We all split up to take responsibility of different areas in the immediate vicinity. My heart is pounding. I cannot believe that this is happening. I swing from feeling absolute rage that I was so distracted by the bloody bathroom mess to a childlike need to blame someone else, and then remember the adult who just needs to be rational to find these children and bring them home.

As I run up the lane on the route I usually take with the children on our walks, I begin to wonder if it was the raised voices in the kitchen earlier that had sent Max and Mia running, when I was trying to find out which boy had been weeing on the bathroom floor and leaving it in such a mess. I don't know why, but the fact that Lily stood there looking at her phone sticks with me. I wonder what that was all about. But I also remember the anger I felt. The trials and tribulations of fostering send you on an impromptu therapy session at the drop of a hat. I'm always trying to evaluate and analyse my own reactions and behaviour, as well as the children's. Maybe I hit the roof because my children are badly behaved and one of them is lying, or because I find mobile phones and the way teenagers seem glued to them annoying. Whatever. It wasn't my finest hour.

I keep walking up the hill with Vincent. He is brilliant: he runs into every field and zooms round all the sides looking in the ditches and hedges. He has much more energy than I do, and it's fuelled by the adrenaline of the emergency. I keep shouting their names, 'Max, Mia!' at the top of my lungs, but hear the words dying in the wind. I start to feel even more nauseous as my head fills with terrible scenarios. I imagine them being loaded into the back of a van with blacked-out windows. Because gangsters or child-trafficking rings would, of course, have been driving by our house just at the moment that Max and Mia ran through the gate. I imagine them hiding in sheds. I conjure a missing persons' campaign, like when you see photocopies of people's missing cats accompanied by messages pleading for people to check their sheds and outbuildings. At what point do I call the police? How long can they have been gone? Eight minutes? Twelve? How far could they have gone in that time?

This is hell!

My phone rings. It's Lloyd. Thank god, he must have found them.

'Have you got them, Louise?' The panic in his voice matches my own inside, and I feel even worse for the momentary flash of hope. I start to cry. What have we done? With every second that passes, there is more time to think. Max and Mia have run away. This is my fault. They were scared off because of the raised voices in the kitchen. That must have been what happened at home – fighting in the family. Perhaps they have suffered trauma from violent experiences in the family home, and my anger at bathroomgate had triggered the memory.

And – oh my god! I gave Angelina my mobile number without really knowing anything about her. Maybe she has mental health problems and has taken them. Perhaps it was all an elaborate ruse to lull me into thinking that she is fine, when she's actually unstable. What have I done?

But, argues the more rational voice inside my head, she doesn't know where we live. I look at Vincent, who is still doing his best to find them. His commitment hasn't flagged at all and he's desperately searching every ditch and hedgerow. I'm going to have to call the police. This is a nightmare. We walk to the top of the hill, repeating the whole walk that I last took with the twins and the flower-spotting book. The dogs run around, looking everywhere, with a similar sense of purpose and urgency, as if they've tuned in to our panic.

I keep checking the time, as we turn round and head back in the direction we've come. They have been gone for the best part of an hour, and nothing from Lloyd or our neighbours. My mind returns to those early, irrational thoughts, and now I really do think the worst. We walk down the hill and ask everyone we see if they have seen Max and Mia. I'm wretched. And, if Angelina has taken them, then it's totally my fault and the end of our fostering career.

I go through the back gate and crouch down, trying to see the world from their point of view, to trace their steps. What would have been in their line of vision? I scan the garden and notice that an area is flattened under one of the shrubs I was cutting back earlier. Just the size for two four-year-olds. Something switches inside me. I wonder if they are hidden somewhere in the garden. That's it. That must be the answer. Vincent and I look around, gently now, not with the mad desperation at the top of the hill. If they are here, then I don't want to scare them.

We find nothing. My panic comes back, times a hundred, worsened again by the false hope.

We walk inside, into the kitchen, and I call out to see if anyone else is back.

'Hellooo?'

I walk up the stairs and into Lily's room. She is sitting on her floor with her back against the radiator, on her phone.

'Anything? Have you checked every room and cupboard?'

She looks at me with a slightly puzzled face. 'Huh?'

I ask again, 'Lily, have you checked everywhere for Max and Mia?'

Her response is a nonchalant shrug of the shoulders. Where is her panic to mirror mine? How can she be so calm and unruffled in the face of what's happened?

Suddenly, I see something in her face that I don't like. A kind of oppositional challenge. A level of defiance that I don't understand. She can't be *jealous*, can she?

I say to Vincent, 'Let's go and have a look.'

He goes straight to the guest room, his own hiding spot from years ago. There they are, fast asleep under the Breton bed.

'Oh, thank god!'

Vincent and I gently wake them. Once their eyes open fully, they become confused and begin to cry. Perhaps they sense my own overwhelming relief after all that heightened emotion. We get them out and I sit on the bed with both of them on my lap. They cry for their mummy, and I feel that we have let them down.

'Vincent, fetch my phone off the kitchen table, would you?'

He brings it up and I unlock it for him to call Lloyd and Jackson and let them know that the twins are safe.

'Get Dad to tell our neighbours that they were under the bed the whole time, and to thank them for all their help.'

My emotions are all over the place. But one thing's for sure. Once this has calmed down, Lily and I are going for a long drive so she can explain to me what's going on.

Chapter Eight

I have a strong feeling that it is Lily who is messing up the bathroom, deliberately and provocatively, and is rather enjoying watching the boys get the rap for it.

I'm seething. I hate this feeling. I am absolutely furious with Lily for what she's doing, but we're in a dangerous moment. I know how this can play out with a foster child. She has hit that teenage hormonal stage of acne and attitude. Maybe she even thought that the twins would be blamed. It wouldn't be the first time that jealousy over new arrivals has led to a deterioration in behaviour. It's bad news, and I don't have the headspace for it. I'm already stressed out from trying to decide how to manage the Max and Mia disappearance. But I saw something in Lily's face today that disturbed me. It was the sense of the enjoyment she got from causing trouble, and that is what I think I'm struggling with the most. It's deeply unpleasant and unacceptable.

On the other hand, I need to put everything into perspective. Everyone is safe, nothing bad has happened, but Lily has been a catalyst for some unpleasant responses and reactions. What I feel like doing is putting my hands on my hips and saying, 'Lily, you are a bad girl,' but it isn't that simple, and she's not a bad person. I can't react that way, because looked-after children have trauma and it's always complicated. It is hard to pull apart the trauma from what seems like bad behaviour. I know that can seem like an excuse, but it's rubbing up against the cocktail of normal teenage boundary-pushing hormones.

My reading of the situation is that she tried to cause trouble and then, when our house was in a state of panic and fear about the twins' whereabouts, she couldn't be bothered to pull her weight and look for them. It's difficult to separate the two events. Every time I think about it, I feel fury. And then I experience every foster carer's dilemma: do I treat her like one of my own, which I do every other day, or do I make allowances for her because of the trauma of her past life? If I let her off the hook every time she does something wrong, am I setting her, and society, up for future appalling behaviour? I know that I will have to report this but again, I am stuck. If I report what is basically a spiteful act of jealousy, it will be on her record forever.

Is that fair?

The permanence of it annoys me. At the end of the day she is just a child, and I don't want her to read about what I consider to be, on some level, natural behaviour, at some point later in her life – recorded in her notes as though it was a crime. She will be hurt and potentially get angry. I don't know, but god, fostering is hard sometimes.

I think I'll sleep on it for a few nights. I don't want to talk about it. I need the pendulum to stop swinging before I decide what to do. I don't even want to talk to Lloyd just yet. I feel too raw. I need to let the dust settle.

Meanwhile, there are the twins to manage. They are, understandably, upset and no doubt confused by the level of tension in the house. I remain certain that it was the tone of the conversation about the bathroom that made them hide, initially in the bush where I saw the flattened grass. I'm guessing that when we had all gone looking for them and it was quiet again, they came back into the house and chose a good place to hide. In a way, it's quite calculated behaviour that would suggest that they've done it before. Maybe their mum and dad would argue, but it must have been more than that, because arguing is what most couples do some of the time. So, what actually happened for them to end up in care? It would be so helpful to know rather than trying to guess, to be able to respond to behaviour that arises as a result of whatever has happened to them in the past.

Yet I didn't sense anything from Angelina other than kindness and love. That's one of the things that's so confusing. Her similarity in age to my step-daughters reminds me that they can occasionally be cause for worry, but still. She seems comfortable in her own skin, is certainly well-heeled, and I imagine that, if she can spend that much on clothes and shoes, she could afford help like cleaners and nannies to ease the load – unlike most of us, who have to do all of it.

The twins sleep well in spite of everything. I sit with both of them, snuggled in, watching *Paddington* (again, it's a winner with these two) and *Cars*. Their thumbs are in their mouths as though that is exactly where they belong. I know that they need the right support more than ever. I go up to check on them throughout the night. I wake every two hours to see if they are okay while Lloyd sleeps. I check on all of the children, since I'm up anyway, and every time I go into Lily's room I feel an awakening of my crossness. That tells me that I am clearly not yet ready to have the conversation I need to have with her.

In the morning, everyone turns up to the kitchen at various times, as though we're all slightly out of sync with one another. I have to remind myself that it's the weekend, so nothing but rest matters for the time being. Max and Mia are early to breakfast, closer to their normal routine. Jackson is up before Vincent; Lloyd comes in and out, and there is food and chit-chat from everyone apart from Lily. I leave her be, assuming that she will appear at some point when hunger gets the better of her. There are no big plans for the day, so we gently pootle around the house, not doing very much. Lloyd looks after the children for a couple of hours while I do the shopping.

He checks and charges the children's old iPad for Max and Mia, so that they can play *Angry Birds*, and has them out in the garden while he finishes repairing the back gate. The reason it was banging to and fro was because it has begun to stick after the recent rain. It needs fixing; I don't want to go through all that again.

Angry Birds is a hit, though I'm still the real angry old bird in this house. Lloyd, like me, isn't ready to talk about what Lily has done. The bathroom we can get over; her infantile jealousy is understandable, too. But not looking for the twins, when they were in the room next to her, while all of us were out searching, hunting high and low and worried sick, is hard to countenance.

Lily's history involves a difficult mother who used to play terrible mind games on her, and her much older sisters. She used to hurt Lily this way, and yesterday I saw Lily mirroring that behaviour – experiencing pleasure in causing pain for others. I think it's this part that bothers me. It doesn't excuse her behaviour, but it does help to explain it. I also need to find a way to stop it.

I walk around Tesco and enjoy choosing all their favourite sweets for the evening, but then I find myself hesitate, my hand hovering over the triple pack of Flake bars that would be Lily's preference.

This is serious. I decide that she doesn't deserve the treat, and walk away. That crumbly chocolate always makes a mess of the floor anyway. A few minutes later, my feet seem to be walking back in the direction of that aisle, almost of their own accord. My arms reach back to the shelf and put a packet in the trolley after all. When I analyse my decision, I discover it isn't because I am feeling reconciled; it's to prevent her from being spiteful again. That's got to be a form of emotional blackmail. Damn, I hate this.

The weekend rumbles along in a low-key way, but I am still not ready to talk to Lily as we approach the end of it.

In training, we were told never to send children to their rooms for more than just a few minutes without checking on them. The thinking is that being sent away will give the opportunity for their shame to hurt them. In this instance, I feel that shame at her behaviour is exactly how Lily needs to be feeling.

On autopilot, I do all the things that I normally do for her. I take her clean uniform up to her and ask her to put it away. She does not look at me or respond to my request. I'm still not in a place to have the conversation that needs to be had, but this situation can't continue. I need to end it now.

'Lily, can you please tell me if it is you that has been making the bathroom dirty?' I say, standing just inside her door. My voice is calm, even though I'm not.

She shrugs her shoulders. It's a gesture I know of old.

'Okay, Lily. I'm going to take that as a yes.'

I stand by the window while she looks at her phone. I know it's a defence mechanism rather than deliberate defiance, but that's not how it comes across.

'Lily, can you put the phone down please? I need to talk to you properly. This is important.' Again, my words are measured and controlled, betraying none of the emotion I really feel.

She puts the phone down to her side, but the action is accompanied by a dramatic eye roll that I'm definitely meant to witness.

I ignore it. 'Lily, I know that things have been difficult lately. I believe you are suffering from jealousy—'

She turns her head away.

'Hear me out. It's understandable, but it's an ugly emotion that achieves nothing but pain. Pain for you and everyone around you. Including me.'

Now her head moves downwards, as if it's too heavy for her shoulders.

'Do you want to tell me anything?'

She returns to the shrug, but she's less sure of herself now.

'Do you want to talk about what's been going on? Do you want to tell me about how you're feeling?'

A swallow. A barely perceptible shake of the head.

'Lily, look, I know that it can't make you feel happier, knowing that you have caused others pain. I know that isn't who you are.'

She looks up at me and all front is gone. She has tears running down her cheeks. I take a step forward and beckon her to come in for a hug. She does. I hold her tight.

'Lily, you are my girl. You always will be. But please stop whatever it is you are doing.'

As I say this, I believe the words. She *is* mine and always will be, but at the same time I also know that it isn't entirely true. Children in the care system are still that: part of a system rather than a true family. No matter how much we want to believe they are ours entirely, they remain children of the corporate parent as well. Even though she is safe for now, I wish with all my heart that she was solely ours. I know her position is precarious. If she carries on displaying negative behaviours, the system may swallow her back up. I have seen great placements break down when the child hits their teens. Unlike birth children, where it's usually just the parents involved in guiding the child through those difficult times, in the system, the foster carers can be hugely undermined by inexperienced or unthinking social workers who see what might be typical acts of rebellion as something more sinister, and intervene, unravelling all the work the foster carer has done over the years.

I hug Lily tight, because I know she is more vulnerable than Jackson or Vincent. Her teenage kicks will be scrutinised and analysed and written about and acted on by others in a way that theirs won't be, and the outcomes will be out of our hands. We stand in silence in the security of our squishy hug. I am silently praying, though I'm not religious, that Lily keeps it together over the next few years so that we can keep that external interference to a minimum.

Suddenly Dotty and Doug break through her door, jump onto the bed and do their happy 'look at us' sneezing and, just by being there, change the mood to laughter. Why wouldn't you have dogs in a house? They're excellent emotional gauges and always know just what's needed.

I leave Lily to their particular brand of love, and notice that the bathroom is no longer a mess. I have some apologising to do myself.

The boys, at first, are a little indignant. Jackson clings on to the 'how dare I accuse them of making a stinky mess?' mentality. But they accept that they have been responsible in the past, and that's probably where Lily got her inspiration from, and where I got my misplaced ideas about their guilt. We spend a good deal of time talking, and I explain to the boys how Lily is struggling with the challenges that life is throwing at her at the moment.

'I know it seems difficult to understand, but I believe that her acts of jealousy are also acts of fear. I suspect the surge of hormones that is upon her is mixed with fears about the new arrivals. There is no doubt that Max and Mia take up a lot of my time. They just do because of their age and because of the fact that there are two of them. That probably feels like a threat to Lily. She must feel that her position in the household isn't as secure as yours is, and that maybe explains why she wanted to get you into trouble.'

I'm proud of my sons because not only do they forgive her, but they don't take these bits of knowledge as tools to use against Lily. They accept Lily as she is, faults and all, and in their own way try to help her by reassuring her that she is still their annoying sister.

After talking it through with Lloyd, we decide to play down the faux twin disappearance. I don't think it is necessary to add in the drama of us worrying that they had been abducted, and that our gate was not safe, or that Lily displayed tendencies that could be aligned to her birth mother's abuse. You could see how on paper, with the added ingredient of an overstretched or under-experienced social worker, this could seem like something more than an unpleasant day of confusions and misunderstandings. That could manifest itself into something unstoppable and out of control.

We are just regular people living regular lives. We aren't superhuman. We make mistakes. I shall downplay it all.

The twins hid in the garden, when I raised my voice out of frustration at the boys, and then found somewhere safe inside the house. The gate had expanded after the rain and not closed tightly, and that led us to draw a wrong conclusion. Lily is going through her first serious blast of hormonal changes and that has led to a temporary regression back into her childhood behaviour.

Let it be!

I will say that the twins hid themselves when the house was noisy. It was nothing more than that, and it won't happen again. Foster carers live in constant fear of allegations. Most of them are angry or mischievous complaints from children, their parents or social workers, each of whom are under different pressures and sometimes need to blame someone else. Sadly, because we live in a society that only values products and services that cost the most, foster carers (who, in the real-world reckoning, generally receive the equivalent of about 30p per hour) sit near the bottom of the hierarchy. We command little respect, so we tend to get the crap. We have been in difficult situations in the past, sometimes as a result of being too honest about what's going on, and now I try to head it off at the pass.

I sit in the kitchen trying to grapple with the next and more immediate problem of what to buy from the supermarket to feed us all over the next few days. It needs not to cost the earth, but also to accommodate all the various tastes and likes and dislikes of all seven of us. That isn't always easy, especially with Lily, who remains the only vegetarian I know who will not eat vegetables. I wonder if perhaps she needs extra vitamins. Maybe that's contributing to her moods and behaviour. I might need to change up her diet a little. And then I need to give some thought to the other issue here: the twins themselves.

Have our unthinking behaviours and preoccupations harmed them further?

Chapter Nine

The children all get off to school this morning with no bother, and I'm happy that, once again, the bathroom is not a mess. I can deal with a few dropped towels and discarded pants decorating the floor, but not the squalor it was getting in before. Lily's room is still in chaos, but one battle at a time, and I'm choosing carefully at the moment.

Max and Mia seem okay. A bit subdued, perhaps. Lloyd has kindly taken them out for the morning. There is a petting farm not too far away that he thought would cheer them up and provide a bit of distraction after recent events, and also allow me to catch up on some emails and work. I'm grateful for the headspace. The phone has been pinging with messages from the flood group, who are as worried about the Met Office storm forecast as I am. Before I settle into my studio, I make sure the sandbags are ready in position outside, along with the big plastic sheet to stack in front of the flood gate. One of our neighbours is quite depressed, as she wants to move but can't sell her house while we are flooding. It's a situation she couldn't have predicted: climate change has exacerbated the consequences of poor planning decisions locally. Nobody's winning here.

The next set of pings come from the foster carers' WhatsApp group. It's not good news. Another carer has decided to leave the world of foster care after 15 years of service, because they are fed up with the way foster carers are treated and can't make the money work. I can't blame them, and I can't say anything that will help. Oh dear. It's a mad world, but I must stay focused.

I put a Joni Mitchell CD on and get to work. I begin sending emails to my agent, publisher, and new gallery in Italy, who I have been in contact with for a while now. I see an email from Bea. She has arranged contact again, but with Dad this time. Again in Salisbury, same drill as last week. Bea is meant to be here every week or so when a placement is new, but I haven't seen hide nor hair of her since she dropped Max and Mia off here. I'm not bothered, as the children are fine and I'm not comfortable around Bea anyway. She can stay away, as far as I'm concerned. Thanks to Joni Mitchell I drift into a better mood, a good zone where I can work on the illustrations for my first children's books.

The next few days go well, and I pay extra attention to all the children, ensuring that I spend time with each one individually, especially Lily. Though we are creeping further into autumn, the light is still holding after they come back from school, giving us a few hours of possibility. I have taken Lily with me on a walk every day. She clearly needs more attention at this particular point in her life. We talk about all sorts of things. I even take the wildflower book with us and she seems interested, though I suspect that might be to humour me as much as anything. She's certainly better at finding the flowers on the pages than her little foster siblings, though the blooms are fewer as the season starts to change.

She opens up a bit more about her early life and talks more freely than ever before about the violence she saw between her mum and her boyfriends.

'Were they *all* violent?' I ask.

She is quiet for a moment. 'Yes, I think they were. But I don't know that mum was choosing violent men. I think she *made* them violent, somehow.'

It's an interesting observation.

The conversation continues and branches into the psychology of human behaviour and the cycles of behaviours that we learn from our parents or caregivers, and those around us with influence.

'Did you ever meet your grandmother?' I ask.

Lily nods.

'And do you remember her story?' I know it, but I don't know if Lily does.

'Nan was with Grandad Barry, who used to hit her and my mum when she was young.'

On it goes, round and round.

'It's up to each of us to break the cycles. It's not easy. It takes a bit of work. The most important thing is to pay attention to our own behaviour and not blame it on the ones before us.'

Lily knows what I mean.

'It takes effort, but we're all capable of changing.'

I say this with love in my heart, and then I confess that I know I need to work harder than I have been doing recently with her; but she has responsibility too. It's the most open, frank conversation we've had in a long time. I only hope it's enough.

I think about the funny, out-of-character little outbursts that the twins have had since they arrived. I think, like Lily, that it's part of a learnt pattern of behaviour, something they've witnessed at some point. Perhaps one of their parents used to drink too much. Angelina seems too 'together' to have allowed that to happen, but we can never know what goes on behind closed doors.

I get a call from Hawfinch Primary School, interrupting my train of thought. It's the headteacher. I already had her pegged as a good woman, and she assures me that the school will bend over backwards to help children and their families.

'The first place will be available next Monday. I know it's difficult, but have you come to a decision about which of them you would prefer to take that first place?'

I let her know that, after lots of toing and froing and changing of minds, we have opted for Mia to attend first.

'I've emailed Bea, the twins' social worker, and Moira, our family supervising social worker with my rationale, and they both agree.'

'Excellent. We'll have everything ready for Mia on Monday. Now for the bad news. I'm afraid that the second place in the other class might be a bit slower than we first thought, as the family who are moving from the area are being held up with their new house. I know that's not ideal.'

She shares a few more details: the usual story about solicitors slowing everything down to make more money while people end up doing a lot of the work themselves. She doesn't actually say this, but it's the interpretation I put together from her words. I have friends in Europe where it takes a matter of weeks to sell a house and move, but here we seem to be utterly fleeced, at the mercy of people's whims, and it all seems to be made as difficult and as stressful as possible. I feel sorry for the family; we went through it ourselves. But this means Max will be here on his own. My heart sinks. Art and writing deadlines burst like balloons above my head.

I try to put a positive spin on it. 'Ah well, it may be a good thing in the long term for Max to be on his own. I think it will certainly do Mia good.'

I talk about how she really is a polite little thing, except when she's fighting her brother, and how she seems to have been in his shadow a lot since they arrived with us. 'So I think she will thrive at school as a solo child.'

'Given that time is short, do you want to bring her in for an orientation visit tomorrow morning, so she's all set for her start on Monday?'

We make the necessary arrangements. I decide that I will work hard with Max to try to bring some calm into his life during our time together. My head is filled with the things I need to do. I must get everything ready for Thursday's trip to Salisbury, and also buy some new school uniform for Mia. Lloyd can occupy Max tomorrow morning. Vincent has kindly loaned him his old Thomas the Tank Engines and tracks, and the anticipation is making him very excited. That will keep him busy for a couple of hours.

The next morning, after the others have gone to school, I get Mia ready for her exciting morning. She will only be doing a couple of hours a day for the first few weeks while she settles in. Max is so excited about the trains that he doesn't really pay any attention to Mia and me heading out of the door together. I can see that Lloyd is enjoying being reunited with Vincent's train set, judging by the sound effects coming from the sitting room. Everyone's happy.

I walk the long way to school, so I can show Mia all the pretty gardens. There are still dahlias and asters in full bloom. There are a couple of gardens on the route that fascinate me, and I hope that Mia will like them too. Two neighbours have become competitive about their hedges.

One has shaped theirs into a battleship and the other has three beautifully clipped dogs. They are quite the spectacle. Mia agrees that they are amazing, and I make a mental note that even though it's slightly further, this will be the walk to school.

We reach the reception area and sign ourselves in. Mia is undaunted so far, from what I can tell. She doesn't seem concerned that she is here without her brother. We are soon met by the very warm and smiling Mrs Jones, the teacher of Ducklings class. She seems lovely: cheerful and welcoming, and more or less ignoring me to concentrate on Mia, which is how it should be. I can see that Mia has warmed to her; she skips along eagerly to keep up, and looks up at her teacher as Mrs Jones points out things on the wall and in different rooms and spaces in the school.

This is the first time I have been with just Mia in the weeks that they have been with us, and I can already see how different she is when she's away from Max.

I walk behind Mrs Jones and Mia as we head along the corridor to Ducklings class, where Mia will be on Monday. It has a lovely feel as we enter the classroom: the children are sitting on a carpet listening to their teaching assistant, who's introduced as what sounds like 'Mrs Shoo-Shoo.' Mrs Shoo-Shoo is showing the children gathered round her a pop-up book.

'That's not her actual name, you understand,' Mrs Jones explains. 'But it's easier for the children to pronounce.'

Mia is fizzing with excitement, and just wants to join straight in with the activity. Mrs Shoo-Shoo invites her to sit down with them, and straight away heads turn and several little hands wave at Mia. Mia tilts her head slightly and I see a little smile appear. She's going to enjoy this. A little girl with long plaits and an eyepatch under her glasses beckons Mia to sit next to her. My heart sings.

I may have got things wrong over bathroomgate, and inadvertently ended up frightening the children, but we've made the right decision here for Mia. Onwards and upwards.

Chapter Ten

Thursday morning comes around. I wake up Max and Mia first. Bea changed the times of contact with their father, without warning or consultation. It's now moved to late morning rather than early afternoon, so we need to get our skates on.

Last night they made cards for their dad, though I played it down and haven't explicitly said that we are visiting today. I suggested that we might post them. I also bought a similar set of sweetie presents for their dad as they chose for their mum, so all is fair.

I pop my head round Lily's door.

'Just reminding you that it is, in fact, morning.'

There's a grunt of a reply. It doesn't fill me with confidence that she's about to leap out of bed.

'Only, I heard your alarm go off fifteen minutes ago.'

Another grunt.

'Perhaps I could entice you down the stairs with the promise of some golden syrup porridge?' It's one of her favourites, and does the trick.

Meanwhile, Mia is sitting up in bed talking to her owl.

'Does Owl fancy a train ride today?' I ask.

She nods, 'Oh, yes!'

Max is already downstairs in the sitting room with the trains, along with Vincent and Jackson, and I suspect that as soon as he comes out of the shower, Lloyd will be there too. I busy myself gathering together ingredients for a train picnic. I can take them to the same place as last time for a little early tea if they're hungry. Or perhaps it will be me who feels peckish; the novelty of being out of my area often seems to make me want to eat.

Lloyd can't drive us today. He's busy with work, so we'll take the car to the station. The local authority won't pay for the parking, I know already, so I'll have to leave it on one of the side streets near the new developments.

They'll accept one receipt for the travel, and have agreed to pay for the train tickets, though I had to negotiate even for that. Moira was supportive, but I had to convince Bea that the train journey might cost a bit more than my 45p per mile allowance for petrol. I had to tell a little white lie and pretend that my car was being serviced. It feels as if the authority is so mean sometimes. We have to negotiate every penny, and sometimes it's like getting blood from a stone. And yet they chuck millions at private children's homes, which could never compete with the care of a good foster placement. It's so messed up.

As before, I plan to tell them two stops before that we are going to meet their father, though they already know that something is up.

Mia is a bright spark. 'Are we going to see Mummy again today?' she asks, as soon as we arrive at the station. I abandon my plan to delay the reveal, because she's too smart.

'Not today,' I say. 'Today we are going to see Daddy.'

They beam, as I hoped they would.

'I'm going to tell Daddy about Thomas and Trevor and Bertie and Edward and James and Donald and Douglas and Henry and Percy,' Max declares, breathless with excitement.

'Anyone else?' I laugh.

'Yes, Diesel, Daisy, Duck, Bill and Ben, and Toby,' he says, giving it serious thought. I keep thinking that Mia is the clever one, but Max is a bright little spark too. He's learnt all the trains in no time at all.

Mia clutches her owl tightly to her chest and repeats 'Daddy,' over and over again to herself. My heart goes out to her, the little poppet.

As the train pulls into the station, Max says, 'It's got red in it. Let's call it James.'

He's right. James is the red engine. I'm astonished.

They sit with me today, rather than on the chairs opposite, and snuggle in. A sure sign that they are feeling comfortable. I am so proud of them; they really are doing brilliantly.

If anyone raises their voice or there is a sudden movement, they still flinch, and sometimes one or both take off to the guest room to hide away under the Breton bed, but I know this now, so it doesn't matter if Lily has her head in the clouds or in her phone – I can find them. We've had a run of dry nights, too, so I'm toying with the idea of trying a night without the pull-ups. Progress on all fronts.

They are both so excited, and happy to talk about their daddy. They clearly love him as much as their mummy. I am so puzzled. Normally in the run up before contact, a child reveals how they really feel about their parent or family member. Sometimes they are angry or nervous, sometimes over-excited (which is another cause for a ponder), but these two are full of joyful anticipation, and I never get the feeling that they have been hurt or beaten or sexually abused. After years of fostering, and with my own childhood experience, I have a nose for these things.

At the third stop, we look out at a field of sheep. They are close enough to the train for us to be able to see their faces.

Max begins to sing, 'Baa baa rainbow sheep, have you any wool?'

I smile and sing with him, and Mia joins in.

I'm enjoying the song very much, but I definitely can't see any rainbow sheep in the field. I love that they can.

In my bag I have some sweets, separate from their father's gift, which of course they happily consume. I am careful that I don't give them too many, lest they overwhelm their father.

They are beautiful children. As an artist, I notice people's faces all the time: structure, symmetry, proportions, idiosyncrasies. Genuinely it isn't intended to be judgemental. I actually find unconventional faces far more interesting to paint. But these two have an old cherubic look about them, like paintings from another time. They remind me of the pictures of Romans that I saw in my Latin textbook at school. I remember how much I enjoyed learning Latin. As someone with dyslexia, I found it a far easier language to learn than some of the modern languages we were introduced to. I wonder how these two will fare at school. It also strikes me as a really big deal. They are taking that momentous step of beginning school, away from their parents and everything that is familiar.

'How do you feel about going to school, Mia?' I ask.

'Excited,' she says, in a voice that sounds as wary as it does enthusiastic. She hugs Owl in tightly to her.

Max smiles. 'Am I going to go to school, too?'

I explain about the places and how we have to wait for a child to leave before he can go. 'But it will be your turn very soon, Max.'

Since all the new housing developments have gone up, school places have become tighter and tighter. They didn't build any new schools or GP surgeries. I sometimes wonder if the CEOs of these property development companies would choose to live in a community without enough doctors or schools themselves. I imagine that the answer is 'probably not'. Perhaps the infrastructure will come soon. We live in hope.

Max takes out one of Vincent's old *Thomas the Tank Engine* books from his backpack. When I turn it over to look at the back, there are pictures of all the different trains. Max holds his index finger and points to each one and correctly names them. He's really nailed these trains. Perhaps it doesn't sound like much, but I find it staggering. He has only very recently begun watching Thomas, and has only amassed a few hours of exposure so far.

They are the most adorable pair, really. Their anger towards each other is just learnt behaviour. I know that. Behaviour and attitudes are reflections of early life experiences from our environment and adults' behaviours. No one is born bad.

Years ago, we looked after a little boy, Connell, who lived with terrible violence. His mother's boyfriend dragged him and his brother out of bed in the night and threw them down the stairs. The boyfriend was high on drugs and had had an argument with their mother. The little boy's older brother died later, after a severe injury to his neck and back from the fall. Connell stayed with us for a few weeks as an emergency placement, and it was a very difficult time. He used to kick me hard in the shin, and it's hard not to react to that. The reality was that he thought this was a way to show love. Each time the boyfriend hurt those boys, their mum would say, 'but he loves you.' The boyfriend was convicted and ended up going to prison for a very long time, I'm thankful to say.

Such experiences are clear indicators of the way that children pick up their behavioural patterns from the key adults in their lives, or sometimes exposure to things on TV. The latter is perhaps more easily corrected. I remember when Jackson was little, he transformed into a little monster for a period when he watched *Horrid Henry*. We decided to stop him watching it, as a result. Vincent, on the other hand, was fine with it; he loved being in the Green Hand Gang. I think that part of our role as parents is to be constantly aware of the ways in which our children respond to things. I have certainly noticed a few triggers and behavioural patterns with the twins. A small, inconsequential spat will escalate exponentially, bringing a great deal of aggression and anger, and that anger is usually directed between Max and Mia. There are outbreaks of venomous swearing, with words that they shouldn't know, particularly given that they haven't even properly started school yet. That first 'I hate you, you fucking arsehole' was a good indicator. Most of the time, though, they are calm, polite and well spoken. It makes those outbursts even more disturbing to witness. I strongly suspect, though, that they are simply re-enacting what they have seen.

I wonder where they have learnt it from.

Their mother certainly didn't present as an angry person, but I wasn't there in their home and I didn't see what happened. Of course, people are not always who they say they are, and things are not always as they seem. We put on our best faces for the people that we meet. I have learnt to keep an open mind, but my gut feeling is that Angelina is a bit lost, rather than dangerous.

The journey passes quickly. Thomas is a good distraction for Max, and Mia, when she isn't singing, reverts to repeating 'Daddy'. It's really very sweet.

We arrive at Salisbury and walk out through the entrance to look for a taxi. I have a feeling of déjà vu, but the children behave as if they have done this a hundred times.

'How are we doing?' I ask as we sit in the back of the taxi. 'Looking forward to this?'

Mia holds Owl up in front of her and looks her toy in the eyes, rather than me.

'I love Daddy.'

Max jiggles about on the seat and pipes up in a sing-song voice, 'Me too, me too.'

In the reception area, Jill is already in position, waiting for us. Once again, she brings a wonderful warm smile for the children and me. You can't beat a genuine smile.

'Is all well?' I query.

She smiles and nods. 'Do you want to take them to the toilet first?' she asks, remembering from last time.

I nod and take Max and Mia in without asking if they actually want to go. I'm well aware that they're far too excited to get the visit underway, and would just say no. I'm right. They do both need to go. We wash our hands and head back to the entrance. Jill opens the doors with a little flourish, as if we are the guests of honour at a gala dinner, and there, on the other side of the room, is the twins' father.

Jill introduces him as 'Ben' and me to him as 'Louise', but the introductions are lost as Max and Mia rush towards him.

'Ben is a train, Daddy!' Max exclaims.

I'm sure the poor man has no idea what Max is talking about, but Ben's arms are wide open, ready to receive his children. He lifts them both up in his hug, almost to the ceiling, and they squeal with excitement. It is another filmic moment, and all the love in the room takes away from the bleak reality of where we are.

Jill has moist eyes and reaches for a tissue, and I realise that I'm shedding a tear too. It's not how I usually feel at a contact visit, but the feeling with Angelina is replicated.

I make a conscious effort to pull myself away from the emotional dimensions of the scene and become a more impartial observer.

Ben is an arrestingly handsome man, though having seen Angelina, I'm not surprised. He's clearly older than her. Quite a bit older, actually. I look at his face and think that he is probably nearer to his forties than his twenties. He has a kind face. He has a shaved head, so I'm guessing by the shine from the lights in the room that he is losing his hair and has shaved it right off. It suits him well though, and fits with his immaculate, metrosexual beard. I don't know whether you can use the word 'metrosexual' to describe a beard, but the husband of a friend of mine, a rather vain but utterly delightful man, explained that it describes a heterosexual urban man who enjoys shopping and fashion. But Ben is also no stranger to a gym. In fact, he looks like he's stepped out of the pages of GQ magazine. Who are these people? I can't emphasise enough how far removed they are from my usual dealings in places like these.

Eventually calm is restored in the room, allowing me to introduce myself to Ben properly. We shake hands.

'Hello, Louise. It's good to meet you.' He is softly spoken and articulate, and he fixes his dark eyes on me in a way that could be disarming. Despite his fashionable attire, he manages to project a down-to-earthiness that is appealing.

'I'll leave you to it,' I say, and sit with Jill in a far corner with the aim of keeping her talking so that she does not interfere. I noticed last time that she has a tendency to try and get a little too involved in the session. I'm sure it's necessary, and welcome it when contact visits are stilted and awkward and the ice needs breaking, but that isn't the case here. This session can be about the children spending time with their father without the contact worker being at the centre of them. It feels like a happy reunion, perhaps after a week away at work – not a family thrown briefly back together after a dramatic rupture.

I pass the time of day with Jill, keeping one eye on the scene, enjoying the dynamic of this little group in their hour of contact. They love their dad, no question. They aren't scared of him, nor are they going out of their way to please him, which can be a sign that they have had to appease an adult. I see Ben look away for a moment and fiercely wipe a tear away, keeping his emotions in check for the sake of his children. I just don't understand it. Any of it. What the hell happened to this family?

He, like Angelina, has bought the children gifts. Again, nothing too ostentatious or showy. A set of Hot Wheels for Max and a box of rainbow sand for Mia. I can tell he has thought this through. Sometimes the parents give their children so much stuff it can overwhelm them, not to mention their bedrooms, when they get home. I have known children arrive back from contact with so much stuff they never actually look at. I also think that children know when it's theatre, and that some parents do this for the audience. One girl once said to me (in front of her dad, which was awkward), 'He never bothered feeding us when we were at home, so what's all this?'

That isn't the case here. It's appropriate to give a gift, of course. And he has the balance just right.

He asks lots of questions, about what their rooms are like, what Mia's school visit was like, how their new big brothers and sister are – he's clearly well informed. But he also listens carefully to their answers, and the conversation flows, as much as conversation between an adult and two four-year-olds can. Max tells him enthusiastically about how we came here 'on James the red engine', and how Daddy has the same name as one of the *Thomas* trains, but there isn't one called Max or Mia. The visit draws to a close, two hours passing by fast, but it has been a resounding success.

Unlike with Angelina, though, I don't give Ben my number.

I feel torn, because it feels unfair, as if I'm being disloyal. Though I'm not sure who to. Angelina? I will think on it. In the final moments, I try to distract Jill once again, in order to allow Ben and his children to say goodbye properly.

Again, I am impressed with how he handles it. Like Angelina, he tries to not upset them. He's careful about what he says, underplaying things so that it's just a gentle goodbye until next time. When they look like they've finished, I walk up to them, holding the children's coats. Ben is holding the cards they made him close to his chest. It's a transparent bit of body language, though I can tell it's natural and not contrived.

The upshot is, I like him. He seems genuine, and perhaps he also seems lost. He doesn't come across as trouble – or troubled. He seems quite lovely, actually. I just can't get my head around this situation.

The children are thrilled with their presents. Thankfully they are the right size to be manageable on the train, though

I don't know about starting the rainbow sand until we're home. We might be alright with the cars.

Jill is in the corner, picking up some books, and that gives me an opportunity to say, out of earshot, 'It'll all work out. I'm sure it will.'

Ben looks at me gratefully. He gives a quick nod. He needed to hear that.

Chapter Eleven

Today, I am mostly very happy – until Bea arrives.

Mia has settled into her first full week of school beautifully and, as I thought (while crossing my fingers), sending her first was most definitely the right decision. She loves it and skips in happily each morning. She talks about various friends – Ruby, Ella and Jessica – and the reports from Mrs Jones fill me with confidence that not only is she fine academically, but she's also sociable and well adjusted in the class. Somehow. Good girl.

My strong hope is that Max and Mia will only be here short term.

I want so much for them to be able to go back home and to be able to go to school locally there.

I think I've known from the moment they arrived that I'm not making a long-term emotional investment with these two. This is unlike my experiences with with some of the other children we've fostered, even the ones who've been the most challenging, when I've known that we might need to be in it for the long haul.

Lily is one such 'long haul'. There is no doubt that she continues to feel jealous and threatened by the presence of Max and Mia, more so than she has done with other foster siblings in the past. Perhaps it's because there are two of them and, therefore, they demand a lot more of me. There is no doubt that you work twice as hard with twins.

Imagine sextuplets. No, I'll bypass that placement if it ever comes my way.

I'm going to have to work even harder at reassuring Lily that we are her family, and this is her home. She is safe. At the moment, as a long-term foster child, the plan is that she will be with us until she is 18 years old. In my book, that doesn't mean that we fling her out after she's blown out the candles on her 18th birthday cake. But on a serious note, it all changes in terms of our status and funding. On paper, we will no longer be her foster carers, and she becomes a 'staying put'. But 18 seems so arbitrary. Children's social care is in a constant state of counterintuition. We learn from the beginning that children who have experienced trauma and neglect have variable emotional ages – as opposed to the conventional milestone developmental ages of children from a 'secure base'. Apart from the fact that I know I now hate this jargon, I am also convinced the system is mad. Once a looked-after child has reached their 16th birthday, they can leave and go into 'assisted living' should they choose to. Don't even get me started. I have known teenagers who have sat on my lap for a cuddle because they didn't have any nurture when they were young, only to be thrust out into a hostel in cheap housing near gangs and drug dealers. Give me strength!

Lily is more than welcome to stay here, but the system acts as if on their birthdays they are suddenly transformed into streetwise, responsible, independent adults, who are capable of running their own lives, walking into a well-paid job, and recognising danger. As vulnerable adults, perhaps more prone to predatory behaviour than the rest of the population, that danger can be cunningly disguised as a friend.

Lily needs to feel safe again. Confident that Lloyd and I aren't going to suddenly bail out on her. I think the mid-teens are tricky years in the care system.

So I *was* feeling happy, but clouds of fear for the children's futures present themselves on the horizon. And that is the lot of a parent. While I gather myself together and rein myself back in from those fears, I continue to open the morning's post and get on with the 'gone to school' room check.

Because the weather is definitely now on the cusp and that little nip in the air is there, especially first thing in the morning, I only open the middle, smaller windows in each room to air them out. I shake out the duvets and do a quick scan for dirty laundry or dirty anything, really. In Max and Mia's room I notice that Max's sketchbook is out on the floor, with pens and pencils and crayons scattered around. I tidy up the colours and put them away, and then pick up the pad and flick through its pages. He's been busy drawing and 'writing' in there. Several sheets are filled with images and attempts at different mark-making.

One page in particular captures my attention. It's a picture of what looks like his mum and dad, a conclusion I draw from the curly red hair on the female figure and a prominent beard on the male. Next to them are two smaller figures, presumably Max and Mia.

I sit down on the chair in their room to take a proper look, holding the book in both hands and drinking in the picture. I flick through the other pages. There is an image of a lovely big house and lots of trees.

Max has put himself right in the centre of the picture.

When I was working as an artist-in-residence at a men's lifers' prison, I occasionally worked with a well-known art therapist called Ron. He taught me that when the artist puts themselves in the centre of the page, that's good news. Even if it's a tiny image, it's full of hope. Max has put his mum and dad either side of him and Mia is to the right, near the edge of the page. Working with Ron, I sometimes felt as if 'reading' art in this way was a bit like reading tea leaves, the ancient art of 'tasseography' – more like divination or fortune-telling than a proper analysis. In fact, some of the things he said used to make me think it was more of a power trip for him, tapping into something mystical that the rest of us mere mortals couldn't see.

Therapists who read this will raise their eyebrows, I'm sure, but that's how it felt. I remember the personality test that was popular a while ago, along with all that psychometric testing that businesses seemed to be paying a fortune for. I recall sitting in staff training sessions at the university where I worked, watching some of the staff and students taking the test. People seemed to 'discover' all sorts of things about themselves, but I wondered how the discoveries were new. It says a lot about how little some people know about themselves. I also saw how some students didn't like what they discovered and re-did the test, supplying different answers that gave them a more flattering reading. Perhaps there are better tests now, but it seemed to me that you could just say what the test needed you to say to get the outcome, and therefore the personality, you desired.

Another 'personality test' became more of a dinner party game. You draw a tree, house, sun, river and snake. Each image corresponds to a description of aspects of you. Maybe the sun represents your father, the snake is your sexuality, blah blah blah. Again, I remember people believing in this rigidly, even though interpretations varied so much according to who was doing the testing.

I have tried to steer clear of anything that feels like an egotistical party trick ever since. Sometimes it even happens right on my doorstep, and I can't avoid it. I've had to sit and endure a psychologist at my kitchen table asking a deeply traumatised child to talk about what they would be like 'if they were an island...'

It didn't seem to be a particularly constructive conversation. I don't like to imagine how many children's lives have been sent down the wrong path because they described the island in a certain way. Anyway, I'm not an island, I've got plenty of other people to think about, and it's time to get on with the day in earnest. And despite my misgivings about Ron's art therapy interpretation, I'm definitely heartened by some of the details in Max's drawing.

It occurs to me that Angelina might like to see it too. It all looks very healthy and homely, and it's quite an accomplished drawing for a four-year-old. I've seen some sights in my time (a child with an axe in their head, a man with shark's teeth, and page after page of erect penises to name but a few) but there is nothing here to cause any kind of concern.

I take a picture with my phone and compose a brief message to Angelina.

Hi Angelina, I thought you would like to see this lovely drawing Max did of you all – Mia is enjoying school and seems so happy to be there. Poor Max is stuck here with me, so we're home-schooling for another week or two until his place is ready.

I hit send, and head downstairs. On my way to the kitchen, I call out to Lloyd, who has been in his studio for hours already. His business clients are all over the world, so he has been up since 5am to accommodate their working hours.

'Don't forget that Queen Bea is coming over this morning.'

I get a pre-occupied 'yeah' in response. By the time I reach the kitchen my phone is pinging, an alert from the Flooding WhatsApp group about a yellow weather warning. Great, that's all I need.

I flip open my laptop, open up all the documents I need ready for the meeting with Bea, and open up another tab for the Met Office weather. Yep, sure enough, a storm is forecast for later today.

I'll use it to my advantage. I'll tell Bea as soon as she arrives, so she panics and goes off to her horses. The thought cheers me up no end. I'm probably a wicked woman who'll burn in hell. But, if it saves me from time with Bea, I'll take it.

I tidy up the kitchen table and try to rein in the bewilderment that overtakes me every time I see a pile of dirty dishes, *stacked up neatly* next to the dishwasher. How is it that Lloyd, or anyone else in the household for that matter, has not yet managed to work out that it would, in actual fact, be quicker to load them straight into the empty, plaintively waiting dishwasher, than to carefully stack them like that?

I squash down the inner banshee who wants to scream out at the top of her voice. Though Gaelic folklore has them as the harbingers of an imminent death, I don't think I would go as far as to actually commit murder for the crime of not thinking to fill the dishwasher. Instead, I sigh, smile and get on with the business of stacking it, remembering to be grateful for the fact that I have a dishwasher, and people around me to create the need for it.

Time for the coffee machine, though I mustn't have too much coffee. My energy levels are rising already without the injection of caffeine.

Within a few minutes, I'm content with the state of the kitchen, and happy with Max as he quietly sits in the front room being home-schooled. By 'being home-schooled', I should point out that today's lesson plan involves *Thomas the Tank Engine* toys. To be fair, the school was very helpful, and some nice person sent me a load of links to different websites, but after five minutes of not being able to log in to some things and being overwhelmed by others, I was so confused I decided to go rogue and just do fun things. 'Engagement' is the idea today. And 'learning through play'. It's all good.

'Right, Max, don't forget that Bea is coming in a minute.'

He looks up and smiles and nods. I know he hasn't taken that in and doesn't give a hoot. He just wants to play with the trains. Also, I'm not even sure he remembers who Bea is, so absent has she been from our lives in the last few weeks.

Here it is, the knock at the door. Dotty and Doug strike up their inevitable lively barking chorus.

I head down the hallway and open the door to Bea.

Once again, she has a bit of straw stuck in her long wild hair. Perhaps it's deliberate: a fashion accessory. Today her hair is tied up in a ponytail. How apt. I note that, once again, she hasn't bothered to change for our meeting. There are the jodhpurs, the riding boots and a tatty green jacket. Perhaps we'd get on better if I let out a little neigh. I'm tempted.

To this day, I have never even sat on a horse, let alone ridden one. The closest I've come was a camel on our honeymoon in Egypt.

Horses are beautiful, majestic creatures, and they make wonderful subjects for paintings. I can admire them, I just don't understand the riding thing. As with sailing, skiing, and perhaps caravanning and camping, I think you have to have grown up with it in order to fully get it. I didn't really have a sailing or skiing sort of background. My adoptive family never even went on holiday, and they never would have paid for me to take up an interest like riding.

It's probably a compensatory reaction to my own childhood that I personally pay for Lily to have riding lessons. She likes it, but it isn't all-consuming, and I suspect her interest will soon die, just as it has for all the girls I have looked after. It has always been a phase, rather than a lifelong commitment. They discover other interests after the *My Little Pony* stage and want to spend their time elsewhere. I never challenge their decision, and the weekly savings are much appreciated.

In comes Bea to the kitchen, like John Wayne entering a saloon. I can almost hear the *How the West Was Won* overture as a soundtrack behind her.

'Where are Lloyd and Max?' she demands, as if they are cattle rustlers pending jail.

She pulls out a chair and scrapes the wooden legs loudly across the stone floor. It's a noise I hate. One that sets my teeth on edge, worse than nails down a blackboard. I've trained the children not to do it by showing them how to lift the chair properly, pulling it gently and slowly. Lily now scrapes the chair on the floor if she is feeling stroppy. It's one of her little signals, and while I accept that all behaviour is communication, it doesn't mean I easily tolerate her behaviour. She knows that too, which is why she does it.

Bea pulls out her laptop from her large brown Aztec-inspired patterned bag, along with a notebook and pen. I see a packet of Marlboro Lights spill onto the floor and watch Bea quickly sweep them back into her bag.

'So, how are they getting on?' is her next gambit.

This is when I know that a social worker has not read any of my emails. Hopefully Bea's read at least a few or I'll have to try and remember what I said days and weeks ago. I've slept since then, so that's not always possible. I'd prefer a slightly more focused question.

I update Bea on Mia's fantastic progress at school, and how she no longer needs to wear the night-time pull-up. She has moved on brilliantly.

'Max still needs the pull-up but, as a mother of sons, I would suggest that there is an element of laziness attached to this scenario.'

She looks puzzled, so I ask if she has children.

'Yes, I have a son, but he lives with his dad, so I'm not sure about things like that.'

Interesting. I'm reminded of the time when a social worker sat in a Personal Education Plan (PEP) meeting at school, a termly meeting held for children in care. As we discussed the improved behaviour of the child in my care, her phone went off. Her son had been excluded and she went into a state of panic. I, along with another teacher at the meeting, ended up having to reassure her that it wasn't the end of the world. I suppose it goes to show that social workers don't have perfect parenting lives either.

'Anyway, the most recent news is the two contact visits with Max and Mia's parents.'

I fill in the details, reporting on how I feel the two contacts went.

Lloyd comes into the kitchen. 'Hi Bea, how are you?'

He moves behind her and points at her hair, so that I can see his gesture but she can't. He's just as amused as I was to see a piece of straw stuck in it.

The coffee machine goes back on, and the meeting progresses well. But as we talk, I detect a tone in Bea's words that I don't like.

'Mum and Dad, as you no doubt saw, are very privileged. It just goes to show that money can't buy you everything.'

I feel my hackles rising. Who is Bea to have an opinion about their financial or social status? Well, she can have an opinion, I suppose, but who is she to be voicing it so freely to me? I have been known to call out this awful, subjective and irrational bias in social workers and other foster carers. None of us are innocent, and all of us have done something that we're not too proud of. It's called being human. Bea's comments anger me particularly, I suppose, because I have been impressed with the dignity that both parents have so far displayed. Child abuse and neglect exists in *all* social groups. It's just that some are better at covering it up than others; some are given the benefit of the doubt because of their faith, some because of their background and education. I genuinely don't give a hoot about someone's social background. I only care about how they are towards the children in their care. If it sounds as if I'm judgemental about Bea, it's because I don't feel that the children are necessarily her priority. It seems that four legs trump two in her case. So, I don't feel as if I can let it go.

'What do you mean by that, Bea?' I say.

I can see the look of dread on Lloyd's face as I ask the question. He knows exactly my view on attitudes like Bea's.

'Well, they have tons of money. He's worth a fortune, so they live in a massive house and have the dream life. Or at least they did until it all went wrong. Angelina is much younger than Ben and personally, I think she's a bit spoilt.'

I try very hard to keep my calm. Even if the words themselves weren't so damning, the 'personally, I think' is a big giveaway. This is just malicious gossip, and totally unprofessional. I want to react further, to make my opposition to this point of view clear, but I also want to keep my powder dry and help this family return to their lives, privileged or not.

Pain and misery can happen to anyone. They aren't exclusive to being poor.

Yes, having more money can help keep some issues away or at bay, but it can also create different ones.

I decide to dig deep and resist letting Bea have my thoughts on all cylinders. I just say, placidly, 'Oh, I see.'

Those who know me well know that when I'm being terribly, terribly polite, it means I have your number and it's just a matter of time. Lloyd's face is clearly relieved, but he is well aware that I want to get Bea out of the house, particularly when I begin to talk about the weather and the yellow weather warning.

'It sounds as if we'll be at the centre of a serious storm,' I say.

She is already alert to this, and goes on to tell me that the riding school where she kept her horse was destroyed by the last storm.

'Eighteen horses were moved at speed to the top of the nearby hill for protection, including my own, a black stallion called Bruce.'

I make a mental note of this story and the location of the riding school, to follow up for more information about the flooding.

'Oh dear. Where's your horse now?' I ask.

'I've had to stable him in another town, which is a pain because it's difficult to get to, but it's only temporary.'

Okay, that explains why she is still in her riding attire; she hasn't had time to go home and change. I'll forgive her for that. Before she leaves, she tells me the next date and time for the twins to have contact with mum. It's another Thursday morning.

'Do you think the time could be rearranged? It would mean taking Mia out of school and I'm not sure that's a good idea just as she's settling in.'

Actually, I don't think it's a good idea at all. Absence like that should be avoided at all costs. Even dental appointments should, if possible, be timetabled around the school day, in my opinion.

'I'm happy to do a Saturday or Sunday. In fact, it would suit me – and Mia – much better.'

'Well, I don't know if that's going to be possible,' Bea answers. 'I need to be there for this contact. I am writing the review for court and need to see how mum interacts with the children. So, I've rearranged things so that I can be there on Thursday.'

'Right.' We agree to the weekday, and to taking Mia out of school, since it's clear that Bea isn't going to be moved on this. 'And do I still need to be at the contact? Jill does a perfectly good job as contact worker. It feels a bit awkward.'

Bea shrugs. I have my eye on the opportunity of doing some shopping in Salisbury during the visit, and maybe even heading to the Arts Centre to see what's on.

The nuts and bolts of our business concluded, Bea finally turns her attention towards Max. She speaks to him in an annoying, patronising way that makes me cringe on his behalf.

'Hello Max. How are we today? Are we enjoying playing with the trainy-wainies?'

It's quite clear that Max just wants to keep playing and not be interrupted to talk to the woman who took him and his sister away from their mum and doesn't know the proper name for a train.

Eventually she departs.

I shut the door behind her and return to the kitchen to find Lloyd making more coffee. He blows out his cheeks. 'Woah, she's quite a piece of work!'

'Isn't she?'

'Well done for not punching her.'

'I have never punched anyone in my life, thank you very much. How dare you.' I smile.

I reach for my phone and discover that while we've been talking, a text has come in from Angelina. I'm glad I didn't tell Bea about our conversations. I don't think it would have gone down very well at all. I'll have to ask Angelina explicitly to keep this between us for now, though I'm sure that she understands. Here we go into the web of cover-ups and white lies to protect the children; and now, in this case, to protect the parents. Notions of 'truth' aren't very clear cut in children's social care. Much of our work is based on lies and deceit.

Angelina is thrilled with the image of the drawing that Max did.

And there's a second message. *Would it be okay to have a chat at some point? x*

I text back. *Are you free now?* No time like the present, and Max is enjoying the company of Lloyd. Or is it Lloyd enjoying the company of Max and playing with the trains to avoid having to work for a while? No matter: they're happy.

Angelina answers straight away, in her delightful Italian accent. I remove myself to the end of the garden, away from the house so that Max won't hear. She wants to know everything about the school, about Max's other drawings, and also, understandably, about our household, and how her children are interacting with my much older children. But she is also very, very frank about her own life, and confides a little about the breakdown in her relationship with her husband. She fills in many of the gaps. I didn't know enough from the paperwork that I was given at the start of the placement to try and understand what had been happening for this family, but I glean a great deal from Angelina. Pieces of the jigsaw fall into place. I have a much better idea now about how this poor woman has suffered, and from what I can gather, she should have had some help long before social services took her children away.

She talks very fondly about her parents, but admits that being far away from them was problematic as a new mother. She opens up about her childhood and how, although they have a good relationship now, her father was violent towards her mother at times. I think about the little aggressive moments I've witnessed between Max and Mia, and I wonder. She talks so much that I wonder if she has had the chance to talk any of this through with anyone. Does she have any friends?

While Angelina is in full flow, Lloyd waves to me from the kitchen window, tapping his wrist, where a watch would sit if he had one, then does eating signals to indicate that Max needs lunch.

I look at my own watch and realise that we have been chatting for an hour. My heart goes out to this poor woman, and I feel as if I could talk to her all day, but with Bea's visit and this unscheduled chat, I'm an hour late for Max's lunch. The poor boy's tummy will be rumbling. I tell Angelina that I must go and feed her boy – a strange conversation if you think about it, but this is foster care: it's all just different degrees of strangeness.

We say our goodbyes and then I send her another quick text. *Thank you for talking to me, and please rest assured that I won't pass on the fact that we've had this conversation.*

I don't add, 'despite the fact that I'm meant to, according to the social workers', but I imagine it will be enough to do the trick. I just don't have a good feeling about what Bea's response might be.

And then I add the same message that I gave to Ben: *It'll all work out. I'm sure it will.*

PART THREE
Before

Angelina and Ben

VII. Ben

Max and Mia are two years and two months old

'Let's have some friends over this weekend.'

Ben has another couple, who also have young children, in mind. He wants to have some fun, but he also thinks that the mums might be able to talk about their experiences. Angelina hasn't smiled in a long time now. He has no idea how long. Has she ever been happy since the twins were born? Perhaps not. When they celebrated Max and Mia's second birthday a few weeks ago, Angelina had talked about bunting and a children's entertainer and children everywhere, but in the end she didn't seem to have the inclination or the energy to organise anything very much. There was no one really to invite, so they kept it a small affair. Just the four of them. It was easier that way. With no one else coming, it seemed silly to have a whole cake or decorate everywhere. They've become so insular.

He needs to make more of an effort. Maybe this will help. It can't make things any worse.

'The weather forecast is good and, even if it does rain, the outdoor room and the canopy will keep us dry.'

Angelina is out of the rhythm of parties and socialising. She hasn't had any visitors to speak of for nearly a year now, and Ben is beside himself with worry, but also running out of ideas of what to do.

He has watched as she has become the clichéd 'shadow' of her former self. But it isn't a cliché when it's happening to your own wife. It began with the gradual reduction in the amount of contact with people she previously spent time with, but it happened so slowly that he didn't notice straight away. And because he was working, he didn't always see that it was happening. Whenever she was invited to something, she always managed to find a good excuse not to attend by saying that one of the children was poorly, or she was unwell herself and didn't want to pass on any nasty bugs to someone else's children. In the beginning, the excuses were convincing, always plausible. These days, she isn't as good at pretending.

He knows how hard she finds it to deal with the twins on her own, but she has also become reluctant for them to do things as a family, or at least things that involve leaving the house. Some days she is a sobbing wreck. The vivacious girl he married has completely disappeared. He realises with a nasty shock one day, when he tries to run his fingers through her hair and she pulls away, that she is in a bad way.

But, 'When did you last wash your hair?' he discovers, is not a good way to begin a conversation.

She no longer wears makeup, or spends any money on clothes. The things that he buys her stay in their expensive boxes and stack up inside her walk-in closet, untouched. The perfume she once loved grows stale in its bottle, and when he replaces it, that grows stale too.

Ben has repeatedly tried to encourage her to visit a doctor, reassuring her that he is happy to go private and that it would be very discreet. In her rich Italian accent, she only says, 'What good would there be in talking to a lunatic?' She has no time for people involved in therapy. 'They are the ones with the problems, not me.'

It is increasingly clear that, despite whatever she may think, she does have problems.

Earlier in the year, he insisted on a nursery place, part-time, so that Angelina could regain some time to herself. They found a local nursery that prided itself on its rural setting within an urban location and focused on outdoor activity.

Angelina had been reluctant at first, but was gradually won over by the small scale and positive ethos of the place.

'Now you can get back to the things you want to do,' he assured her. 'At least for a few hours a week. What about getting that yoga woman back?'

But it seems that there is nothing that Angelina wants to do. She has completely lost her mojo. And the nursery experiment didn't last long. The children would have benefited enormously from attending but, after a few weeks, Angelina drifted away. She blamed the other mothers, but they seemed happy and friendly as far as Ben could see.

He's sure that she received coffee invitations from them while the twins were in nursery, but to his knowledge she never accepted.

Instead, he occasionally finds her in the garden, alone with a large glass of wine. And sometimes a cigarette, which is strange because, as far as he knew, she was never a smoker.

He's tried to talk about their non-existent sex life, and worked out, from the things that she has said, that she is scared to become pregnant again. They'd always talked vaguely about having lots of children, but the reality of having twins seems to have suppressed all those thoughts.

Maybe her fears contribute to the way she presents herself these days, as drab and uninterested. The flowing, feminine designer outfits she wore previously have now been replaced by jeans and sweatshirts. He remembers the desire he had felt for her in the early days of their relationship. He wants the closeness back. He misses her touch, her breath on his neck in the night. Now, somehow, she seems to be asexual.

It breaks his heart to see the way she has changed. This is not the family he wanted; far from it. For a man used to being able to get whatever he wants, it is destroying him, too. He tries not to be angry, but sometimes he wishes she would just pull herself together. Suddenly, Ben realises how much he misses his parents too. He knows that he is too old, in his forties, to play the orphan card, but sometimes he just needs them. He wishes desperately that they could have seen the children, even just once. They would have loved the twins so much. Perhaps things would have been different if his parents were around to support them. The pain is almost too much to bear.

Now is one of those times. Damn it, why can't she just cooperate?

'Go on. Think about it, at least. We haven't seen Gus and Silv for ages. Let's have them round.'

'I don't know—' She bites her lip.

'I do,' he says, as gently as he can. 'Come on. What harm could it do?'

'It will make me unhappy.'

'Then see the doctor, Angelina. This can't go on!'

'I don't want to see the doctor. I don't want to take "happy pills".'

'But you're happy to drink wine all afternoon?'

Ben watches her flinch, as though he has physically hit her with that remark.

'I'm sorry. It's only the other day when I came home, and saw you with a glass—'

'It's hard being at home with the twins all day. What? Am I not allowed to relax with a glass of wine?'

He shakes his head. 'I'm sorry. I didn't mean that. Forget I said it. Come on. What about it? Gus and Silv over this weekend?'

He is relieved when she finally nods in agreement.

'I'll take charge of the cooking. You won't have to do anything. Let's make a list of what we'll need. Will you help me do that?'

The sudden burst of activity that the idea generates is a welcome distraction. As Ben drives to the supermarket, he realises with a jolt that this boring task of getting the groceries for a barbecue feels normal, like their old life. He fills the boot of the 4x4 up with bags of children's goodies. He makes sure that there are plenty of healthy snacks, but also some colourful treats. He knows which will be the preferred option. Yes, this will be good. They have known Gus and Silv for such a long time. Of course, they won't be entirely aware of the situation between him and Angelina, and Ben realises with a slight sinking feeling that they will never be able to sustain 'normal' for the duration of the afternoon, but it definitely feels like a step in the right direction. He realises that he is already quite emotionally invested in the success of this weekend. He wonders, for a moment, about giving Gus and Silv a heads-up about how Angelina is these days, but then chooses to let things be. They are old friends. They will understand.

Ben only wishes he could understand himself what was going on.

VIII. Angelina

The same day

He can't possibly know about the wine. She has been very careful. But he made that comment. How can he know? She feels a momentary panic. She had located a wine supplier who delivers during the day, and she pays for it using her own account. She hides the wine bottles away in a suitcase in the dressing room, where Ben never goes, and they only go in the recycling on the day it is collected and once he has left for work. He comes home hours after the bins are emptied, so there is no way he could know about that.

He can't know about the other way she has found to relax either, courtesy of Ainsley, one of her neighbours' sons. Ainsley is studying International Relations at the University of London, but also works part-time as a DJ and, more importantly for Angelina these days, has access to drugs. Through him, she regularly buys weed. But again, she is very careful. She keeps the long silver rizlas, a ticket card for the roach, a small pair of scissors, a lighter and a pouch of tobacco in a Tupperware container in one of her many handbags in the dressing room. Ben would never come across it, even by accident.

When he is out late in the evenings and the children are asleep in bed, she sits in the garden inhaling on a joint until her mind feels free from the mundane thoughts about caring for her children.

It has become a simple but necessary pleasure. Her life has become small – tiny, in fact. After putting the twins to bed, she just needs to sit down. She remembers her old self and her old life, but she cannot remember herself *in* that life. Energy, enthusiasm and joy. They are no longer actual things, just words. She has not smiled or laughed in so long. She isn't even sure if smoking weed is helping anymore. At least it transports her somewhere else. Provides a feeling of numbness against the nothingness.

Every so often she catches sight of herself in the mirror and barely recognises the face that she sees. Her features seem dull and flat. The only suggestion of depth is given by her forehead, which is beginning to house deep lines, as if someone has used a sharp pencil to draw a crude suggestion of age. Beneath her eyes are baggy, loose pockets of skin.

Some days she catches the smell of herself, of her own body. Those are the days when she is too tired to wash.

But, as the weekend garden party approaches, Angelina finds herself with a growing sensation of excitement. The feeling is unfamiliar. It has been so long since she has looked forward to anything. Instead of sharing her anticipation with Ben, she channels her energy into locating the perfect outfit. She has plenty to choose from, though she is completely out of the habit of coordinating pieces to wear.

Max and Mia seem to pick up on her mood shift. Perhaps they sense that their mother is a little happier than usual. They leap around the dressing room giggling as Angelina pulls out different items of clothing, holds different combinations against herself, tries things on, twirls in front of the mirror. Energy and happiness are infectious. Angelina begins to feel a tiny buzz of life once more.

It is so strange that she can barely acknowledge what it is she is feeling. She watches the twins tumble across the enormous bed and realises that it has only seen restless nights for the last few months. Angelina has not slept in their marital bed for nearly a year. At first, she said it was because she needed her sleep for the children and that Ben snored, which was disrupting her sleep even more than the twins themselves were.

It is true that Ben snores. But it is more than that. They are living very separate lives. Angelina can no longer connect with the talk of Azure, even though it was once her workplace. Angelina has taken to eating earlier with the twins and so, each night when he comes home, he eats the meal that Angelina has made for him on his own. Their evenings are spent apart. Angelina generally just lies in her bed all evening with the TV on. During Ben's lonely meal, he generally consumes a bottle of wine. If he doesn't finish it with his food, he takes what's left of the bottle to his home office and drinks the rest alone. Who is he to talk to her about drinking? Perhaps it is the extra drinking that causes the snoring. But, anyway, the snoring is not the real, or at least not the *only* reason that she doesn't want to share his bed.

She has been hiding herself away. All her *joie de vivre* has been carefully packed up. She doesn't want Ben to want her. He can't fall for her again. If they ever have sex again, she might fall pregnant. And then they would be back in the hospital screaming for the lives of their babies. Or screaming for her own life. She can't talk to Ben about this. She can't imagine a world in which that conversation could take place. He would just try to reassure her, but there are no reassurances. It is easier to play a game of avoidance. The default setting for her and Ben is to be distant. It is better than the alternative, which is to be angry with each other.

It is all such a muddle in her head.

She thinks about things too much. She can't remember the last time she lived 'in the moment'. Most of the time she is trying to get *out* of the moment, but the tumbling tots are forcing her to smile. She suddenly has the urge to play a song, to hear some music of summer. Anything.

'Alexa, put the radio on.'

There are speakers throughout the house, and within a few seconds music starts. It is a song she vaguely recognises, a fluffy song filled with happiness and light.

'That was Lady Gaga with "Summerboy", the DJ says over the closing bars.

As the music fades, so does Angelina's mood. Everything is fleeting, everything is temporary.

'Stock up on those barbecue coals, because the Met Office are telling us that the sun is going to shine all day on Saturday!'

He's too upbeat, this loud man. It's too much to cope with.

'Alexa, turn off the radio.'

She decides on expensive skinny jeans, a cream gypsy top, huge gold hoop earrings, and a pair of Manolo Blahniks. She has plenty of designer gear to choose from. Ben has always been incredibly generous, but the Manolos she picks out are not ones that Ben bought her; these are ones she paid for herself, with one of her first pay checks. It feels better, somehow. Not making a statement exactly, but finding some self-worth. Even if it only comes from shoes.

Saturday comes.

The sun shines as it is supposed to. As well as taking care of her own appearance, Angelina decorates the garden, placing beautiful, oversized green cushions on the patio furniture. Tom suggested these particular seats as a personal recommendation. He had them in his country home in Devon, which has featured in several architectural and lifestyle magazines. Even in her mind, the outdoors resembles a set that wouldn't be out of place on *Love Island*.

What irony, she realises.

IX. Ben

Saturday

Several bottles of champagne are on ice, chilling to the requisite temperature. Their friends live only a 20-minute walk away, so there will be no need for anyone to drive. Ben has lined up some summer garden party music: Zero 7 and Moby. It is perfect.

Ben looks out of the window and watches Angelina in the garden as she fluffs the cushions. His heart skips a beat, the same way it did the first day he met her. She is beautiful. Beyond beautiful. She could easily have become a model.

She pauses for a moment, standing still to survey her work. The sun is behind her, illuminating her mass of red hair.

Could today be different? Could today mark the start of a return to their old life? Ben dares to wonder, to hope even.

He turns his attention back to Max and Mia. The children are happily playing inside in the living area. The TV is on in the background, but they are chasing each other and occasionally having a harmless tug of war over a toy. Their current favourite programme, *Bing*, comes on and their game stops abruptly. They stand still. Both put their thumbs in their mouths and there is silence, apart from the few joyful sounds of laughter.

For a moment, Ben thinks this is what family life should be like.

He checks his watch, which is racing round to 2.30pm. The time has been carefully chosen to allow a good party for both toddlers and adults. Ben has a trick up his sleeve for the children. In the back of his car is a teepee that he picked up from an expensive shop in Camden, near the Azure recording studio. He fetches it and puts it up in the garden. Angelina loves it and immediately begins to fill it with cushions and toys.

'Ah, this will help to amuse the little ones,' she murmurs.

This is the Angelina that he remembers. He dares to hope some more.

Gus and Silv have three children, but one is older. Around 11, if Ben remembers correctly.

He checks his watch once more. They are due anytime now. He hopes that the 11-year-old will help the younger ones to play, but he doesn't want to just make that assumption, nor does he like the idea of the older girl being exploited just because she is the eldest. He has bought a few bits and pieces for her too. A quick trip to Flying Tiger saw him walking out with a load of art materials and a big sketchbook, and then, for no reason in particular other than that they were just there, a giant calculator and a pair of sunglasses covered in plastic daisies.

When Gus and Silv ring the doorbell, he and Angelina greet them with a twin each. Exuberant hellos and kisses are exchanged. Ben gently ushers the children into the garden with a protective hand.

'Come on through, come on through. It's so good to see you. They've grown so much. Remind me of their ages, Gus?'

'Betty is four, Sam is seven and Katie here is eleven, going on about sixteen, it seems like!'

'Wow. She's nearly your height, Silv! Where does the time go?'

'Nearly my height and she can wear my shoes. It won't be long before I'm borrowing clothes from her,' Silv jokes.

'And Katie's off to secondary school in September. Primary school's all done and dusted. Enjoy it all, mate. Every second. It goes by in the blink of an eye.'

The children troop into the garden, excited by all that somewhere new offers. Even though it has been designed and landscaped to within an inch of its life, there are still places to explore and things to look at. The teepee is a hit and Katie is delighted with the daisy glasses. A bottle of champagne doesn't go far between four, and Ben is soon opening a second. He is an assured host, convivial and attentive, and the atmosphere is relaxed. Their friends are affable and up for the party. Angelina is on good form, full of chatter and smiles. The day is going well.

With their guests settled into seats in a shaded part of the garden, where they can still keep an eye on the children, Ben sets about topping up glasses and offering various nibbles. Gus and Silv, like most working parents, seem pleased to be out and happy to be looked after. Conversation meanders around. Angelina is much chattier than Ben has seen her in a long time. She reaches for the champagne bottle without waiting for him to refill it, and her action is a little clumsy. He wonders if she has had more than the two glasses that he has poured for her. All that openness and good humour, perhaps they are wine-fuelled. As soon as he has had the thought, he dismisses it from his mind. Enjoy the moment, he reminds himself.

Angelina instructs Alexa to turn the music up a little, and begins to dance to the music. This encourages the children to follow, for a little while at least. When they tire of this, Katie, the eldest child, takes on the mantle of organising the younger children, as predicted. It happens quite naturally and she seems to enjoy it, evidently used to taking care of her own siblings. She is delighted with the thoughtful presents from Ben.

'And now for the food,' Ben announces. He has prepared fish and salt beef on the barbecue, along with plenty of sausages and burgers for the children.

The wine continues to flow, and Ben finds himself noticing each time Angelina tops up her own glass.

With young children, the unspoken assumption is that the party will break up in the early evening to allow space for the bedtime routine. Angelina may have neglected herself in recent months, but she is a stickler for the evening duties and, on an ordinary day, would have the twins fed, bathed and ready for a bedtime story by 6pm. But that time comes and goes, and no one looks like they are going anywhere. Angelina seems to not notice the time. So relaxed for the first time in a long time, how could Ben break that spell and remind her?

In the early evening sunshine, the twins look a little red. It has been a warm, sunny day and they have been running around the garden, in and out of the teepee, around the play area and seating area. Not all of it is in the shade. Ben reaches out to Mia's flushed cheek.

'Did you put suncream on them?' he asks, and the words come out more sharply than he intends.

There is a sudden shift in the atmosphere, nonetheless.

Angelina shakes her head, looking at him pleadingly.

'No, I don't think I—'

She has no explanation. Just shakes her head again.

'Or their hats? Where are their bloody sunhats?' Ben says, desperately.

'It's a bit late for that, now,' Silv says in an effort to lighten the mood. 'They'll be all right. God, I don't even think my parents had heard of sun cream.'

'Angi, why didn't you put cream on them?' Ben says.

'Why didn't you?' Angelina hurls back.

Max and Mia, exhausted by the afternoon's fun, are both lying down on a giant beanbag by the teepee. Their pale skins seem to be reddening further by the minute. There is an awkward silence.

'Perhaps we should make a move,' Gus says.

'No, no. Please don't break up the party. Have one more drink,' Angelina says, reaching for the bottle. 'I insist!'

Ben can see now that she really is drunk, as she tries to top up Silv's glass from an empty bottle, and takes a moment before she notices and works out that there is nothing left.

'Silly me! I'll be back in a moment. I'll just go and grab another bottle.'

Ben catches her wrist as she goes by. 'Angelina, you've had enough,' he whispers, through gritted teeth.

But Angelina shrugs him off and carries on walking back towards the house.

Just as she reaches the glass doors she raises her right arm, sticks up her middle finger and shouts, 'Fuck off, you controlling arsehole.'

'O-kay,' says Gus. 'We'll be off, then.' He busies himself collecting the children's debris from the garden. 'Katie, can you help pack up Betty and Sam's things?'

Ben looks across and both Max and Mia have their eyes closed. That may mean that they missed Angelina's little outburst. Ben has no idea what she is playing at.

At that moment, she reappears at the glass doors, bearing a tray laden with four clean flute glasses and a fresh bottle of champagne. 'Darling—'

She ignores him and seems to be talking to herself. It is all in Italian, and not for his benefit.

Just as she tries to step down from the patio area to the grass, she misses her footing and goes flying. As, if in slow motion, the bottle and the glasses smash all over the patio.

She loses one of the Manolos in the fall, but rights herself and then steps straight onto the broken glass. Her foot is cut to shreds and there is a gash across her hand. Suddenly, it seems as if there is blood everywhere. Silv dashes to her rescue and helps her to a seat and then, once Angelina is taken care of, she starts to clear up the mess.

Ben sits back in the rattan chair with a face like thunder.

After Gus, Silv and their children have gone, Ben and Angelina stand in the kitchen facing one another.

'What the hell did you think you were doing?' Ben snarls.

'Fuck off.'

'You're a mess, Angelina.'

'How dare you? You did this!' Angelina hurls herself at him, lashing out as if possessed, beating her fists against his chest in a drunken rage.

After a moment she hobble-runs out into the garden to retrieve her shoe, blood showing through the improvised bandage on her foot.

'I fucking hate you!' she screams, throwing the shoe at Ben. It hits him squarely in the back, the heel catching his shoulder bone.

'That fucking hurt! I hate you too, you unhinged fucking troll.' Ben's self-restraint has disappeared with Angelina's outburst. He looks around for the nearest thing for him to throw, sliding his hand across the work surface and launching a heavy cookery book in Angelina's direction.

For a few seconds they both grab whatever they can get their hands on and throw it at each other. Books, plates, cutlery, glasses, a pot plant.

There is screaming, slamming, shouting and crashing.

Neither has given the twins a thought while they perform their dance of anger and hatred.

Suddenly, Angelina points. Standing in the glass-framed doorway, holding hands, are the twins. Both are tear-stained, crying.

'Mummy! Daddy!'

Angelina watches helplessly as Ben dashes over and scoops them up. He clutches them both to his body and carries them into the house, settling them onto the sofa. Blood drips from their feet and seeps into the oak floorboards. A blood stain to match the dark patch that remains from when Angelina's waters broke before the birth. Now an emergency of a different kind. Both twins evidently have glass trapped in the skin of their soles.

Ben swallows. He is too drunk to drive them to the hospital.

Angelina, sobering up now, runs to grab the first aid box from the kitchen cupboard. She is crying hard, but in a different way to the way she was a few minutes ago. She is as devastated as Ben is.

Ben knows it is their collective selfish behaviour that has put the children in danger. He watches as Angelina dresses their wounds. She whispers, over and over, '*Miei bei bambini, mi dispiace così tanto, la mamma è così dispiaciuta*': 'Oh, my beautiful babies, I am so sorry, Mummy is so sorry.'

She doesn't look at Ben at all.

Ben knows that she feels the same pain that he does. What has happened to them? Where did it all go so wrong? How did they become so lost? So broken?

X. Angelina

Three months later
Max and Mia are two and a half years old

'So we'll book our flights to arrive on the Monday, yes?'

'Great,' says Angelina. 'Can't wait. See you.' She waves cheerfully before ending the call, a feeling of dread rising up inside her. Angelina's parents always come for Christmas, arriving at the beginning of December, in time for the 'Great Feast' on the 8th, in honour of the Immaculate Conception of the Virgin Mary. Angelina's parents remain devout Catholics, and use this date to mark the start of the festivities.

They generally stay with Ben and Angelina for the first few days before disappearing off for a week of visiting the Cotswolds or Stratford-upon-Avon, and then returning to Ben and Angelina in plenty of time for Christmas. There are parts of England that Massimo and Emanuela love and, of course, they love being reunited with their grandchildren. It is usually a time to look forward to. Angelina's mother is a fabulous cook and makes all sorts of delicious meals and treats for them. Ben jokes that one of the reasons he married Angelina was in the hope that her culinary skills would one day match her mum's. But this year, neither Angelina nor Ben is looking forward to the visit. Up until the disaster of the barbecue, there had been distance between them, an unspoken area of No Man's Land within the marriage. Those first acts of aggression on that fateful day seem to have triggered a declaration of war, with regular open hostilities. The atmosphere in the house won't stand the strain of house guests. Yet how can she put them off?

Angelina knows that her parents will be sad if she tries to suggest that they don't come this year. And she isn't ready to face the barrage of questions that such a request would inevitably provoke. She no longer knows how she feels about Ben. She isn't ready to have that conversation with herself, let alone her parents. Since the barbecue, they have reached a kind of false impasse. They both put on artificial 'everything is okay' faces and voices, when it so clearly isn't. Angelina has become robotic, distancing herself from Ben even more than before, disappearing to her room as soon as he returns home in the evening. It is rare for them to be in the same room together. Usually, it is staged as a quick wave in the background when Angelina is speaking with her parents, as in this instance.

'Them coming here is the last thing we need,' Ben says. 'We could use the building work. We could bring it forward, start before they get here. That way they'd have to find somewhere else to stay.' For some time now, he has wanted to convert the sprawling basement into a recording studio. The original plan was conceived so that he could work from home more and be there for the children, to help Angelina around the house and to see them grow. But that was before he began to use the recording studio in Camden as a reason *not* to be home. He had already sought planning permission for the project, and the approval was granted several months ago.

'I'll give Tom a call. Get him to start asap.'

It is an appealing solution on paper. It is also as if some kind of truce has been called between them. The terms are unspoken, but there is a shared understanding of the requirement to present a united front in the face of the visit from Angelina's parents. The threat of a different kind of invasion has galvanised them into acting together.

Within a week, Tom has enlisted a team of Eastern European builders.

'More skilled and hardworking,' Tom explains to Angelina and Ben on the first morning.

'And, knowing you, cheaper!' Ben retorts.

'It's your money I'm saving,' Tom shrugs.

The builders arrive each morning by 8am and the house quickly becomes a building site once again.

'We'll have it finished by Christmas,' they assure Ben, cheerfully.

'No hurry, no hurry,' Ben keeps assuring them. Having builders in is the perfect excuse for Angelina's parents either not to stay at all, or not to stay so long.

Meanwhile, Angelina has been good at pretending all is well. She has maintained the weekly Facetime calls with her parents. She times them so that she can show them the twins in the bath or having their tea. She makes sure to show them the work taking place in the basement, and pretends that she and Ben are fed up with the pace of it.

'It is a nightmare!' she says, making sure that the innocent builders are out of earshot. 'The noise, the dust. I wonder, *madre mia*, perhaps you should find somewhere else to stay.'

Angelina knows how much her parents enjoy their creature comforts, so they will be easily persuaded to stay in a nearby hotel. Her parents need never know about her deteriorating relationship and disintegrating life.

After the barbecue fiasco in the summer, Ben has become more insistent than ever that they hire a nanny. He would like to have someone installed in the house during the day to protect the welfare of his children while he is out at work.

Angelina has continued to refuse the nanny, but she has compromised and booked the twins into a new day nursery, a 15-minute walk from the house. They can do the morning slot, finishing at 11.30am. Ben drops them off in the morning and Angelina collects them. He would like the session to be longer, but there aren't two places available for the afternoon session at the moment, and they don't want to separate the twins. They are on the waiting list for the longer day session, though. If the weather is good enough, she walks them to the nearby park afterwards. There is a lovely new playground funded by the efforts of local people, some of whom were her friends before she had the twins. Gus and Silv were part of that project. She feels a stab of shame when she thinks of them. Neither she nor Ben have seen them since the garden party. The only communication was a cursory thank-you card from them which arrived in the post the following week.

Today, she manages to get herself together to collect the twins at the allotted time. She no longer drives. Since she has been smoking weed and drinking during the day, she has avoided the car – it is always a walk. It has just become a habit. Better that than putting the children at risk with her behind the wheel. She has been more careful since their feet were cut at the barbecue. It gave her a fright, made her remember how fragile they are. It also made her realise that she is truly alone. There is no way she can be friends with anyone or rely on anyone else. She certainly can't rely on Ben. She can't even speak to him. Her world, which grew so small after the birth of the twins, has shrunk even further in the last few months. The builders are pretty much her only contact with the outside world. She tries to avoid speaking to anyone at the nursery unless it is absolutely necessary; she has perfected a technique where she waits until another parent arrives and goes in just behind them, hoping that they will take up most of the attention of the nursery staff. That way she can usually get away with calling out a quick 'thank you' on her way out. Today, though, Max and Mia's nursery teacher corners her at pick-up and seems determined to talk.

'I'm glad I've seen you. I just wanted to say that they both seem much more settled these days,' she says. 'They're doing really well. Max, in particular, is a lot more confident than he was in the beginning. And Mia is socialising more, too.'

'Oh, that's good.' Angelina is caught off guard and doesn't really know how to respond. There is an awkward pause.

'So, I just wanted to let you know that they're making good progress.'

'Right, well, yes, thank you.' Angelina takes the children's bags and makes to turn away.

'Don't forget Max's coat!'

It is a meaningless exchange, but Angelina found it stressful nonetheless. The teacher's comment has also made Angelina feel guilty. Does it mean that they were unsettled before, lacking in confidence and not socialising? Should she have known more about this? She tries her best to not drink during the day but, sometimes it helps to have a little glass before she leaves the house. She is going to try even harder now not to do that. Then again, actual interactions with people are hard. It is easier to feel slightly numb, to inoculate herself against unwanted intrusion.

Still, for a while she makes the effort to get up earlier and take the children to nursery in the morning as well as collecting them.

It feels good.

It's a start.

XI. Ben

A few weeks later

In the run up to the arrival of Angelina's parents, Ben has been happy for the builders to work more slowly and, in fact, has actively engineered delays by encouraging them all to take time off and go Christmas shopping in the afternoons. It is something that the builders are not used to at all, but they are more than willing to oblige, and it means that the house is a calmer place in the afternoons.

'Papà! Mamma!' The reunion greetings are genuinely warm on all sides, but the plan has worked, and Angelina's parents will only stay at the house for a total of five days while they are in England. He and Angelina will be able to keep up the semblance of a relationship for that time, if they both play their parts well.

Ben is still working long hours, far longer than he used to, but, for the duration of their stay, he makes a big effort to be home earlier and to spend more time at home.

Angelina's parents adore the twins and have missed them since their last visit. They are joyful and bring love and warmth back into the house. Without realising it, they help restore the love and affection that both parents have failed to provide in recent months.

Angelina's parents insist on going to the nursery to collect the children each day, taking them to the park and to a café for hot chocolate and cake. Thoroughly spoiling them the way only grandparents are allowed to do. Max and Mia quickly bond with them in the flesh. Old connections are easily re-established when they are used to seeing them so regularly on a screen.

Ben realises that he has actually enjoyed playing house with Angelina. In such beautiful surroundings, it is easy to pull off. On the surface they are the perfect family. The five days pass quickly. Ben is there to see them into the taxi at their departure. They insist that he not bother taking time out of his busy day to drive them to the airport.

But, perhaps, the underlying tension has not gone entirely unnoticed. He watches as Angelina's mother holds her daughter's hands and says, '*Sei sicura di stare bene?*'

'Yes, Mamma, of course I'm alright. Why wouldn't I be alright?'

But her mother gives her a longer, more searching stare than most would find comfortable before she gets into the taxi.

Ben puts his arm around Angelina's waist as they wave the cab off, but drops it as soon as the taxi has turned round the corner. He can't get the look on Angelina's mother's face out of his mind. *She knows*, he thinks, as they turn round to go back inside the house.

In spite of the deliberately engineered delays, Ben's basement studio is finished by the end of January. It is stunning. Tom has done a good job. Ben smiles to himself when he looks at his new state-of-the-art studio and thinks back to where it all began: in his tiny flat in Ladbroke Grove that he once shared with Tom and two others. Tom had helped to plaster the walls of Ben's room with egg-boxes to create soundproofing. What a long, long way he has come.

Arms folded, surveying his new kingdom, he feels amazing. The only problem in his life is his marriage. He no longer knows how he feels about Angelina, after their cruelty to one another. Is there any kind of chance left for them?

Surely he isn't imagining that there has been a shift in atmosphere since Angelina's parents' visit. The expression 'fake it till you make it' comes to mind. Perhaps there is still some faint hope that they can pave their way back. Perhaps he should approach the counselling subject with Angelina once again. She has always been so resistant in the past, but perhaps she can be persuaded, for the sake of the children.

Max and Mia also seem calmer since their grandparents' visit. Before that, he had begun to worry that they might have ADHD. They seemed so restless and unsettled at times. He had even begun to approach the subject with Angelina before Christmas. Money might buy the answer. Paying for therapy or behaviour and learning specialists would ensure that the children would be cured of whatever it was that might not be right, but perhaps they don't need to go down that route at all, given the recent progress they seem to have made. It would be a relief. It doesn't occur to him that the mood and responses of his children might be directly influenced by his own behaviours.

By February the basement studio is busy. There is a steady stream of clients using Azure West Brompton, as well as Azure Camden. It operates as an extension of Azure Recordings, and it's excellent for the business to have more than one location. Ben has had to hire an additional producer, so there are now three of them to handle the new swathe of artists in the industry. Ben's clients tend to be younger and less well known. He likes to take a risk with new talent and, in spite of his problems at home, his reputation within the industry has continued to grow. In the music business, he feels unstoppable, regardless of what might be happening in his private life. His public presence has been augmented in no small way by the new, young but very skilful PR co-ordinator called Philippo that Ben hired. Actually, Philippo was born 'Philip', he confides in Ben, but all agree that the 'o' adds an appropriate edge.

Ben is excited about the new signings and the way that business is booming. If only he could get things right on the domestic front too. In a rare burst of conversation, he tries to tell Angelina about his vision for the next stages of Azure's inroad into the music industry. He's got a new signing from Nashville, who's going to be the next big thing.

'Good for you. It all sounds great.'

Angelina says the right words, but the emphasis is emotionless and falls flat. Ben knows that she is still unable to find motivation in anything. He wishes that he was able to communicate with her the way that they once did.

His hope for reconciliation with his wife fades. They can only ever play at being husband and wife.

XII. Angelina

Six months later
Max and Mia are three years old

Even in her semi-robotic state, Angelina can't help but pick up on Ben's intense enthusiasm for his new studio, and for one new signing in particular. Before the twins were born, Ben had been to Nashville to meet a bunch of new artists that had been brought to his attention by his network of talent-spotters. Nashville, she knows, is a tough place for artists. It's easy to be missed in the midst of so much talent. Ben had been particularly impressed with a singer called Verley Lee. Angelina vaguely remembers mention of her at the time. Now she's back in the picture as one of his new young talent signings at Azure.

'Twelve new songs, all written by her, all brilliant and all ready to go.'

He babbles on. She lets it wash over her.

'Her manager got in touch with *me*. Can you believe it? I didn't have to go chasing this time. They're coming over to record them. It's a major coup, I'm telling you. A really prestigious contract. This could be the artist that catapults Azure to the big time. She's got an amazing voice. Husky, with a real, unexpected level of maturity given that's she's only young. And a great stage presence. It's a winning combination. Let me play you something.'

Angelina couldn't care less what this Verley Lee person sounds like. She hasn't listened to music properly since the twins were born. But something about the way Ben talks about her strikes an unpleasant chord. It's beyond the usual hype for a new signing. Ben seems mesmerised by her.

'She has a level of talent that is electrifying. She can play a multitude of instruments, anything you like, but her first love, after singing, is the banjo, can you believe that? It sounds crazy and old-fashioned, but that's the point. It's an instrument which gives her contemporary lyrics a nostalgic edge.'

He goes on and on and on. It's all he can bloody talk about, and Angelina has never seen him so talkative. In fact, she can't remember the last time they really spoke about anything – apart from the practicalities of the children.

As Verley Lee's imminent arrival consumes him, Angelina feels even more excluded and detached from everything that is going on. She musters enough energy to look up 'Verley Lee' on the internet, wondering idly what all the fuss is about this time. She's a bloody banjo player, for goodness' sake. She remembers that there was sometimes a buzz about new artists when she was working at Azure, but she can't really remember what it felt like to be caught up in it all. That was a different world, a different lifetime. She can't even imagine being involved in that business again, if she's honest. It is as though it happened to a different person. She wishes she could feel something the way Ben does. Get excited about anything. She would love to be driven the way Ben is, to have some focus. It is like he is in some sort of fever.

The images that Google throws at her surprise Angelina. This new singing sensation is not what she expects a female country singer to look like at all. Country music isn't a genre that has ever particularly interested her, though they'd always had a few country artists on the books at Azure. She classified it as music for old-timers, without much to say to the young. Full of lyrics about pain and despair, and nothing to do with her. Poverty-filled misery wasn't something she'd ever had to think about. It was sung by wizened, careworn Kenny Rogers and Dolly Parton wannabes about lives lived badly. With its roots in the Southern states of America, and a long, complicated history with racial issues, country music was a predominantly white domain, as far as Angelina remembers, and actually a white *male* domain at that. Much more Kenny Rogers than Dolly Parton.

But she's been out of things for a while, and it shows.

One click has Angelina sitting upright in her chair. Verley Lee is a woman of colour and she is stunningly beautiful. There is no button-down flannel and cowgirl denim in sight. She is wearing the obligatory cowboy boots, but they serve to accentuate the length of her silky legs. Just, wow, Angelina thinks. There is nothing careworn or wizened about her at all. She has a smile that is seductively inviting. Her pout has nothing to do with pain, rather suggesting that she might actually be all about pleasure. Having worked on the front desk at Azure, Angelina was once used to mingling with the beautiful people, the good, the bad and the angry of the music industry, but Verley Lee, judging by these pictures, would be just as at home on the catwalk as on the Pyramid Stage.

The shock of Verley Lee's appearance combined with her husband's uncharacteristic fervour are enough to galvanise Angelina into feeling *something* at long last. She realises that it is time to up her game. She takes a long, hard look at herself in the mirror. It is enough to make her book an appointment at the hairdressers for the first time in over a year. She also takes time to leave the house and go shopping for some new clothes.

Perhaps she is going to need to lure her husband back. Perhaps Ben is worth fighting for. Whatever is about to happen, she needs to be prepared.

The arrival of Verley Lee is a big deal. Ben drives to the airport to collect her and her manager himself, even though the flight comes in at an ungodly hour of the morning. He has never done this for a client before, as far as she knows.

'Why not just book a cab for them?'

'This one's all about the personal touch,' Ben assures her, though to Angelina's mind it looks less professional to meet them from the plane.

'Trust me,' says Ben.

Angelina's anxiety is precisely because, for the first time, she isn't sure if they have gone too far for her to be able to trust him.

But they are speaking, at least. And civilly. Angelina puts effort into making sure there is daily communication in the days leading up to Verley Lee's arrival.

Verley Lee and her manager, Elijah, are booked into a smart Chelsea hotel, closer to the West Brompton address than to Azure: a practical arrangement based on the idea that the basement studio will be the more desirable recording venue.

'It will give them total flexibility while they're here, and we can record around the clock. And it will give me a chance to test out all that state-of-the-art equipment,' Ben explains. 'Some of that stuff is better than what we have at Azure.'

A number of session musicians have been booked to work with the artist, and a provisional studio timetable has been agreed. Even Max and Mia seem to want to meet Verley bloody Lee.

Angelina tries to analyse her feelings. This is Ben, at work, doing the thing that he's always done. Why, suddenly, after all this time, does she feel these surges of jealousy, when she herself hasn't desired Ben in so long? There seems to be more at stake. Perhaps it's fear of losing her lifestyle, as well as her husband. And Verley Lee seems to take up every bloody waking minute of every bloody day, and some of the sleeping minutes of the day too. Recording hours are long and, even though they are taking place in her own basement, there is no legitimate reason for Angelina to be around. As well as steps leading down from the hallway, the basement has its own separate entrance from the main front door of the house too, so there is no real opportunity for Angelina's path to cross with Verley Lee's. Nevertheless, Angelina tortures herself trying to catch a glimpse of the American beauty. From what she sees through the bay windows, her fears are confirmed. Verley Lee is just as stunning in real life as her media profile presents.

In the early mornings, when the studio isn't in use, Angelina peeps inside. Somehow it feels transgressive, even though she reminds herself that this is, in fact, her own house. She is disturbed to see that Ben has had some beds moved into a couple of the rooms down there.

'Babe, it's practical. For those nights when Verley Lee and her manager want to take a break for a few hours. It's intense in that studio space.'

Another of the rooms is converted into an office space for Ben. When he isn't asleep, he seems to live in that underground world.

Angelina suddenly feels the need for company. She wants to reach out to old friends, but it has been so long. Where to begin? She sends out some tentative messages to a few names in her contacts list. In the end, only Silv replies and reaches back out to her. It is mortifying; thinking about her again makes Angelina relive that horrible afternoon last summer. But it is better than this endless isolation. After a period of being easier to manage, the twins are up in the night again these days. Both have begun to wet the bed. They're still quite young, she supposes. After sleepless nights in the early days, it doesn't seem fair to have to go through it all again, and this time, the bulk of the night-time duty falls to Angelina. Ben is either still working when they wake or has only just gone to his room. Angelina feels as if she is putting more and more time into their marriage and the children and getting less and less out of it.

'Ben is very busy with work, but it would be nice to catch up again. I'll organise some drinks and nibbles.' She deletes 'I could use a friend', fearing that it makes her sound too needy. Busy with work is an understatement. Ben has always had a good work ethic – that's how he made his breakthrough in the beginning – but this is borderline obsessive. The studio walls are soundproofed but Angelina still hears, or imagines that she hears, the trace of music day and night. They put a date in the diary for a few evenings' time.

Whenever Verley Lee is in the house, which is pretty much constantly, Angelina is drawn to the basement. In some ways, this possessive inclination over Ben and jealousy of Verley Lee is a good thing. Something long dormant has awakened inside her. She finds herself moving through her days with greater energy and purpose, even if that purpose is channelled into suspicion and negative thoughts. The rational side of Angelina knows that nothing untoward can be going on. Ben and Verley Lee are not alone. There is a team of professionals down there. Session musicians, publicists, Verley Lee's manager.

'There's no downtime,' Ben assures her. 'It's all work, work, work.'

And while Angelina knows this to be true, her paranoia is steadily increasing. She tries to talk herself out of dark thoughts. It's not as if she suspects that a mass orgy is taking place in a room in her house. It's just that the whole idea of that woman being under her roof, in her basement, in close proximity to her husband, never mind their years of estrangement, is difficult to deal with; the whole situation is strangely disconcerting. It twists up her insides and eats away further at any self-esteem that she has left.

The first thing that is odd this evening is that the interior door is locked, even though the recording light isn't on. This is something they've already argued about. It made Angelina cross that Ben had wanted a lock at all.

'It's standard, babe.'

Once a term of affection, the word 'babe' seems to have acquired a barb all of its own.

'Even when the studio is in your own home?'

'Especially when the studio is in your own home. Just think about when Max and Mia are a bit bigger. We wouldn't want them down here with all this wiring and voltage.'

Since their feet were shredded by glass at the barbecue, any mention of danger to Max and Mia has been an immediate trigger for Angelina, and Ben knows it.

'Or they might ruin a recording by barging in.'

He has a point, but still, the idea of a locked space in their house makes Angelina uneasy. And to be locked now, when no actual recording is in progress? Is that a message to her? What secrets might lie beyond the door? Although, she has to admit, perhaps that question is the result of her own guilty conscience. Her life is full of little secrets and deceptions, bottles stashed in locked suitcases, hashish hidden in the top of her shoe cupboard, assignations with a drug-dealer, surreptitious deposits in the recycling bin at strategic times, and Mummy's 'special cup' in the mornings when she needs something more than coffee to start the day. And that Oscar-worthy performance of marriage in front of her parents at Christmas. That was a masterclass in deception. Though the penetrating look her mother gave her at their departure momentarily suggested that the pretence might not have been as convincing as they thought. Ben had been her supporting actor then. What other duplicity is he capable of? What lies might his life contain now that she knows so little about it?

She tries the handle of the recording studio once more, just to make sure. Definitely locked.

'Ben, can I come in?'

The nature of the soundproofing means that her knocks fall only as deadened thuds behind the musical rhythms.

'Ben? Let me in.'

But there is no answer. Just as in every other avenue of her life, she feels shut out and powerless.

She has taken to lurking about in the darkness of the basement stairs once the kids are in bed. She doesn't even really know why.

But the second thing that is odd this evening is the laughter when they all troop out at the end of the session. Laughter that stops abruptly when they see her standing there. She catches only a snatch of an utterance, but it sounds something like, 'I hope she doesn't listen!' Followed by, 'You'd be in trouble, mate!' and more laughter.

Already in a heightened state of alert about Ben's imagined infidelity and adulterous potential, Angelina pounces on the words, assuming that she herself is the 'she' who they hope doesn't listen.

She knows enough about the workings of the studio to be able to play back the latest tracks laid down. Ben seems to take an age to leave the house the following morning, and is still there after Angelina has dropped Max and Mia off at the nursery. When he finally goes into work, she heads straight to the basement.

The studio is a mess. Beer bottles sit on surfaces and in corners of the room. Ashtrays spill over. There are the remains of a spliff in one, and Angelina would know. In the stereo sound of the headphones, Verley Lee's vocals are as honeyed and seductive as her pout. Lyrically, the songs are compelling too. She sings about the hardness in ordinary things, the avenues cut off as you make different decisions in life, thwarted ambition, thwarted desire. Stuff that Angelina can relate to. It is good. Very good. No wonder Ben is excited about this young artist.

And then it comes.

Right at the end of the recording. Not a full track, just a mess-about jam from the end of the session. The words half-sung, half-whispered in a mocking chorus:

If only there was no Angelina. If only there was no Angelina. If only there was no Angelina.

She has to play it back several times. She tells herself it is to make sure that she isn't hearing things, but it is also partly to feed her rage, and enjoy her bitter triumph at having her suspicions confirmed. This is what they were laughing about behind her back.

If only there was no Angelina.

She'd be well within her rights to sabotage the whole recording. But she doesn't do it. She stops herself. She needs to be in this for the long game. She surveys the scene, tortures herself by imagining the final hours of the evening before, escalates her own exclusion from it. The words echo away inside her head long after she has stopped replaying the recording.

If only there was no Angelina.

XIII. Angelina

The more upbeat Ben is about progress on Verley Lee's album, the more Angelina seethes. On the one hand, those lyrics were childish and petty, but on the other hand, they sound like a threat.

Angelina sticks to her morning routine of taking the children to nursery, avoiding the staff, particularly since she recently had to sign a form one day after Max bit another child. Ben has taken to sleeping in later and later anyway, as the recording sessions seem to go on longer and longer. How long does it take to record an album?

'It takes as long as it takes, babe,' is Ben's unhelpful answer.

But, having had the daytime drinking back under control for a while, she has taken to drinking a can of cider on the way home from nursery after dropping Max and Mia off. The cans are an obscure brand, and discreet, as far as Angelina is concerned. They look like a fizzy drink rather than alcohol. None of the neighbours or other parents from the nursery could possibly suspect.

Silv's visit rolls around. The evening is artificially polite and therefore uncomfortable, serving to remind Angelina of how friendless she really is. Conversation is stilted. Under the microscope like this, Angelina realises how very little they really have in common. There is no way she could begin to communicate her fears to Silv. They are very different people. Silv is the editor of a fashion magazine, her career on the rise. She also manages to keep her feet on the ground, perhaps as a result of her Yorkshire roots.

'You seem distracted, Ange. Anything you want to tell me?'

Silv seems to cotton on to the fact that she is being used to occupy Angelina, because she makes her excuses early and prepares to leave. Seeing Silv out provides Angelina with an excuse to walk past the studio.

'Is something happening down there?' Silv gestures towards the basement door. 'You keep looking in that direction.'

'What? Oh, no, I don't think so.'

But something about Angelina's tone alerts Silv.

'Seriously, is everything alright?' Silv asks, putting her hand on Angelina's arm in a kind gesture. 'You can tell me.'

'Of course, everything's alright,' Angelina says, gruffly, shrugging her off. What was meant as an affectionate action on Silv's part only fires a wine-fuelled Angelina into a rage. Once she has closed the door behind Silv, she finds herself banging on the door to the basement with both fists.

'What the fuck are you doing, Angelina?' Ben barks.

Angelina pushes past him to see what's going on.

Nothing, it turns out. Three of the session musicians are sitting around sharing a spliff and casually strumming the guitars. There is no sign of Verley Lee.

'Happy?' Ben snarls.

Angelina doesn't know what she expected to find, but now she is embarrassed as well as angry. She continues to rage at Ben, when he eventually comes upstairs after the musicians finally depart.

'Jesus Christ, Angelina. Look at yourself. You're a mess. It would be easier for me to stay down there and not bother to come up here at all, for all the grief I get.'

'Oh yes, you'd love that, wouldn't you? To have no responsibility for your fucking children.'

Ben walks away. Perhaps Angelina's remark has hit home. It gives her no satisfaction.

A couple of days later, Angelina snoozes on the sofa in the afternoon while Max and Mia are taking a nap. Since upping her cider intake, she has also taken to having a nap with the kids to sleep it off a little. Today, though, she doesn't wake up when they do. She's jolted awake when a loud commotion downstairs interrupts her slumber. Is something going on in the basement? But it is the twins thudding around as they charge up the stairs.

'Mummy, Mummy,' Mia calls. 'Come quickly.'

'We went to look for Daddy, and we found him, but Daddy's fighting,' Max says.

Angelina is a little disorientated. Her mouth is dry, and she must have stale booze on her breath. She wipes a dribble of saliva away from her mouth as she tries to pull herself together.

'Fighting? Oh, my precious babies. That doesn't sound like Daddy.' For all their rowing, they have tried very hard to keep it away from the kids. Ben is generally very mild-mannered in public. 'Who is he fighting with?'

'A woman!' Mia declares.

A surge of triumph hits Angelina. Perhaps Ben has had a falling out with Verley Lee. Perhaps the obsession is about to come to a timely end. She grabs hold of a hand of each of her children and runs down the stairs to the basement. The handle moves in her hand; it is unlocked, for once.

Ben and Verley Lee spring apart as she bursts in with Max and Mia. Whatever they had been doing, it wasn't fighting. Verley Lee's buttons are partially undone, and her lipstick is smudged above her lip. Ben wipes his mouth with the back of his hand and has the decency to look shamefaced.

'Don't worry, my darlings, I think the fight is over,' Angelina says calmly, looking directly at Ben. And the words are for his benefit rather than the twins, because then she seems to forget the children altogether, as she drops their hands and begins screaming and hurling whatever she can find at the couple. Drumsticks, cables, a beer bottle and a music stand all go thudding across the studio floor. 'You bastard,' she screams. 'And you bitch. You're no better.' And then the language morphs into Italian.

Verley Lee grabs her jacket and bag and makes a flying exit, ducking out of the way, while Angelina is still throwing everything in sight. The door up to the street is left wide open. With Verley Lee gone, Angelina's full attention is focused on Ben. She runs towards him, possessed, still screaming a diatribe of Italian rage, thumping and kicking him. She is a woman scorned and she has, in that moment, no thought for the children and where they might have got to.

She finds out later that the rain was heavy as the children ran out of the house onto the street, away from the horrible exchanges between their parents. They are holding hands, and they are so little to be out and about by themselves that it doesn't take long for someone to intervene. They haven't gone far before an older couple, who recognise the twins from their nursery commutes, walk them back along the road.

'What brings you outside without your coats in this weather? That won't do at all. Let's get you home, shall we?'

When they knock on the door, Angelina is horrified to discover that a crowd has gathered outside, drawn by the commotion – which has quickly escalated to the kitchen, then the front steps – as the hysteria mounts when they realise the children are gone.

Neighbours crane their necks to see the story of some lost children and the promise of more drama.

There are blue flashing lights. A woman is standing on the steps of their home, talking into her mobile phone. Three police cars arrive.

Angelina finds herself and Ben being arrested.

'But you can't take us away! The children!'

'You should have thought of that before you let them wander the streets alone.'

Angelina doesn't have a chance to say goodbye.

She is bewildered and aghast by what has just happened. How could things have gotten so out of hand that police officers are waiting with her children for social services to arrive?

XIV. Angelina

Though Angelina and Ben are both released quite quickly, it is to discover that their children have been driven off to an emergency placement in Battersea. It takes several days to organise a multi-agency meeting with social workers, the police, and a mental health professional, but it is agreed that the twins should stay with their parents, though with some conditions to adhere to. Angelina is so relieved. She has been beside herself thinking about what might happen. She has heard horror stories about children being permanently removed by social services, and it seemed like a serious possibility for a while because of the involvement of the police. But, of course, having your children taken away for ever is the sort of thing that happens to other people. Perhaps it is because Ben is wealthy, and they live in a nice area, that they receive a lighter judgement and better arrangements than might otherwise have been the case.

She has had to agree to counselling, something she has steadfastly resisted in the past, but it is one of the terms of the children being allowed to remain in her care. It's also not the kind of counselling that might have been on the table once, before the intervention of social services, when Angelina might have had free choice about which expensive therapist to visit. The counselling services that are stipulated are housed at the back of a community centre in Fulham. Most of the clients are not wealthy women struggling with the noise and upheaval of the new extension to their multi-million-pound property. Angelina feels sullied just through attending the bi-weekly sessions of separate and joint meetings, and does not take them quite as seriously as she should. She, like Ben, rattles through the meetings with an assurance that they hope fools the counsellor, treating it as a formality. They talk about how loved the children are, how much their arrival was anticipated, they joke about 'the *cicogna*'. They point out how Max and Mia have their every need provided for, how wonderful their play area is at home, how successful Ben is in the music industry. They cite that pressure is a contributing factor, but manage to suggest that they are 'over all that now'.

Beyond the four walls of the counselling room, Angelina is angrier than ever with Ben. His attitude that having nothing more than a snog with Verley Lee 'hardly counts as the greatest of crimes, under the circumstances' has not gone down well.

'I didn't even instigate it. I was always very polite and professional.'

'*Porca miseria*, Ben!' Angelina snarls. She slips into Italian more and more when she is in a heightened emotional state. 'Don't give me that! It didn't look very *professional* from the view I had.'

'Look, she threw herself at me. It just happened. And it was always going to happen, given that you have ignored me, physically and emotionally, since the twins were born. That's more than three years of celibacy, Angelina. Three fucking years. I'm entitled to some sexual fun. I wasn't going to say no, was I?'

This kind of conversation does not take place in front of the counsellor.

Deep down, Angelina agrees. She knows that he has a point, that she has systematically pushed him away. But she also doesn't want to lose Ben, or the lifestyle, and that fear makes her reluctant to admit any culpability.

They mark the occasion of Max and Mia's fourth birthday with an expensive afternoon tea at an exclusive London restaurant, but with only the four of them present, the atmosphere is strained.

At least some consistency is maintained for the twins by the nursery, who continue to support Max and Mia in spite of their behavioural deterioration. The pattern of biting and hitting other children escalates, they both return to wetting their pants despite having been dry for many months, and they fall asleep as soon as they sit on the story rug in the afternoons, but Angelina doesn't regard this information as too problematic. They will grow out of it. All children take steps backward at times, don't they?

XV. Ben

Ben manages to keep the performance with Angelina going for the better part of a month. Verley Lee returns to the US with a great album and a good story, whereas Ben's life is never going to be the same again. He goes through the rigmarole of the ridiculous counselling sessions, spouting the spiel he knows they want to hear. Inside he knows just how much of a lie it all is, though, and it feels as if he is living on a knife edge. And why? For whose benefit is he doing all this? It certainly doesn't feel like his.

He arrives home early one afternoon. Angelina is in her usual position: outside in the back garden, working her way through a bottle of white wine. Who knows if it is even the first of the day? Something snaps inside him. He pulls back the grey-framed glass doors, and the words are out of his mouth before he even knows he is going to say them.

'I can't do this anymore. You're a fucking mess. It's over. I'm leaving.'

She doesn't move. Perhaps she hasn't heard him. He doesn't have the energy to waste another breath and check. He closes the door and goes upstairs to pack. He decides that he will check himself into a hotel that Azure uses for clients. It makes him furious that he has paid for a recording studio with two guest rooms but can't be near Angelina anymore, because, he admits to himself, he hates her.

In his room, he gets out a couple of suitcases and begins throwing things into them. He hears Angelina's tread on the stairs, but ignores it, focused on packing what he can to get out. The next thing he knows is that a glass is flying by his head. It smashes into the mirrored wardrobe and cracks that too. Yet again, he is drawn into a physical fight with the woman he once loved. She launches herself at him, punching and kicking and screaming, and he finds himself retaliating. At first in defence, but then he too lashes out. He isn't aggressive by nature, but some primeval instinct kicks in. A rush of blood to the head. He doesn't stop, even when the twins come running up to the bedroom door to see what must look like a massacre. There is blood on the walls. He is not sure if it is his own or Angelina's. They are both covered in scratches. He has a gash down the side of his face. He doesn't even stop when Max wets himself, the stain darkening his trousers.

Angelina, in a Herculean effort, launches a bust of Artemis towards Ben.

'I've always hated that fucking statue,' she screams.

It misses him, but sails through the bedroom window. The outlook is to the front of the house, and the expensive artwork smashes onto the street outside. Once again, the beautiful house becomes the centre of attention for all the wrong reasons, as neighbours and people passing by begin to gather at the commotion.

Ben hears a male voice shout, 'There are two young children in there!' and it brings him to his senses for a moment. He gathers Max and Mia in his arms, both now shaking and crying, and sweeps them out of the room.

'Don't you dare,' screams Angelina after them. 'Don't you dare paint yourself as the better parent, you bastard adulterer!'

The brawl erupts out onto the West Brompton pavement as Angelina chases after him. 'Come back here! Come back here with my children!'

History repeats itself. The police are called. Both he and Angelina are arrested again, then quickly released. Social workers arrive and remove Angelina and the twins to a women's refuge.

This time things look much bleaker for Ben and Angelina. This is clearly no one-off. All the memories of the previous incident are fresh in the minds of the professionals. And this time, one of the police officers, a female officer trained in domestic violence, takes the trouble to visit the nursery and collect the evidence that the nursery staff have collated, over many months, about the behaviour of Max and Mia. The nursery school have kept excellent, detailed records of the children's behaviour and disclosures.

Ben is shocked. He had no idea that any concerns had been raised.

The police officer raises her eyebrows. 'I find that very difficult to believe, sir.'

'But it was my wife who had all the dealings with the nursery.'

She explains to him that the nursery manager also contacted children's social care a number of times in the last 12 months.

'But we've never heard anything from social services before.'

'Apart from when your children were removed from your care on the previous occasion, Mr Martell?'

Given everything that's happened, Ben can't believe the decisions that the authorities come to. It is suggested that Angelina may have been suffering from serious postnatal depression. It's a diagnosis that makes sense because, when he looks back, he can see that Angelina changed almost from the moment of the twins' birth. The woman who came back from the hospital was completely different from the loving wife who went in. The mixture of low moods and manic behaviour are a classic symptom. He knew it too. He just didn't do enough about it. It is normal for mothers to have some baby blues.

The fact that Angelina's went on for years is partly his fault. He must shoulder some of that blame. The fact that her condition went untreated and unsupported means that the social workers look on Angelina's actions more leniently and empathetically.

Angelina is placed in a nearby refuge centre with the children, with access to the agencies she needs to recover. He overhears a police officer tell her colleague it's ironic that if they had been poor, she would have been more likely to get the help she needed. Ben is painted as the big bad wolf because he came close to infidelity with Verley Lee, because he didn't see that his wife needed help, because he was complicit in neglecting the children, because he enabled her burgeoning alcoholism.

The other officer tuts and agrees that it's a great shame, commenting that 'it's a mad world we live in.'

As Max and Mia are taken away from him, his marriage irreparably broken, his beautiful home empty, no one feels that it is, indeed, a mad world more than Ben.

XVI. Angelina

Things go from bad to worse.

Angelina, understandably, does not enjoy the conditions at the refuge centre, but Ben is providing financial support, which enables her to make sure that Max and Mia don't go without. She can't live in the style she's become accustomed to, but she still has a case full of nice clothes for her and the children. What she can't do is shake off the air of privilege that those years of plenty have given her, and that goes down like a sick sandwich in the refuge centre.

'Oh, here she comes, Mrs La-Di-Da with her Gucci and her Dolce and Gabbana. They won't help you in here, love.'

They aren't designers that Angelina particularly favours, but the other women in the refuge are aiming to be mean rather than accurate. They take an instant dislike to Angelina. Perhaps her accent makes her seem exotic. She has enough self-awareness to realise that her attitude towards the other residents doesn't do much to help her cause.

After less than a week, a fight breaks out in the refuge. It is two against one.

The refuge manager calls both the police and social services, and refuses to keep her in the centre for her own safety, as well as for his own peace of mind.

The social worker is shocked when she sees the state of Angelina, whose face is blotchy and scratched from the clawing blows of the other women, as well as tear-streaked from the sheer horror of what she's experiencing.

'This is hell!' spits Angelina, venomously. 'How dare you do this to me and my children!'

She is not to be reasoned with.

The social worker checks with her manager.

'I think the best solution is that we give Angelina a break and put the twins into foster care.'

Angelina registers suddenly what is happening to her. 'No!'

The decision causes Angelina huge distress.

The emergency call out is made. Angelina and the twins are put up in a nearby Premier Inn. Angelina hears the name 'Louise Allen' for the first time; the name of the woman who will be taking care of her children for the next few weeks, possibly months, possibly longer. The children are collected by a social worker called Bea, who drives them 'to the countryside.' Angelina feels as if her life is ending.

Sobbing, she phones her parents in Italy to break the news about her broken heart and her broken life.

PART FOUR
Louise

Max and Mia are four years old

Chapter Twelve

Max seems to be calming down more and more while Mia is away at school. I'm so pleased with my decision to start them that way round, even if I do say so myself. Because it's right both ways: Mia is absolutely thriving and – this is the most exciting bit – she has been invited to the birthday party of someone in her class.

Their independence from each other has begun in earnest.

I suspect, while they have been in the care system, and perhaps before that, they have been spending too much time together. There is an assumption that all siblings should be placed together. I imagine that twins are a different story, but after many years of fostering, I can confirm that keeping siblings together is not always a good idea. The previous life history they have shared may contribute to creating a dynamic that is unhealthy for both of them. I once looked after one of three siblings, because that sibling *pleaded* to be separated from the others because he was being bullied. Sometimes individuals need a bit of space to thrive.

If there was a violent relationship between their parents, then it's not beyond the realms of possibility that the male-female twin pattern somehow recreates a model of the children's perception of their parents. This could explain why Max and Mia argue and fight so much; perhaps they enact the routine behaviours they have learnt from their parents. It's only a guess. I don't know because I wasn't there, but I do have a strong feeling that children who are near violence, whether it's verbal or physical, carry on the pattern in their own way. Why wouldn't they? What else can they do if that's what's been modelled to them?

It sounds strange to say, but since Max and Mia have had space from each other, they have become better friends. Mia has joined Max in the circle of the trains a couple of times, and seems to be as excited as he is to drive Edward and James, choo-chooing and chug-chugging them around the track with gusto.

Sometimes I think we all just need space from those we are closest to.

I remember when I was a child, listening to an interview on Radio Oxford with Paul and Linda McCartney, and hearing about how they had never spent one night apart. Though it sounded sweet, even as a child I knew that could never be me. I still like my own time and space. For twins, I wonder how much is assumed about their emotional needs just because they shared the same womb space. We tend to only hear the stories about how close twins are, you know the sort of thing: 'I knew something was wrong even though my twin was on the other side of the world.' I'm not convinced. What about triplets or quadruplets? Do they share that same level of clairvoyance? Not that I've heard of. So, in my usual sceptical way, I choose not to believe everything I hear. What I see is two independent little people, who might very well share bedding and cutlery, but that doesn't mean they're the same.

I follow up Bea's mention of a riding stable of 18 horses online, and find news of a lady whose life was destroyed by the flooding. Her riding school, her home and her income are all gone. She and her family are living in static caravans on her yard.

Ironically, perhaps, I also learn that not that far away, on another equestrian yard, a number of little caravans have children living in them. Yes, children, because there is a shortage of foster carers. It's not hard to see why. I'm not shocked that foster carers leave in droves when the authorities shell out hundreds, sometimes thousands of pounds a week for a child to live in a children's home, but the foster carer is restricted to a matter of pence per hour. Maybe I should tell the lady who's in the static caravans to get more, and put our most vulnerable children in them.

Moira checks in. I really must change the spelling of her name in my phone.

'Give me the headlines. How are they doing, really?'

I give her a genuinely healthy picture of progress.

'Listen, I had sight of an email exchange between Bea and the children's psychologist, and it looks as if the psychologist won't make the deadline for the court hearing.'

I'm shocked. All the professionals, surely, have a duty to make sure they meet whatever deadlines are set for these children. 'Why not?' I ask.

'Between you, me and the gatepost, I genuinely don't think the psychologist has had enough time.'

'Why not?' I ask again.

'The hearing's next week.'

I'm even more shocked. I had no idea it was so soon. Given Bea's casual references and generally laid-back approach, I'd just assumed it was a month or two away. 'So, what can be done?'

'I'm not sure.'

'But this isn't on. The children are thriving. I will be sorry to see them go, but things need to move on for them. They feel safe and happy about their lives through being here, and they're all the happier for seeing their parents. The courts need to know that.'

'I know.'

'Is it Bea holding things up? Because I tell you, I have a bad feeling about that woman.'

Moira is very professional and doesn't take the bait, flipping my comment back. 'I'm sure she's probably just busy.'

I snort at that and remind her that Bea works for an independent fostering agency, an IFA. 'She told me that she has nine children in her care, and six of those are in long-term placements, so not too demanding. That leaves one other beyond Max and Mia. She's not as busy as you.'

Moira doesn't go as far as telling me how many children she's responsible for, so I fill in the numbers for her. As a supervising social worker, she only has foster carers on her books, and she's also part-time. I guess that she has about 12 families, including us. But the average social worker has a much bigger caseload.

'You have more families to see than she does. Tell me that isn't true. And social workers I know working for the council have up to thirty children or sibling groups on their books, and rarely are they as settled and straightforward as Max and Mia are, so come on?'

She doesn't deny it, so I assume that I'm close to her working load, and that of her colleagues.

'The psychologist needs to meet the children and see them, talk to them. They are thriving and I really think—' I bring myself up short, because I nearly spilt the beans about my long conversation with Angelina. I must not reveal that link, because I didn't tell them at the start. I might have done, if it had been a social worker that I had a better relationship with, but I haven't been sure about Bea from the off.

I know that foster carers can get too involved with the birth family, but usually that's about the foster carers' personalities and a bit of the old 'mother hen' syndrome, which I don't have. Usually, I am looking for ways back into my studio, not making more work for myself.

'Bottom line, Moira. Can you broker some sort of deal where at least the psychologist has the chance to talk to us – to me and Lloyd, that is, if not the children themselves – and not just Bea? We're the ones who've been looking after them and getting to know them, whereas Bea has hardly been involved at all. We've only had her at the house twice in six weeks, and one of those visits was with you to drop them off!'

I tell Moira that Max has successfully done two nights now without his pull-ups. She is congratulatory about that.

'And Mia is going to a party, so we have some shopping to do. She needs a party dress and a present for her school friend.'

I explain the ways in which I now do activities with them individually. 'They still sleep in the same room, they see each other every evening and weekend, but I genuinely believe that this is good for them. They've both come out of themselves. Watching these two thrive in their own skins is an utter joy.'

'I'll see what I can do, Louise. But I make no promises.'

'I'm back to Salisbury in the morning with Max and Mia to see their mum once more.'

I let Moira know the arrangements for contact tomorrow and explain that I might leave them to it. 'Otherwise, there will be too many adults and, no matter what Bea thinks, this is still a contact visit for the twins and their mother. It's not just an observation session for the benefit of Bea. This little family aren't a bunch of lab rats.'

I don't know where it will get us, but I feel better for the conversation. I hang up and look to the skies. I hope it doesn't storm today or tomorrow, as I'll be busy in Salisbury and not able to 'defend' the house.

The weather is heavy and grey, and the clouds look full to bursting.

Chapter Thirteen

The kitchen is filled with the sound of sizzling from the frying pan and the alluring aroma of bacon. How Lily can resist the temptation as a vegetarian, I don't know. I fry rasher after rasher and chop up tons of fruit into bowls. There is more sizzling as the pancake batter hits the oil in the pan.

It's a Louise Allen special 'build your own' dinner. It's an easy option, but the children actually love assembling their own meals this way because they get exactly what they want, and it's a lovely, sociable way to eat. I fry pancakes as quickly as they eat them. Maple syrup flows over bacon and fruit. My adopted mother would turn in her grave at the notion of mixing bacon with anything other than mustard. I smile at that thought. Max and Mia also embrace the fusion food – though I'm not quite sure this is what the swanky chefs in London think of as 'fusion' – perhaps 'confusion' food describes it better.

Whatever. We all love it.

We love it even more when it comes to pudding. I bring out a fresh container of vanilla soft-scoop ice cream, which is the preferred way to complete a 'make your own' dinner, and everyone's favourite bit. I place the tub in the middle of the table and leave the ice cream scoop next to it, then pull five bowls out of the cupboard. I can't help tutting when I notice another chip on the side of one. I watch with contentment as the children all dive in. My work is done, and it has required very little preparation.

It's also interesting to see the way they approach the food. Lily finds it the hardest to be patient. I see, once again, that the twins have some great manners. They've been here long enough to feel settled and not hold back, but they are very polite and wait their turn, despite being the youngest at the table. The boys are well trained at the table, and are generally very well mannered. To be fair, they do employ them most of the time – except when they're gaming. Then I think they are possessed, and all civilised responses go out of the window. Jackson offers to help Mia get hers, but she has no need of his assistance.

For a moment the only sound is the tapping of spoons on crockery.

'Hey, careful there. Don't scrape off the glaze,' I beg, as their enthusiasm to devour every last drop of ice cream overtakes them. Once the bowls are empty, the children all disperse to the sitting room.

I grab their used dinner plates and start placing them in the dishwasher. 'Please note, my darling husband, that this is how it is meant to be done,' I say.

'Alright, I'll finish off,' he says, reaching for the ice cream bowls, so clean that they don't look like they even need the dishwasher.

I don't need asking a second time, and head to the sitting room to see how the children are getting on. They are all playing with the trains, even Lily, whose behaviour is much better these days, though I can't help feeling that we aren't out of the woods just yet.

Despite all the sugar, natural and processed, they all toddle off to bed quite nicely. I remember to wake Max up before I go to bed and get him to have a wee. He obliges half-asleep, or at least goes straight back to sleep, but with an empty bladder.

Lloyd and I chat for a bit about tomorrow's contact visit.

'I'm planning to leave them to it and take the two hours as a treat to do a bit of shopping.'

'Good, you do that.'

Lloyd, I know, is looking forward to having the house to himself, though he doesn't say that. He doesn't need to. We are definitely not Paul and Linda.

In the morning, the boys and Lily get off to school with no complaints at all – not even the usual script of me being blamed for them not knowing where their PE shorts are. That scene regularly unfolds even though I have washed said PE kits, folded them, placed them neatly on their beds and said at dinner, 'Make sure you have your PE kits ready for the morning.' It never seems to work, but I live in hope, and today that hope pays off.

I ask the children to choose their own clothes today. I always try to offer choice, but usually it's a choice between two things to keep it simple. Today I tell them, 'Choose whatever you want.'

'You choose, Louise,' Max says. He doesn't want to waste precious seconds when he could be downstairs playing with trains. I notice, though, that he's already wearing a *Thomas the Tank Engine* jumper that Vincent donated. The cheeky monkey has pulled it out of the laundry basket and teamed it with his underpants.

Mia though, ponders more carefully. She likes purple and looks striking in it with her red hair. In the end she picks a purple jumper and denim skirt with red tights.

'Fair enough.' As I'm thinking about clothes, it dawns on me that, while in Salisbury, we could choose an outfit for the party.

I let them play while I pack bags and gather food. Lloyd's work diary is too crammed for him to be able to give us a lift today, or so he says, so I put the children on their booster seats and drive to the station. I decide not to walk another half a mile from the new housing estate where I parked previously to save the council a few quid. Today I am buying a whole five pounds' worth: an entire day's parking. I'm just going to put it through the authority's books and see what happens. And if they want to argue with me about that, I'm ready. Just let them try. I'm sure I'll think of something. Though why I should have to 'think of something' to justify what is actually part of the journey, I don't know. It was their idea, after all, to home the children this far away from their parents.

Mia has her fluffy owl, but Max has ditched his teddy for three *Thomas the Tank Engine* books and a few trains to run across the dining car table. The Thomas thing is bordering on obsessive now, but it certainly keeps the boy happy.

Mia is very chatty, telling me all about school and her new friends. Max is only half listening, genuinely more interested in his Thomas books. It all feels very relaxed. They seem like totally okay children to me and, once again, Max alerts me in plenty of time to needing the toilet. Mia is way past that stage in her life and behaves as if it never even happened. They already seem more grown-up in the space of just a few weeks.

Being on a train is ridiculously exciting for Max these days, fuelled no doubt by his *Thomas the Tank Engine* passion. The children settle into their play, and this gives me a chance to reflect on the long telephone conversation I had with

Angelina, and the way she spoke about Ben. How things had gone so dramatically wrong.

'Oh Louise, we loved each other so much, once. I can't tell you.'

She talked openly about what had happened between her and Ben, how she had pushed him away.

'After the birth of the twins, I felt as if I was losing my mind.'

Her words echo those of another friend of mine. She was actually a headteacher, very successful and accomplished. She confided in me that after the birth of her first child, she had postnatal depression which escalated. It was much more serious than a case of the 'baby blues'. It's a serious mental illness and should be treated by medical professionals. I remember her describing her condition as exactly what Angelina said: feeling like she had lost her mind.

'I felt as if I didn't know myself, who I was. I wouldn't let Ben come anywhere near me. So perhaps it's not surprising that he had an affair.'

She pauses.

'I *think* it was only in the early stages, but I caught them red-handed. I don't think it had gone very far, but I saw red.'

I picture her red hair, and imagine a fiery Mediterranean temperament.

She also talked about the horror of living in a women's refuge: the shock to her system brought about by such a contrast to her life before, and how she had got herself into a fight which led to her being evicted and the children being taken away.

'Before the fight happened, I talked to other women and heard some of their stories of abuse. It made me realise what I was inflicting on my own children. I felt overwhelmed with guilt and shame. I'm terrified that I have hurt Max and Mia, damaged them, because they witnessed our appalling behaviour.'

I have looked after enough children who have grown up witnessing domestic abuse, verbal and physical, to know that we can never underestimate the damage that it does to a child or a young person's view of the world.

I know that, for many abused people, work needs to be done to stop the cycle. Otherwise, it gets passed on to the next generation. This happens too often, because replicating the patterns is easier than breaking the cycle. It isn't called 'work' for nothing, and it can be a lonely journey.

Trust me, I know.

I am mulling all of this over, while at the same time admiring the way Max and Mia are happily occupied with their play. They know exactly where they are going today. There is no need to pretend that we are on our way to somewhere else; emotionally, they are in control. I reflect on how much better they have been since they started to have time apart. The tell-tale detail that both have stopped wetting the bed is a good indicator of the progress they have made.

I don't feel as if Angelina was trying to play me when we spoke. Actually, it seemed that she needed to talk in order to try and understand what happened. She never said it outright, but I'm sure that she desperately wants her family back.

I look up 'severe postnatal depression' on my phone. The first few websites I look at are shocking. It sounds awful, and my heart goes out again to my dear headteacher friend who shared her story with me. I don't think, at the time, I knew enough about it to have any idea of what she went through.

I know that she has since recovered, and career-wise, she is amazing. She has totally transformed a large primary school during her tenure there. I know that my friend is supportive of the mums at her school. I see why, now. She is an incredible woman. Even if Angelina's experience wasn't as catastrophic as hers, severe postnatal depression is a serious issue.

Before I know it, we are drawing into Salisbury station. We are used to the drill by now. Max and Mia head straight for the taxi rank, leading the way, hand in hand. At the family centre, we greet Jill, just as Bea comes out of the toilet, which is where we are heading ourselves.

'Hi Bea,' I say cheerily. She looks much more professional today, dressed in a smart suit. Though she is top to toe in black; maybe she's going to a funeral.

We all congregate in the foyer and chat about how the session is going to work.

I feel a little uncomfortable. I'm not sure it's appropriate, given that the children are standing with us, listening. I desperately want to say hello to Angelina, knowing how much she has confided in me, and what strength that must have taken, but I also have the strong sense that Bea does not want me in the room. She stands so that she is practically barring my route through. Jill stands to one side. As a less-well-paid member of staff than Bea, and probably without a social work degree, she kowtows to Bea.

I decide to ignore Bea's very obvious body language and walk past breezily with the children.

The children are excited to see their mum once again.

She holds them in a big warm group hug and gives me a grateful nod over the top of Max and Mia's heads.

Bea reaches for a clipboard, which never goes down well with me, particularly not in a situation such as this. Give someone a clipboard and you give them a false sense of power.

I lightly touch the backs of the children and look Angelina in the eye.

'Have a lovely time. I'll see you all later.' I'm going to carry on with my plan to head towards the shops.

Then I turn and smile what I think of as my fake 'I'm being paid to be nice' air hostess smile to Bea and Jill. I do like Jill, but I'm annoyed by her obvious subservience to Bea.

I leave the room, knowing that actually I really don't want to intrude on this little scene of love. Those children are back, for a couple of hours at least, where they belong.

Chapter Fourteen

I get a text from Angelina.

Louise, would it be okay to speak? X

It is a few days after the contact visit. Everyone is out and I am just about to start my penultimate illustration for *Ask the Seahorse*, the children's book that I'm already late on the deadline for. Normally, I would try to postpone a text or call until my headspace is clear of creative work. I usually make sure that my phone isn't even with me in the studio. I tend to leave it on the kitchen table, so it's there when I stop for a coffee but not interrupting the flow or providing a distraction. Avoiding distractions is crucial. In fact, I always have short fingernails, with no polish or jewellery, not even my watch, when I'm working.

I know myself too well. Even a piece of jewellery might act as a sparkly distraction. I'd rather see my hands as tools for my work than as a place to exhibit precious stones or a fine manicure. I used to do those things before I took my work seriously. These days I have to be disciplined, or nothing will get done. I've carved out this time. I must use it.

But something makes me think twice. This is Angelina, and I didn't really have a chance to speak to her at the end of the contact visit. All seemed well when I went back to collect Max and Mia in time to catch the train; Bea had gone by the time I arrived, so I never got to speak to her. I will confess to not being too disappointed about that. Jill was very pleasant, as always, but has no responsibility for any kind of decision-making or report-writing. If you think about it too much, which obviously I have, this is a kind of madness, since she is usually the only adult overseeing contact. Given that she has no real jurisdiction over what happens, I'm sure some parents could run rings around her and their children.

Nevertheless, she, Angelina and the children all seemed happy at the end. Max and Mia sang and chatted for most of the way home, before nodding off for a bit. Everything pointed to it all being a success, even though I hadn't witnessed this meeting directly.

So what could Angelina want?

The art will have to wait a bit longer.

I sit down and ring her number.

'Oh, Louise, thank you so much for getting back to me. I am so sorry to call you, but I didn't know what else to do.'

Her voice is sad, tearful, as if she is struggling to speak.

I sigh. I know this will not be a quick phone call, so I turn my chair to look out of the window at my front garden. Already the trees and shrubs are almost empty of their leaves; the hazy morning sun behind them makes them appear like rough pencil-line sketches on a canvas.

'What's happened?'

Angelina needs no further invitation to begin her narrative. Her voice takes on a frantic tone as she explains, 'They are going to recommend that my children stay in care. The social worker even mentioned adoption. Louise, I may never get my children back.'

I feel my own heart breaking a little as I hear the anguish in her voice.

242

She gives me a few more details and, as I listen, I wonder once again how the hell they have arrived at this decision. There is a piece of the jigsaw puzzle missing. There must be something that I don't know. I'm aware that I'm only getting one side of the story, but Angelina has been frank about her mental health and about the deterioration in her relationship with her husband. What else has happened? Might Angelina have tried to murder her children? Was she a heroin user? Was she an alcoholic? Had Ben abused or sexually abused the children? If it has reached a stage where they are talking about adoption, then something pretty serious must have occurred.

But none of it adds up with my own experience of Angelina, of Ben or of the children themselves. None of this rings true. None of it quite makes sense.

My first reaction, after the shock of hearing her news, is one of rage on her behalf. Then my brain moves to doubt about Angelina. Have I got her all wrong? Is she, in fact, a brilliant actress, covering some horrible character flaw? Or is it Ben who is hiding something? I also begin to doubt my own observations of the children. Am I painting too rosy a picture of their progress because in my heart of hearts I feel that this family should be back together?

But no, that can't be it. I keep such careful notes, daily, about what they get up to. And I'm very experienced at this. Why am I doubting myself?

Then I rock back to rage again.

This poor woman is going out of her mind.

'Ok, slow down and start again from the beginning.'

'The social workers have got it in for me. Bea and the first social worker from here, the one who took Max and Mia away in the first place. They're friends.'

243

'Ah, yes. Bea. I have some thoughts about her.' Though now definitely isn't the moment to share them.

'Together they have written a report about my parenting skills and been totally damning about what type of parent I am. They know nothing!'

She begins to cry again, and I wait for her to compose herself and come back into the conversation.

'They said that I am a cold, distant mother who could not give my children the love and attention that they need.'

She breathes heavily down the line and blows her nose. I hear paper rustling. She is reading from her own notes, or perhaps she has a copy of the report.

'They say I am into myself and that I display narcissistic tendencies. I am only interested in myself and fashion and how I look.'

My blood is boiling.

I want to put the phone down and head over to Bea and this other sour old bag's office and give them a piece of my mind. How dare they make a judgement like that from one meeting? I have seen nothing but love and care and attention. Max and Mia were in the best of health and very clean when they arrived. Their bags were beautifully arranged, packed with a great deal of thought and care. I have looked after a lot of children in my time, and these two looked like they were coming for a little holiday rather than being thrust into the care system. Their teeth were in excellent shape, which is always one of the first things I look at when I meet new children. They both had good-quality clothes and polite manners.

As Angelina sobs down the phone, my own theorising goes into overdrive. I wonder if something else has interfered with the judgement of these social workers.

Yes, Angelina looks amazing. There is no denying that. I was very taken with her appearance myself when we first met. But it's almost as if she achieves that with very little to no effort. She certainly wasn't caked in makeup or done up to the nines. Quite the opposite, in fact. In many ways her look was totally understated. My impression was of a very natural kind of beauty, one that emanates from her striking looks, certainly, but is accentuated by her elegance and style. I don't recognise the Angelina that I have met at all in the description she has offered. Could it be Angelina's appearance that has ignited one of Bea's insecurities? The description of a 'narcissistic woman', 'only interested in how she looks', strikes me as being far more applicable to Bea herself than to Angelina.

I'm also now clearer that Angelina and Ben went through the nightmare of undiagnosed severe postnatal depression, a condition that should be treated by a perinatal mental health team. I know too well how our society is not kind to women. It judges especially harshly women who struggle with motherhood. There is a kind of innate belief that we're all wired and programmed to know what to do, how to respond, how to feel, and that simply isn't true. There is a backlash against any woman who isn't instantly maternal, or who dares to insist on having a career and a life and not making continual sacrifices. Perhaps Bea has some strange views about parenting herself. She certainly didn't seem to know much about raising her own son.

Perhaps it's the family's wealth that has upset Bea and her colleague. I know that Angelina is, or at least was, very wealthy. I know that they lived in an amazing house. Perhaps Ben still does. Bea had some pretty interesting views about that, I seem to remember.

So, could it be as simple as good, old-fashioned jealousy?

A nasty characteristic, one of my most despised (along with self-pity), but one that I definitely wouldn't put past Bea. And if this other social worker is a friend of hers, then perhaps they are just a pair of embittered women, taking their various insecurities out on someone vulnerable, like a pair of playground bullies.

That's the conclusion I draw: Bea is jealous and is acting on her jealousy in a brutal, vindictive and – for Angelina – life-changing way.

Chapter Fifteen

Sometimes we need to listen to our gut instincts.

I liked Angelina the moment I met her. I felt a kindness radiating from her, but also sensed vulnerability. It seemed to me that she was lost and scared, had made mistakes but was trying hard to do the right thing.

When I met Bea, on the other hand, I took an instant dislike to her. My first grudge was the simple fact that she works for a private fostering agency, a very successful enterprise that floated on the stock market for £100 million. That's wonderful for the shareholders, but the reality is that all that money comes from the taxpayers and should be destined for the children – to enrich their lives, not to make millionaires. I was put out by the way Bea seemed to feel that she didn't have to appear professional when she came to my house. From my understanding of the situation, this was because I was 'only' a foster carer. I note the way she could very much manage the suit when she was at the family centre, but looked like she'd been mucking out at the stables every time she arrived with me.

The fact that she loved the sound of her own voice did little to endear her to me. Snide comments that she made had put my back up at the time. She strikes me as an egomaniac, and listening to one does get tiresome very quickly.

So, my allegiances are clear. But I need to make sure that I have things in perspective, and that I'm not allowing my judgement to be clouded. When I get like this, I need to settle, just like the weather, which, as I glance out of the window, looks ominous. Those clouds look like thunder, lightning and heavy rain. And heavy rain means flooding. I draw a few parallels between the weather and Max and Mia's situation. In both instances, some of the resulting problems are rooted in incompetence.

But those threatening clouds remind me that I should take the dogs out before it rains. The mood I'm in, I could do with a good stomp up that hill, and it will give me the time and space to think about what to do.

The fresh air helps to clear my head. The dogs, as ever, cheer me up and what seemed like a hopeless situation on the way up begins to feel more surmountable on the way home. As I descend the hill, my plan forms. I see a way forward that might just manage to help me to stay calm, but more importantly to help this little family.

As far as I can see (and my stomping time has given me the opportunity to consider all sides and angles), Ben and Angelina are being punished by the system for being beautiful and rich.

I know that, when I think back to my friend who suffered from severe postnatal depression, the language she used and the feelings and symptoms she described sound so much like Angelina's experience. I'm convinced that Angelina was seriously ill following the birth of the twins. It also seems as if that all went largely undetected, and that may go a long way towards making sense of this whole situation.

Angelina also hinted that her own childhood had contained violent episodes, acts of aggression against her mother carried out by her father. As with Lily, it could be the old story of patterns of behaviour being passed on, creating a never-ending cycle. I have witnessed the sudden angry flare-ups that can take place between Max and Mia. It's time for the chain to be broken.

It is possible that Angelina's behaviour, and in particular, the paranoia about what her husband may or may not have been getting up to, were not exclusively the result of her being a privileged young airhead, which is the impression that Bea seems to be giving. The level of paranoia she described to me can be associated with postnatal depression. The fact that Bea's report bears no resemblance to anything I have seen, and I'm the one who's been living with and caring for Max and Mia, makes me think that the social workers have the wrong end of the stick. This family shouldn't be being punished by separation. Rather, they should be supported. But that isn't what is happening. Nor can I see any evidence of any kind of support before the removal of Max and Mia. Two social workers, who should be trained to know better, can't get past their own prejudices, bias and jealousy.

How many other women in this day and age are being subjected to similar treatment for this reason?

I have an old friend, who is a lawyer. She moved to Boston in the US, but thanks to the miracles of modern technology and social media, we keep in touch. She and I met years ago, when I first began campaigning for the rights of children in the care system. She fell in love and married an American. It was great, and I was so happy for her, but of course it took her away from our regular London lunches, where she'd happily join me in dissecting the latest twists and turns in children's social services. She would list all the laws that were broken on a daily basis, and I would slump into my chair and shake my head in despair. I know that she'd have a view on this case.

It's 10.30 am here. She'd be fast asleep in Boston, so I can't ring. Instead, I fling her an email outlining the bones of Angelina's situation, and what I think is going to happen if something isn't done soon.

What I really need right now is to speak to someone. I go to contacts and find 'Mowra'. It's time to give her a call.

'Hi Moira, how are you?'

I play dumb as we chat. 'I was just wondering if you had any news on how the run-up to the court case is going for Max and Mia. I mean, especially as the psychologist never got to meet the children, or chat to us.'

If that sounds a little bit passive-aggressive, it won't hurt.

Down the phone line, I hear Moira making the sounds of someone looking up something on their computer. There are the tell-tale taps along with her, 'Bear with...'

After a moment, she says, 'Aah. Oh, that's a surprise. I really wasn't expecting that.'

I continue to play stupid. 'What's up?'

'Well, it seems the social worker is recommending that they stay in long-term foster care or be put up for adoption.'

'And how do you feel about that?' I ask. 'Given that it doesn't accord with anything I've reported to you?'

'I have to confess, I'm surprised. I thought all was good, and that a plan to return home may have been on the cards.'

I decide not to pull any more punches. Given that Moira is of the same mind, I offer some of my observations and my hunch about what might be going on.

'And, frankly, I have never liked or trusted Bea,' I finish.

Moira maintains a professional demeanour. 'Are you prepared to say why?'

I explain the unpleasant comments about Angelina's wealth. 'I can't remember the exact words now, but she said something along the lines of, "For all that money, they can't have it all." It was something like that, and it just sounded vindictive. It was saturated in loathing and jealousy, as if she just had it in for Angelina.'

'I see.'

'Surely, though, it's not her role to judge.'

'I suppose it's inevitable. You know as well as I do that we don't often get the offspring of wealthy people ending up in children's social care.'

'Perhaps not, but that doesn't mean that the authorities should be prejudiced against them.' I remind her about equality and diversity, and how we are not allowed to express a bias about people's religious beliefs or backgrounds. 'I mean, it's none of our business if people are rich or poor. We do what we can to support the children, regardless of the circumstances.'

I go a little bit further than I intended to, but then articulating all of these thoughts has inevitably fired up my rage on Angelina's behalf once more. 'Perhaps, if we actually supported families in the beginning and helped them through difficult times instead of penalising them, we wouldn't have so many children in the care system. Nor would we require so many social workers or foster carers. Then those greedy vulture capitalists wouldn't be able to take so much money away from the children.' The last bit all comes out in a bit of a rush. In for a penny, in for a pound.

I brace myself for the telling off. But instead, I'm surprised to hear Moira say, 'I totally agree, Louise.'

That's pretty unusual. Normally, social workers and supervising social workers like Moira, in particular, try to smooth everything over to keep the peace and the current status quo. Her supportive utterance spurs me on.

'So, what can we do, Moira? What can we do to stop this car crash?'

Moira is very calm. 'There's nothing much we can do, I'm afraid. We have no powers at all. All I can suggest is that you can submit a report about the children and what you have seen at contact visits.'

That will not be enough for me. I am in a fighting mood.

'And what would be the point in that? It literally wouldn't be worth the paper it's written on. It would never see the light of day, in any case. You know as well as I do that all it would take is for Bea and her fellow social worker to casually forget to submit my report. How would I even know? Then there would be nothing, no record at all.'

'Louise—'

'I'm so cross. And what about Ben? Nobody seems to be gunning for him in quite the same way. He had a bloody affair—'

Whoops. I've overstepped the mark there. I'm not supposed to know that. I repair what I can.

'—I mean, I imagine he did. At least that's the impression I get. Why is his character not being demolished in the same way?' I don't pause to let Moira answer. My question is entirely rhetorical. 'I'll tell you why. Throughout the whole of time, women and the conditions that come with being a woman – having periods, menopause, premenstrual tension and having babies – all of it has been framed from a male perspective.'

'Louise—'

I'm off on one, and barely hear her attempt to interrupt me. 'All of it has been commented on and written about by men. Not women, men. So now we are finally moving towards an enlightened age part two. And it's definitely part two, because part one, the historical Age of Enlightenment, all that intellectual and philosophical stuff in the seventeenth century, that was all men, too.'

'Louise—'

'And so, the only way for some women to survive it all is to put other women down. Instead of women in authority holding out a hand to reach out to their fellow sisters, there are some bitter, sour women who will kick the boot in to attack other women.'

'Louise, I'm not sure—'

'Well I AM! It's so much a part of our history and culture that women – as well as men – are guilty of it. I know it all too well because I experienced it myself when I was teaching at the university. I naively thought fellow women would be supportive and we could all help each other succeed, but no! It was just the opposite. As we hung, uncomfortably stuck in the lower, middle rungs of the career ladder, male colleagues just seemed to stroll by us. The opportunities were so few and far between that the knives were in the back as soon as there was an opportunity for women to shine. Only a few got to make it to the middle.'

'Louise, where are you going with this?'

'I'm trying to say that there are parallels. That's when I left the university. I just couldn't face the rest of my working life stuck in the lower middle because I wasn't prepared to stab a colleague in the back. Angelina is not on a career trajectory, but she is on her life trajectory. It should be hers to have. It shouldn't be taken away from her by a jealous, back-stabbing bitch!'

Chapter Sixteen

Rant over, I realise that I meant every word of it. Deeply ingrained misogynistic attitudes abound, and sometimes where they might be least expected. I feel a tiny bit better for voicing it, even though that alone isn't going to help Angelina. I try as hard as I can to leave it all behind me for the rest of the day and get on with my other tasks. Even if I'm not thinking about Angelina and her predicament and Bea and her misogynistic jealousy, I know that my subconscious will still be busy mulling it all over. Meanwhile, there are practical things I need to concern myself with.

Next week Max will finally be at school, so there is a uniform, a school bag and all the other bits and pieces to sort. It will only be for a few hours in the morning, just as Mia did at first, but it's a start and all is going in the right direction – in that avenue of their lives at least. Mia loves school and, by any measure you could possibly choose, is thriving. I couldn't have hoped for a better outcome. The increased confidence has turned her into a real chatterbox, but she also loves to be helpful and is very kind.

Since the children have had more contact with their mother and father, they have calmed down and are less angry. Of course they have. It's good for them. I am so cross that the psychologist didn't meet them. That alone makes it feel very personal and vindictive on the part of Bea and her sidekick.

See – I can't stop thinking about it, even though I'm trying so hard to think about other things. But my subconscious has definitely been hammering away in there. I have a sudden brainwave connected with school. I call the headteacher and ask if she has submitted a report to the court.

She has no idea what I'm talking about. So, not only have the children not seen the psychologist, the school haven't been asked for their perspective either. That seems to me like two very significant gaps.

The storm warnings continue, so we are standing by for flooding – literally hour by hour. The news in our Facebook flood 'resilience' group depresses me. I'm not sure how much resilience I have left.

The twins are busy playing downstairs and I find myself drifting towards their bedroom. I justify this to myself by saying that it needs tidying up, but actually it only takes a few seconds to pick up a few toys and clothes. The reality is that I just feel like I need to be in here. I need to be close to their safe space. I'm full of worry for them. The waves of sickness and stomach-churning feelings that have beset me all day are all on their behalf. I'm so fearful for their futures.

Adoption, in this instance, is not the answer. I'm sure of it. In any case, adoption doesn't always have a happy ending. It can be a way of a local authority 'parking' a child, or in this case, children, out of fostering because it's financially savvy. Adoption is cheap – or free. David Cameron introduced his plans to speed up adoption in 2015. The sentiment was admirable, but the implementation, like so many other things, has been less effective. Since then, scrutiny has been reduced. I wonder how many adoptions have failed because crucial work is being messed up with this goal to 'speed up' adoption. We will never know the data on that, I'm sure. It's all carefully tucked away. But it's happening right now to Max and Mia and Angelina and Ben.

I'm so scared for this family.

Later, when Lloyd comes home and the younger children are in bed, I talk to him about the whole situation and my fears for the family. We sit on opposite sides of the kitchen table. Normally, in any situation where I hold a strong opinion about something (and there are a few of those), Lloyd likes to play devil's advocate. I'm not sure if it's a helpful strategy, the playing out of a power struggle, or just him being annoying. But, today, he doesn't do any of that. Today he looks as horrified as I am, because together we've seen enough over the years to develop a feeling for what might be the best outcomes for the children in our care. Instead of trying to convince me that Bea must know what she's doing, will be party to more information than us, has a social work degree, has sight of the bigger picture, blah, blah, blah, he simply says,

'What about Ben?'

He's right. Even if Angelina is deemed 'unfit' to parent her children, why is he? Moreover, all my sympathy has been for Angelina as the mother. He's just about to lose his children too.

I'm increasingly minded towards breaking all the rules. By that I mean the 'make it up as you go along rules' used or not used by children's social care according to some lunar calendar I'm not privy to.

So I text Angelina and ask how she is.

She responds straight away. *I'm with Ben.*

Hey presto. Just like that, Lloyd's question may have the opportunity to be answered. 'He's there with her now!'

How are you getting on? I mean it both ways – how they are getting on with each other, and how they are getting on with the issue of what may happen later after the court hearing. Angelina can choose her interpretation.

We are worried and scared. Ben does not know what to do. Neither of us can believe this is happening.

The moving dots tell me that she's still typing.

It's a nightmare.

'Will you talk to Ben?' I ask out loud.

Lloyd nods. 'Yes, why not?'

I text Angelina back once more and suggest that, if Ben is happy to give us his number, Lloyd would be happy to chat. *Believe me, we know how difficult this must be for you both.*

So far, I have been raging on behalf of Angelina and, if I'm perfectly honest, until Lloyd said it a few moments ago, I haven't given Ben much thought. I do now. The poor bugger must be in a similar state of fear, just as devastated as Angelina.

I set a plan in motion. I'm well aware that we have to work quickly, as the court hearing is in one week.

Vincent pops into the kitchen. 'I'm going to bed.'

I'm surprised. He often needs a prod in that direction, and it's still early. I look up at the clock. It's not early at all: already 10pm. Blimey, where did that time go? He squeezes my shoulder and waves as he says, 'Laters,' which is about as tender as it gets these days.

I scoot upstairs to do a little goodnight round. Jackson is lying in bed, propped up with pillows, laughing at *Hell's Kitchen*. Lily is on top of her bed looking at TikTok videos of cats and kittens.

'Bedtime, missy,' I say. Over her shoulder, I spot a black-and-white cat on her screen. It's wearing a box and walking round a kitchen and Lily is laughing her head off.

Strange old world.

When I get back downstairs, I see that my phone has another text from Angelina containing Ben's contact details.

'Lloyd, Lloyd, she's sent through Ben's number!'

'Great. I'll message him tomorrow if I get time.'

His level of *carpe diem* mentality can't quite be said to match mine. And I can't hear his less-than-enthusiastic response without reacting to it. I manage to keep my temper in check (just about), and suggest that Ben is likely to be feeling very anxious right now. 'And we only have a week. Perhaps a little text back may help him feel better and get some sleep?'

Lloyd looks at me as if I have asked him to catch a flight to Timbuktu and give an impromptu lecture on the future of humanity. He does his 'oh I'm busy/I'm tired' procrastinating man-thing, then clocks the expression on my face.

He texts Ben back.

Chapter Seventeen

I wake up to learn that Lloyd stayed up chatting to Ben past midnight. Excellent. Although, I didn't realise because I had nodded off reading one paragraph of a book called *Meditations: A New Translation* – a series of spiritual exercises and practical and ethical guidance for life, originally by Marcus Aurelius. It's supposed to make me wise. I do try to be highbrow, but every time I start to read something intellectual like that, I seem to fall asleep.

Still, some of it may have rubbed off, because I feel calmer today. I've woken up with less hatred towards Bea and more determination to take action for this little family. Some may say that I'm allowing myself to get too involved, and they'd be right, but the one thing I kept on hearing myself say in the book about my own childhood, *Thrown Away Child*, was, 'Why didn't anyone keep trying, why did no one dig a bit deeper into what was going on?' I've never been able to understand how some of the cruelties and abuses that my brother and I experienced were allowed to take place.

So, I'm determined to keep trying and to dig deeper. And, to be honest, when Moira agreed with me that it wasn't fair, it kind of felt as if I was being given permission to carry on. That's my reading of it, anyway. Never mind that I barely let her get a word in edgeways.

The children are hard to wake up this morning. All of them went to bed late, apart from Max and Mia, and on a school night too. I must have been very distracted last night. I tempt Vincent downstairs with the smell of bacon frying and brownies baking in the oven. A heavenly combination of smells.

I crack an egg into the frying pan too, and add some baked beans to a saucepan on the next ring. That boy has hollow legs. Lily comes down and sniffs the air accusingly.

'If he's having bacon and eggs, what are you going to cook me for breakfast?'

As one of the world's fussiest eaters, she generally turns her nose up at almost everything, but when I empty out her school bag, I find crisp packets and sweet wrappers. Evidently, she finds a way to supplement her diet.

'Anyway, I wouldn't want what Vincent's having. His breakfast is unhealthy.'

Oh, we're in one of those phases.

'In that case, perhaps you'd like some fresh fruit and yoghurt?'

No, it transpires, she wouldn't. She turns her nose up at the carnivore's option, but also the herbivore's. She does, however, spot the new box of 'chocolate cushions', or whatever nonsense those cereals are called. I bought them for Max and Mia as a treat, but they're probably better off without them.

Lily settles on those, and somehow manages to fit half a box into one small cereal bowl. There's barely any room for milk, but never mind.

They get off to school somewhat sluggishly today. Once the house is clear of teenagers, I put everything in the dishwasher and gather up the twins, who go for a bowl of chocolate cushions each after seeing Lily tuck into them.

Lloyd's busy in a Teams meeting with his clients in the Netherlands, so I leave him alone and walk both children down to school. Mia is in her uniform and Max is in his civvies, for another few days at least. I'll take Max to the outfitters later today to buy his sweatshirt and tie and school PE shirt and bag. If I pay a little extra, he can have his name embroidered onto his bag. He'll like that.

I think it's a good idea to walk him down with us this morning to get him used to the journey, and it won't hurt to watch how happily Mia goes into class. Every morning, she skips down the lane so enamoured with life, in spite of all her emotional upheaval. She's far happier since the regular contact visits with her parents. It's hard to even understand what they must have felt and known. The poor things must have been so worried. They were taken away from their 'proper' home, bedroom and surroundings, and then taken away from the women's refuge where they'd been staying, and then taken away from their mother. Then they endured a long car ride with Busy Bea, Busy, Bossy Bea. That journey must have been strange. I haven't seen much natural warmth, or even interest towards children. Why on earth did she become a social worker? Perhaps she doesn't like children and her career choice is an act of revenge. No, that's harsh. Maybe she would be better at being a social worker for horses. All the way down to school I keep up a running commentary for Max.

'This will be you next week in your uniform, walking down to school with Mia. How exciting that will be!'

He holds my hand and listens, but instead of asking about school, asks me lots of questions about Thomas the Tank Engine. I am a bit 'Rusty'. Pun intended.

When we return from the school run, Max is straight back into the sitting room to get going on his 'Thomas' world. For extra ambience, I put on a Thomas DVD in the background, which means he can keep listening to the music and integrate the storylines into whatever his versions of train adventures are today. He thinks this is amazing, and is in Thomas-heaven.

With Max suitably occupied, I head to my studio to check my emails. The one that leaps out is a reply from Kate in Boston, though it isn't her private email, it's her corporate work address, with a Kirkland & Adams law firm logo and signature. I wonder if Kate is a partner. It's not beyond the realms of possibility, given the career trajectory she was on, and her surname is Adams. I read her message very carefully. She sounds very professional and serious and not at all like my friend of old, but she must just be in full-on work mode.

She states Angelina's options and offers details of a colleague of hers in the UK, based in Manchester. The long and the short of it is that Angelina and Ben need to provide evidence of their side of things, and I need to provide a statement about what Bea has said about Angelina, as well as supplying all the emails I have, clearly dated, highlighting the comments from Bea about not having enough time for us to talk to a psychologist. In addition, she thinks the dates of missed or postponed meetings with Bea will be helpful. She also suggests including communication from the school to confirm that they haven't been spoken to at all about Mia or Max.

Ok, Marcus Aurelius, here is some practical guidance I can follow. I text Angelina with the comments and the contact details for the lawyer in Manchester. As soon as I've hit 'send', I feel a little bit lighter.

In cases of bullying, as I believe this to be, life can be a bit 'my dad's bigger than your dad'. Having the support of a senior lawyer in Boston, and potentially one in Manchester, feels quite weighty.

I'm not even the one being bullied, but I have no intention of sitting back and letting it happen. I intend to stand up and support Angelina and do everything I can to make sure this ends right.

With most of the day ahead of us, I take Max to the beach to do some fossil hunting for a couple of hours. It's a break from the trains, and perhaps a bit more in the spirit of home-schooling than reading about, playing with or watching *Thomas the Tank Engine*. Though in truth, perhaps the activity is as much for me as it is for him. Not only is it a satisfying way to explore the natural world in uplifting landscapes, but wallowing in thoughts of ancient and prehistoric worlds provides a great distraction from life's minutiae. I think it's also something that appeals to my inner, obsessive nature.

We park the car in the big car park and find it almost empty. I much prefer coming here in the off-season, during term-time. It can be hectic in the summer. I offer Max a bucket, hammer and safety goggles.

'Now, my little archaeologist, it's important that you wear these for safety when chipping at the big rocks. You have to protect your eyes. You've only got the two of them.'

I know he's not listening, and I know I'll need to say it at least another 40 times before he begins to understand.

I watch him say hello to the dogs coming the other way. Their friendly owners smile and comment on his mission today.

'Oh, best of luck. I do hope you find some fossils, young man.'

Max beams.

'What a lovely thing to be doing with your son!'

I don't bother to correct her. In any case, Max is already running off along the shoreline with carefree abandon, his bucket clattering at his side. He reminds me of my own boys when they were his age. Except, it seems almost impossible that Jackson and Vincent were ever that small. I wish everyone could understand and find a way to appreciate just how precious this time is. We are constantly shaping our children for their futures, even in the myriad moments when we forget that we're doing it.

I've looked after children who have had terrible or sometimes even no parenting in early life; but I can see that Max and Mia have had parenting. They have been loved and cherished. Their early flare-ups would suggest that they've been exposed to some ugly scenes, but I'm also aware that they were worried and scared to be away from their mum. There haven't been any recent repeats of it, which means that it's been 'unlearnt' pretty quickly for learnt behaviour.

I follow Max to the waves. He jumps over the frothy white tips in the shingle and laughs. He, like Mia, is a happy little soul at heart. We spend a good hour trying to extract a few shapes that look like fossils. I take photographs and send them to Lloyd, who is far better at these things than me, just in case we inadvertently miss an important archaeological find.

'No, we can't carry that enormous rock to the car, or I might fall over and hurt my back,' I explain. Never mind it has what looks to me like a perfect fossil embedded into the back of it. He is insistent for a moment, but then generously agrees to let go of the idea when I mention the chip shop over the other side of the car park. Result.

Again, I'm not sure which of us is more pleased.

I say a silent thank you to the area's local town planning for allowing the placement of the chip shop as the perfect ending to our little outing.

We buy a portion of chips to share and a hot chocolate for Max. We sit down on the bench facing out to sea. There are ships on the far horizon, and we make up names for them, though I notice that they are all repurposed names from *Thomas the Tank Engine*. The beach is empty and it's a peaceful spot. I chat away to Max about the sea and tides and anything else I happen to know about the location. He takes none of it in.

Instead, he puts his hand in mine and says, 'I want to see Nonna. Can I see Nonna and Nonno?'

He hasn't mentioned Nonna and Nonno before, or not that I've noticed. I think for a moment about who these people could be. It doesn't take a linguistic genius to work out that they must be his grandmother and grandfather. Google confirms that they're the Italian words for grandparents.

'Please, Louise. I miss Nonna and Nonno. Almost as much as I miss Mummy and Daddy. When can I see Nonna?'

Not only has this child got parents who love him, he also has grandparents. Why has no one investigated this? Why are words like 'adoption' even being used?

It must be the wind off the sea making my eyes water. I blink a few times. These poor children have lost so much.

And they're on the verge of losing so much more.

Chapter Eighteen

When we get home, I go all continental and make Lloyd, Max and myself a Croque Monsieur for lunch. Though it's only a glorified (but very lovely) French version of a ham and cheese toastie, calling it a Croque Monsieur makes it seem like an event.

My culinary efforts go largely unappreciated, though. Max cannot wait to get back to the train set.

'Let him go, Louise.'

Lloyd is clearly itching to tell me something.

'So, while you were out giving Mary Anning a run for her money, I've been talking to Ben again. We had a long chat.'

I look at him in astonishment.

'Yeah, he's a great guy. He's really interesting. We talked about music for ages. Do you remember The Mekons?'

I nod, recalling going to see them at the student union in the early 80s. I also remember John Peel, the now deceased DJ from Radio 1 who hosted a late evening show, playing them and enthusing about them. He discovered and supported so many good bands, giving them airtime on a mainstream station. 'Didn't they record sessions for John Peel?'

'Yeah, yeah.' Lloyd is flushed with excitement that he has a new music friend. Lloyd, like a lot of ex-punks, seems to drill down into music in a way that I never did. I was never a music snob, unlike many fellow punk and post-punk friends of mine. I'm not ashamed to admit that I know all the words to *Living on a Prayer* by Bon Jovi. Lloyd knows them too, but you'd never catch him owning up to it.

He tells me that he spent a good hour or so talking to Ben, mainly about music.

'He's a producer. He works with some big, big names.'

'Right. What does this have to do with The Mekons?'

'Well, nothing much. We were just talking about them. They were one of the first bands he got into.'

'Oh, right, good.'

'Just that one of their lyrics cropped up in our conversation: *Everybody's so in love, but they don't touch or meet*. Seemed fitting.'

'Right.'

Sensing my growing annoyance, Lloyd tries to appease me by talking about The Freakons; a mix of two women from Freakwater and two members of The Mekons, one man and one woman. Lloyd always talks up the women when he is concerned that I may not be impressed by something.

'Right, and did Ben work with them?'

'Well, no, but – never mind. He really knows his stuff. First hand. He's worked with all sorts. He started with punk bands, but now handles lots of different genres.'

'Great.'

This is all very lovely, but I don't see how it's going to help their cause of getting Max and Mia back. I tell Lloyd as much.

'Well, maybe not. But I'm getting there. I did find out a bit more about his dalliance.'

Lloyd fills in some of the gaps that Angelina had left tantalisingly unclear.

'There was this Country and Western singer from Nashville that Ben was raving about. She was the main reason he and Angelina argued and fought. But it was just a kiss, nothing more, and the woman threw herself at him, so you can't really blame the guy.'

I raise one eyebrow.

'Okay, okay, you *can* blame the guy. I'm just trying to say that it didn't go any further than that. We spoke about the lawyer in Manchester too. Ben's already contacted him.'

'Good. Let's hope something positive happens as a result of it.'

I don't know the ins and outs of Angelina's and Ben's current financial situation, but I do know that parents of children in care are entitled to free representation in court. However, if a foster carer or an adopter ends up going to court about something to do with the children in their care, they aren't entitled to representation. They're entitled to diddly squat.

I text Angelina with the information that they're entitled to representation.

She texts me back immediately. *Thank you so much, Louise. Ben and I can afford a lawyer, so we will fund this ourselves.*

That's good, and I totally understand, I write, *but you are entitled to the same support as all other families.*

There's a little pause, then the moving dots tell me she's typing more. *After being in the hostels, I met women who had nothing. That was partly why they were in the situations they were in. Hopefully, the money we do not take out of the system can help another family.*

I pick the phone up and give her a ring. These endless text messages are hard work.

I tell her about our brilliant time at the beach, and about Max starting school on Monday. 'I thought you might like to know that Max asked if he could see Nonna and Nonno. He said that he missed them.'

'My parents.' She sounds tearful, suddenly. 'When we went to Italy, we would go to the beach for picnics. I miss my parents too.'

This feels so sad. I don't want to change the subject abruptly, so I ask her how much her parents know about the situation.

'Not all of it. They only know a little. I didn't want to tell them everything. I'm so ashamed of the mess that we have ended up in.'

I suggest, as gently as I can, that maybe her parents would like to help. 'Maybe that would be good for everyone.'

I stick my neck out a little further. 'Sometimes, we end up in situations that make no sense to us, and we behave badly because we don't know what to do.'

'Like my father,' she whispers. 'And like me.'

'It's not excusing the behaviour,' I go on. 'I found, with my own childhood, that once I understood more about my adopted mother, I was in a much better position to move on. I could put her in her time and place, and I could see how society was partly to blame. All the pressures of what a marriage is meant to be.'

'Yes.'

I tell Angelina that, as I grow older and see the ups and downs of my friends' relationships, and my own, I know how much pressure marriage can be. 'After all, marriage is a male religious construct. It can be a terrifying and harmful place for women who, even these days, can lose their rights.'

'I still love Ben,' Angelina blurts out. 'I was stupid. It was all my fault.'

That's probably not a helpful attitude either, but I don't say that. 'Angelina, in my experience, it's rarely any single person's fault. It's almost always more complicated than that.'

'You are very wise.'

Marcus Aurelius, eat your bloody heart out.

'Look, I'm not a doctor or a psychologist, so I don't know, but I think that you may have suffered from postnatal depression. Have you heard of it?'

'Yes.' And now she begins to sob. 'I didn't know it at the time, but they suggested that may have been the case afterwards.'

She cries on the phone for a good ten minutes. Every few seconds I find myself making soothing noises. 'It's okay, Angelina. It's okay,' or 'Shhh, it's really okay.'

I find myself crying, too. This poor woman, this poor family.

How many other mothers have been punished because of postnatal depression, a chemical imbalance that's no fault of their own? I'm sad, angry and I don't know what else.

'After the twins were born, I felt so threatened and insecure by Ben's work, and who he was working with. He had a lovely new receptionist, and I was his lovely new receptionist once. I felt so ugly after the birth. I was worried that I would lose Ben to another woman.'

She tells me how they have talked it all through, since. 'I was stupid and shallow to think that, and I can see now how I drove my husband away.'

She explains how, since the diagnosis, she has been undergoing cognitive behavioural therapy to help her break the negative cycle of emotions that she was feeling, to rid herself of the unhelpful and unrealistic thinking and expectations about what being a new mum should be like.

'Every mistake I made, however small it was, broke me a little bit more.'

Amidst the heartache and heartbreak, I'm developing a persistent little stress headache. These revelations are all important, but they may have come too late. The clock is ticking for this family. Court is next week. There is no time to get everything in place. The whole future of this family is dependent on the opinion of Bea and her fellow social worker, neither of whom I trust to do the right thing.

I have written my report and cc'd it to Moira and Bea, for what it's worth. I tell Angelina this. I don't hold out much hope that Bea, who seems to be on a mission to destroy this family, will do anything with my information. Having gone down the line of 'freedom of information' requests in the past, I'm well aware of the propensity for crucial documents to go missing, be tampered with, or be lost among the filing. I don't tell Angelina this part. Eventually she recovers enough for me to feel that I can end the call.

Someone has shut poor Pablo Picasso, our beautiful huge black cat, in our bedroom, and, amidst all the stress and tears, it must have gone unnoticed for some time. When I go past the door to fetch something out of Max and Mia's room, I hear the scratch of a sad paw on the inside of the bedroom door.

I open the door to be met by the stink of cat poo.

Not only is it cat poo, but worse, it is cat poo *on our bed*. The duvet is too large to put in the washing machine, so now I have to take the stinking quilt to the dry cleaners. I pull the covers off. I might possibly use some curse words. Luckily, it hasn't gone through the mattress topper onto the mattress itself. The mattress topper will just about squeeze into my washing machine, but it'll probably need two washes to be rid of the stench and the stain. Timing, Pablo, timing. My head hurts!

I bring the soiled linen downstairs to the kitchen, to discover that we have run out of washing powder.

The horizon, as framed by my kitchen window, looks as if it's being weighed down by the sky. A sky that is turning the nasty dark grey, my least favourite shade, that signals 'rain from hell'.

I want to stop today and get off.

Could it get any worse?

Yes, it could, and it does. I read an email from Bea, cc'd to Moira, informing us both that, *sadly, all the paperwork has gone to court already and your report was not there in time. A very great shame.*

Oh yes, Bea, it is. A very great shame indeed. Your shame.

Chapter Nineteen

I can't even begin to communicate quite how furious I feel right now. There aren't the words. I have to physically stop my hands from typing out what I want to say to her.

'Well, bitchface, you could have bloody well asked me in time, couldn't you?'

One of the strategies I have seen with local government organisations is an almost infantile approach to communication and information. Sometimes I think they just about manage to hold back from typing 'na-na-ni-na-nah!' at the end of their toxic, petty little messages.

Bea could have done this properly and ethically, but she has used the system to try and get away with her own nasty plan. I'm running out of ideas on how to battle her bitchiness. Right now, she holds all the cards. I feel very, very stressed. It's a fight against the clock, and a fight with one hand tied behind our backs.

That information is going to the court for the judge to review, and it's not complete, nor is it fair.

It is unforgivable.

That a professional can allow it to happen – worse, *engineer* it to happen – is shocking. I know first-hand what tardy incompetence can do to the trajectory of a child's life. This is worse than tardy incompetence. This is deliberate, calculated and vindictive. Social workers can end up playing God, and that is not right.

I go to bed worrying about Max and Mia.

I wake up worrying about them.

This is horrible.

If I feel this awful, how do Angelina and Ben feel?

Moira, I can tell, is not impressed. But what a supervising social worker really thinks and what they're paid to think are two different things. It's the injustice of it all that's hurting me the most.

My blood rises to the boil in cases when I know it's the adults who are the problem.

I have a meeting with Bea scheduled for a couple of days' time. I don't want to give that woman the time of day, but I have to get over myself and manage it properly for the children. I have to think about something else. Better things. I need to find a different focus. I head to my studio, but work is impossible. I can't write. I'm too unsettled to describe any situation objectively. Thinking about writing makes me panic because I'm so behind with deadlines.

Art, then. Illustrations. Expressing myself creatively is good.

But no. At the moment, art makes me feel like a failure, because it's so hard to get recognition in the art and creative industries if you are not male.

The illustrations make me panic, because I know I need to rework at least four of them.

What's left? What else do I have that can help take my mind off this turmoil? I think about my beautiful, blended family. I'm so lucky to have them all. But thinking about them doesn't work either, because I have an image from the supermarket earlier of all the tubs of Quality Street, Roses and Heroes piled up. We're being urged to get ready for Christmas already. The tubs are on special offer. They're two for £7 now. The special offer makes me nervous. I worry that I have to find the money to provide possibly five children with Christmas presents and do the whole festive thing. There's nothing relaxing about thinking about family when Christmas is on the horizon.

My dogs. Yes, that's it. I'll focus on my darling little doggies. Not the cat, because Pablo's in my bad books after he pooed on our bed.

Actually, nothing is working at all. I am so emotional about the injustice for this family. The only good news is that the clouds have lifted a little and the sky is white, not that heavy grey, so maybe I don't have to deal with a flood situation today. Well, not a literal one, anyway.

In the end, I'm like a cat on a hot tin roof all afternoon, not quite settling to anything. Even the hill walk with Max in the afternoon offers no inspiration or calm. I decide to make lasagne for dinner and biscuits for when the children come home. I will be Ma Larkin for the evening and try to calm down that way.

I hear the sound of my phone vibrating from somewhere, and eventually track it down to my bag hanging up in the hall.

It flashes up 'Mowra'. I could change that for starters. That would give me something to do.

'Hi Moira, how are you?' I ask wearily.

'You'll never guess what.'

No, I won't. My children do this to me all the time. 'Mum, guess what?' and I always say, 'How can I?'

But Moira sounds happy. 'The court case has been postponed for two months.'

Two months? Wow!

'What? How? Why?' I babble out to Moira.

'Bea wouldn't say, but I'm guessing that something has been challenged.'

I wonder if it could be the ripple effect of Angelina and Ben speaking to the lawyer in Manchester. Perhaps things have been kicked into action.

'And there's more good news.' Moira goes on to tell me that during half term, which is only another week away, the children are allowed to go and have contact with their grandparents. 'They're coming over from Italy and will be staying in an Airbnb in Cornwall so that they can all have a break.'

I'm suddenly so excited I could burst.

Just what Max wanted. Just what he asked for, to see his Nonna and Nonno. But even more importantly, two months gives us a chance.

I check my email and frown when I notice that Bea has cancelled our meeting. Well, surprise, surprise. But even that can't do much to dampen my mood after this sudden surge upwards.

No worries, I type back, hoping that the tone sounds airy. And then I can't help adding a P.S. at the end: *At least the delay in the court case means that my report can now be added, though!*

I put the very worthy Ma Larkin lasagne back in the fridge and get a takeaway instead. I feel uplifted, and these days when I feel like this, I go wild by ordering fast food. In my younger days, such a lift in mood would probably result in me going down to the pub and then ending up in a club somewhere at ridiculous o'clock in the morning. These days, I eat chow mein instead. But I keep some of that old partying vibe by getting the children to put their music on and join me for a kitchen disco. We have a wonderful evening and it's still a school night. Woohoo.

I send Angelina pictures of Max and Mia dancing round the kitchen with Lily and the dogs. The dogs don't mind a boogie either. I also send a lovely picture of Max and Mia both waving at the camera. When I have cleared up and Lloyd has put a film on to settle everyone down, I sit at the kitchen table and look at my phone.

I look at the reply from Angelina, who loves the pictures of her babies. Now that the court hearing is postponed, she too sounds much happier. None of us really know what's made such an impact, but Ben has engaged the services of the lawyer from Manchester and is paying top dollar for them – and lo and behold, matters have now dramatically changed. If there is one thing that the senior management in children's social care are scared of, it's a court case where they are in the dock.

I have no idea what's really going on, but it's interesting how quiet Bea seems to have gone.

Chapter Twenty

Max takes to school as much as his sister did. His first day goes smoothly. He makes friends, even though we're almost a half term in and those first friendships are already established. Though he sees his sister in the playground, the teaching assistant explains that he didn't gravitate towards her, but instead chose to hang out with his new friends. He completes the week of mornings, taking it all in his stride, getting ready each day as if he's always done it.

But it adds an extra dimension to their talk at home. Now that Max can join in properly with the school chatter, they're at it non-stop. Though the talk is, of course, accompanied by train play. It's the first thing Max does when he gets through the door, straight back on the train set.

I smile to myself. They don't know yet about the visit from their grandparents, or the fact that they're going to get to spend a few days away with their mother next week for half term. That surprise is still to come. Could things get any better? Yes, they could – because while the twins are away next week, I'll have a chance to get my sitting room back at least for a few days, and I'll be able to clean it properly if the train set's away.

Yep, it's the little things.

I still can't believe how quickly things have changed. I think it probably just goes to show what a difference being able to afford a top lawyer can make. Having said that, most parents who find themselves going to court about their children have free representation, so it's not that they don't have access to lawyers. But the speed of this intervention to a court hearing that was imminent does make you think. The legal world is a small world; its members often know each other or can find out. I wonder what this lawyer is like. Pretty good, I suspect, given what they've already achieved.

My emotions at the moment resemble a ping-pong ball. Backwards and forwards. Now I have to plan for their little half-term trip, and I'm full of joy for them. At the same time, I feel a tiny bit sad because I'm going to miss them. They have so quickly established themselves as part of the household, and have been, for the most part, an absolute delight. I will need to fill the half term with things for the rest of the family to help them (me) get over it. Maybe a trip to London for the children, while the twins are away. That would mean dinner in Chinatown. Always a winner. That's good. I'm feeling better already. All I had to do was plan for tomorrow and stop dwelling on yesterday and today. It's so much easier advising others.

Soon, I find myself driving the twins to Truro, with their little suitcases all packed for their trip. We stop at a service station nearby, our allotted meeting point. Jackson is in the car with me; he fancied a day out. So did Vincent, but he gets carsick, so it's just the four of us. Lily is out with her friends, swanning around town in her new H&M attire.

As soon as we pull in, we can see Angelina and her parents standing at the verge, waving at us. What a sight the family make. Like Angelina, her mother has a natural elegance. Though her hair is grey, it is long and thick and tied back away from her olive skin. I see where the red hair comes from. The twins' grandad has thick curly hair, a faded hue now, but I imagine it was much redder once. He is open-armed and smiling as Max and Mia escape from the car. Both twins run up to hug him and then their grandma.

Angelina steps forward and the children squeak with delight.

Jackson looks at me and smiles; he gets it.

'Shall we all come inside and have a coffee? There's a Starbucks,' Angelina suggests.

I can tell by the look on Jackson's face that he may find that a bit too much, so I politely decline. 'We're going to go to the sea for a walk and to find somewhere nice for lunch, so we'll leave you all to enjoy your time.'

We say our goodbyes and confirm arrangements for the end of the week, then head out to find the sea. We have to drive another ten miles or so to reach the coast, but it's worth it when we find a gorgeous beach of sandy dunes.

Water has a contemplative effect. Jackson asks many questions. We talk about Max and Mia, and their family. Like me, he hopes that these lovely people may soon be able to put their troubles behind them. But he seems mainly concerned about the unfairness of things. Why 'life' happens to some more than others. The sorts of questions that I don't really have answers for.

I'm proud of my boy. For years, I was scared that being a fostering family would harm my sons. I felt guilt about exposing them to certain situations, individual children that were challenging. I worried that some of the moments they experienced and scenes they witnessed would be too much for them. Today I know that not to be the case. I feel good because my son is growing into a wise and empathic young man. That is a warm and wonderful feeling.

When we get back, windswept and philosophical, Lloyd announces that, while he's in London on Thursday, he's arranged to meet up with Ben at his studio in Camden. A little bit of me knows that Lloyd is loving this: music and music-related chat on tap. It seems that men talk about things very differently from women. Years ago, I went on a work trip with two male colleagues from the careers department at the university where I taught. I listened to two days of football chat. It occurred to me that the trip had actually been organised around football stadiums. When we got into taxis, driven by other men, the conversation was always about football. Men do things differently, and hopefully Lloyd and Ben will be able to explore some of the issues that have been so difficult for Ben and Angelina. Having been responsible for Ben's children for the last couple of months, he's in a unique position to offer counsel, I think. If they can get beyond music!

When Thursday comes, Lloyd arrives home from London on the last train. It's the 'skin of your teeth' train, before the wait for what used to be called the 'milk train'. It's very late, and so I don't even hear him come in. I'm fast asleep after a busy day with my darlings, sorting out their bedrooms and trying to convince them that a clear-out of old toys is not the end of their childhoods, but a way of creating more space with Christmas around the corner.

As well as sorting my precious sitting room and temporarily removing all trace of train tracks and trains, I have also managed to clean the whole of the upstairs, including the dreaded cobweb-battle.

In the morning, though, I'm impatient to hear all the details about their meeting, and don't hold back.

'Well? Come on, then! How did it go? What happened?'

Lloyd, of course, takes his Lloyd-time to get round to telling me the important bits. First, I have to listen to a list of all the musicians that Ben has worked with. I can see Lloyd is impressed. Eventually, though, I'm able to pick out of him what Ben said about their situation.

His version of events matches Angelina's. They were happy before the children were born. Angelina was the love of his life. Ben thought life could not get any better when he learnt that he was going to be the father of two, after losing both his parents and being an only child. According to Lloyd, he still loves Angelina. He accepts now that she had severe postnatal depression, though he didn't know it at the time. He regrets his behaviour. He said he should have known, because there were times when he just didn't recognise his wife. He thought she was crazy with jealousy and didn't realise that he was fuelling her pain and insecurities.

'He cried a lot,' Lloyd says. 'He kept saying "I've fucked up", over and over again. And "it's my fault". I think he was relieved to have someone to talk to about it all.'

Lloyd explains that they went for a drink and, after the initial music chat, Ben just talked and talked about their relationship. Then they got back on to music and design. Lloyd would have been in his element with those subjects.

'So, how has it all been left? What's going on with the legal angle?'

'You already know that Ben appointed the lawyer, the one you sorted out, from Manchester. That did halt the court hearing. Since then, he and Angelina have booked couples' therapy, but with one of the leading therapists. The best that money can buy. I think they're both hoping for a reunion. Ben certainly is.'

He explains that Ben and Angelina have been out for dinner a few times and things are much better between them. 'Angelina's stopped drinking, apparently.'

'Ah.' She didn't mention that part, and she doesn't look like a drinker to me. I didn't get that vibe at all, but people are capable of hiding so much. 'Is she an alcoholic?'

'I think so. Or heading that way. She's having some sort of cognitive behavioural therapy for that too, I think.'

'Has he seen the grandparents since they've been back in the country?'

'Yes. He met Angelina's parents at the airport, and they all went to Ben's house – the actual family home in West Brompton which he's still got – for dinner and a very honest and open conversation. Ben's funded a flat for Angelina somewhere and is paying for all the therapy. They aren't sleeping under the same roof while everything goes back to court.'

I squeeze Lloyd's hands across the table as he wipes away a tear of his own. Then he laughs and says, 'I don't know why I'm crying!'

I smile. Perhaps men and women aren't so different after all.

Chapter Twenty-One

Max and Mia return to us after the best part of a week with their mother and their grandparents. The children don't settle down well at all. Of course not – they have, no doubt, been thoroughly spoilt, and they want to be with their family.

'We saw our daddy too,' Max tells me, proudly. He came to have lunch with them on Friday, driving all the way to Cornwall from London and then back again. He would have been driving late into the night. That's a hell of a journey in a day.

Luckily, Max and Mia have the distraction of school to keep them occupied, but that brings its own little issues. They bring home some little friends, and not the two-legged kind. The nits cause a bit of a stir, as Lily also acquires some lodgers.

We manage to keep it light-hearted, an amusing anecdote; but Lily is far from amused, and I don't want to give her any opportunity to turn the headlice incident into a bigger thing against the twins whenever she's in a bad mood. Her nose has erupted into spots, and that doesn't seem to be doing much to improve her humour.

Max now seems much easier than Mia; it was the other way round when they first arrived. But now Mia cries sometimes that she wants her mummy and daddy. The quiet stoicism that characterised her arrival seems to have disappeared. And why wouldn't it? She's four years old. It pulls on my heartstrings, I can tell you.

Life carries on in a mood of quiet uncertainty.

Moira keeps in touch by email, but her words lack warmth. They feel officious and perfunctory, not at all how she would normally speak. Her emails have quite a negative effect on me. I thought we were getting to know and understand one another, but now it feels as if she is too important to let me have any information in case I can't be trusted. Perhaps I can't be. It's true that I'm technically breaking the rules by talking to Max and Mia's parents, but she doesn't know that. Something about our relationship has changed, though. Perhaps she's just being bound by the restrictions of the organisation she works for, but it takes a long time to establish a good relationship with a supervising social worker, and right now I feel as if I'm a child in detention who isn't quite sure what they've done. I know I should be grown-up about it, but emails like this just leave me feeling a bit paranoid. I have stopped overthinking stuff as I once did, when I questioned everything as being related to my abusive past, or worried that I had weird attachment issues. I know the reality to be that all foster carers feel like this when the children's social care staff try and pull rank. Perhaps I'm not that grown-up, because my gesture of retaliation, which I recognise as being childish but which makes me feel much better, is to give them the middle finger from my kitchen.

The uncertainty has an impact on the whole family. It's very unsettling not to know what's going on, or what the likely outcome is going to be. The court case is still another month away. Before it was moved, when it came upon us suddenly, I wanted it to go away. Now I am wishing for it. I want all this to end well for Max and Mia's family. I want these children to be able to exit the care system and go home, to be able to put their nightmare to bed.

Bea has cancelled three meetings now, and no other social worker has appeared in her place from the independent fostering agency. As part of an IFA, she'll have access to big fat lawyers herself. I imagine the local authority solicitors will be terrified of that kind of legal battle. All of which means that if 'dark work' has gone on here, as I believe, much is at stake. The fostering agency will want to preserve their public image, as well as protecting future commissioning from the local authority. It's commonly accepted among foster carers that it's these private companies who are in charge, not the local authority. The reason is finance, as ever. The local authority is short-staffed and broke, mainly because the managers keep commissioning private fostering agencies rather than recruiting and retaining their own good foster carers. It isn't rocket science to know that investment in better and more cost-effective service is good for everyone, and yet they are forced to keep on outsourcing.

I'm heartened that Lloyd and Ben have struck up such a good friendship; they're actually not too dissimilar in age, and Lloyd is quite a good listener. I can tell that Ben must be appreciative of his counsel. They seem to be in regular text communication. I also keep sending Angelina pictures, and have learnt that one way of settling and reassuring the children is if they can actually say goodnight to their mum.

Of course, I haven't told the social worker because Bea isn't available to tell. That's my story and I'm sticking to it. Of course, explaining quite how that situation has arisen in the first place would also land me in hot water, so for now, I'm just getting on with it. I'll think about the consequences later.

Angelina too, seems much calmer. A nightly video call check-in with her children is as soothing for her as it is for them. She has come totally clean with her parents now, and there is a great deal of talk between them all. It must be doing a power of good alongside the other talking therapies she's undergoing. Not only have they talked at length about the breakdown of Angelina's own relationship, they've also opened up as a family about what her father was like years ago. Angelina told me how her dad cried as he talked about his own violent behaviour towards Angelina's mum in the past.

'I am the lucky one,' he said to Angelina. 'I have no idea why your mother is still with me.'

They have spoken about cultural influences, and how 30 years ago, perhaps men in Italy weren't as enlightened in their attitudes towards women as they are now. He has been very apologetic and shouldered plenty of the blame that is flying around in that family.

Angelina's mother has also spoken about her own pregnancy: how hard she found it, and the aftermath. Finally, they have compared symptoms and shared experiences frankly, rather than pretending that everything was fine. That's something that too many of us are guilty of, and something that isn't helpful for anyone in the long run. There's still a long way to go for us all to achieve actual 'enlightenment'.

Ben and Angelina have been taking their relationship slowly and have stuck to all the rules and requirements laid out by their lawyer. They are doing absolutely everything by the book, determined to get their children back and to get their lives back.

I admire them enormously.

It is the Friday before the week of the court hearing. I am standing at my drawing table in the studio, deciding if I have enough time to lay down some ink before I have to leave to collect the twins from school.

My phone lights up with a call from Angelina. Nothing out of the ordinary there, as we speak daily now, but it's much earlier than usual.

'Louise, Louise, it's done!'

Her voice is charged, and she can't slow down enough to tell me properly what's happening. The stream of largely incomprehensible words is punctuated with Italian phrases that I don't understand. There's something about 'Lyme Regis' and 'no court case' and none of it makes any sense.

I endure a couple of minutes of this breathless babble from her until Lloyd walks in making the thumbs up sign. 'Do you need me to get Max and Mia? You seem pretty occupied there.'

I give him the thumbs up and a nod back.

'Angelina, take a deep breath and tell me what you mean.'

But she isn't capable of doing that. I hear the sound of the phone being passed over, and Ben comes on the line.

'Hi Louise, what *my wife* is trying to tell you is that it's over.' He pauses. 'We're bringing our children home.'

Chapter Twenty-Two

'Lloyd, wait! Come back!' Now I'm the one who is squealing and inarticulate.

'What is it?' Lloyd asks.

I point at the phone and punch the air and find myself making 'woohoo' noises, while laughing and crying at the same time, so Lloyd suggests that we all go onto speaker phone so he can join in the conversation.

Angelina has calmed down enough now to explain. 'Everything has been resolved prior to going to court, so the children are being returned to us!'

Ben takes over to fill in some of the blanks. 'I'll tell them, babe. Our lawyer has put together lots of evidence that shows that, as a family, we have been badly treated from the beginning, because no one bothered to ask the right questions, so the children are being returned to us.'

'Oh, congratulations, mate!' Lloyd's response is a little bit less emotionally overwrought than mine, although he then follows up, 'Champagne is never cheap!'

It seems such a non-sequitur that I look at him as if he's utterly mad, until Ben answers, 'But I could pay someone to drink it for me.'

It's like they're talking in code, and I'm as bewildered as I was when Angelina was delivering her stream of consciousness.

Lloyd shrugs. 'The Mekons,' he says, nonchalantly, as if that explains everything. He then signals to me that he'll fetch the children so that I can continue with the conversation.

Ben continues with more explanation. 'Our lawyer said she'd go public with her findings about incompetence and victimisation.'

'Victimisation?'

'Yes, because we have money and are outwardly doing well in life – the lawyer's words – apparently that has gone against us. We have been made victims.'

I make a huge, satisfied, 'ha!' sound. 'I'd call it a case of the green-eyed monster.'

Angelina doesn't understand that particular idiom, so Ben has to explain it to her and the way he does it is both tender and playful. It sounds as if they are good friends again, and it's lovely to witness.

'Since it hasn't gone to court, all the legal fees will apparently have to be paid by both the London local authority and the independent fostering agency. They can fight it out between them. As you can imagine, they are wriggling and protesting about it, but we'll leave that to the lawyers to settle,' Ben continues.

'And, Louise, we read your report. That was a big help, too. The lawyer said that was one of the convincing pieces of evidence. We're very grateful for that. And for everything else you've done.'

'I can't tell you how happy I am for you all,' I say. I'm also happy that report must have had some sort of sway. I don't mention, although I'm more than delighted with this outcome, that I'll also be sad to lose Max and Mia from our household. 'When can you all be a family again?'

'From now,' Ben says, 'but I understand that's a bit quick from your point of view, and we want to make the transition as smooth as possible for Max and Mia.'

I can't stop smiling. 'Whatever you want.'

'Well, my Signora Redilocks and I were wondering if the children might stay with you for a few more days, which will give us a chance to properly organise ourselves and also arrange for Max and Mia to be enrolled in a primary school so that their education isn't disrupted.'

Signora Redilocks is cute. But the idea of taking time to prepare for the return of the twins is so measured and thoughtful. I think I'd be tempted to grab my children back the minute I was allowed to, but this makes much more sense. 'We'd be more than happy to do that.'

We carry on chatting for a while, discussing the logistics of the handover. Then, 'What's Lyme Regis got to do with it all?' I ask, remembering what Angelina said at the start of the conversation.

'Oh, yes, that. We've decided to buy a holiday home there, which means we can potentially drop in on you from time to time – if you wanted us to.'

And now my happiness is complete, because I know that I won't lose touch with my darling little twins, or this lovely family. I'm not sure how Lloyd would cope without his new best friend, either.

All of a sudden, I hear the front door go and two little voices chiming, 'Mummy! Daddy!' in unison. Into my studio run two very happy little people. Lloyd must have briefed them and taken the short-cut home.

I leave my phone on the drawing table and leave them all to it. Joyful voices ring through the house.

Even the sight of a pile of dishes stacked right next to the dishwasher can't intrude upon my happiness today. Lily, also just back from school, mooches into the kitchen. Strangely, she's holding her teddy bear, which looks kind of odd for a teenager-type, but suggests that she is feeling more child than teenager and is in need of a little bit of reassurance.

'Are Max and Mia going?' she asks, moodily.

'Yes,' I say with a brave smile, assuming that she will be relieved to regain a little bit more attention in their absence.

Instead, she begins to cry.

I walk over and give her a big squidgy, hug.

Life is hard to fathom.

Afterword

This story is very different from most of the cases that I've been involved in. On the one hand, prejudiced assumptions about wealth and privilege came close to needlessly tearing a family apart. On the other hand, that same wealth and privilege meant that avenues and opportunities were available that might not be to families in less secure financial situations. It wasn't quite as straightforward for Ben, Angelina and Max and Mia to overcome all that they had been through as the ending might sound. Months of counselling lay ahead, and the path was rocky at times.

Both Ben and Angelina were in emotional and psychological turmoil. Ben saw the arrival of his twins as a kind of compensation for his lost parents, but hadn't had time to grieve properly for his mother, so he, himself, was not in a stable place. Angelina's story is heart-breaking to me. To change countries and experience a whirlwind romance; to stand in her designer home, no longer the receptionist at Azure, but as a wife and mother; to be in her mid-twenties and have it all, must have been magnificent. She had a lifestyle most of us could only dream of: a talented, successful husband, every luxury money could buy, and beautiful children with the same red hair that she and her father had.

And yet none of that could override the feeling of melancholy and emptiness that poured through her in the throes of postnatal depression, laughed off sometimes as baby blues. But severe postnatal depression is no laughing matter. It can require specialist treatment. Some women, like Angelina, experience complex mental health needs during pregnancy and after giving birth. Some women need to be admitted to hospital or a mental health clinic in a specialised mother and baby unit. Given what I now know about Angelina's situation, I think this is possibly what she might have needed.

I broke the 'rules' by getting in touch with Angelina privately, exchanging numbers and communicating by phone and text message 'off the record'. In our modern age it is very easy to make contact with anyone, which is why 'closed' adoptions are no longer an option.

I took a calculated risk that, if things had gone differently, could have got us all into trouble. It's not a course of action I recommend. Another foster child's birth mother (whom you can read about in *Sky's Story*) got hold of my number against my wishes, and that caused a world of problems.

We still stay in touch with Angelina, Ben, Max and Mia. Their little holiday home in Lyme Regis means that they still call in to see us on the way. It's always an absolute joy to see them and to watch them all grow as people. Angelina and Ben are a great partnership and have a strong relationship. Angelina has recently finished a degree in Social Work at Goldsmiths University in London. We talk a lot about our experiences of children's social care and how the system should shrink and be simplified. She got a first-class degree, and I think, after everything she's been through, she will be an amazing social worker, already aware and in tune with the system that is so clearly flawed.

Ben and Lloyd have remained friends, and Lloyd occasionally heads up to London to gigs with his 'muso' mate. Max and Mia are amazing: at the time of writing, heading towards Year 5 at primary school. They have become their own very independent people. Though they argue as siblings do, they get on well. Their parents have kept them away from the mystic narrative that can be used to describe two people who shared womb space. Max seems to love sports and art, while Mia has followed her father's love for music and already plays three instruments and sings in the school and community choir. When I spend time with them, I feel energised and happy. Ben and Angelina give their time and money to a charity that helps women and their families who have experienced postnatal depression.

But the outcome isn't really what the story is about. As ever, the real story is about the people, the personalities, the accidents, the loopholes, the what-might-have-beens.

And of course, there are some recurring themes.

I'm well aware that I can launch into a rant from time to time about the often-contradictory mentality of children's social care, but it regularly makes me cross, and I feel that, with my multitudinous experiences on both sides of the system, I'm entitled to a view. The language and terminology around children's social care changes all the time, but there are always clues in that language use about the current priorities. I struggle with the idea that those in charge in both the council and the private sector call themselves 'CEOs' and 'regional managers' as if they were running a chain of pizza restaurants.

My experience in this particular instance highlighted several other things.

That no one thought to consult with the nursery the first time the children were placed in emergency foster care, for example, says an awful lot about how the nursery, and young children generally, are regarded by the 'system'.

If you've read any of my other books, and even if you've only read this one, you'll know that the financial burden of raising a child isn't covered by the allowance given to foster carers. When I got the call about Max and Mia at the airport, of course Lily was with us. We paid for Lily to go on holiday; the alternative was for her to go for a week's respite with strangers. It simply wasn't an option, because she's part of the family. I largely have to ignore the sums, because they don't make sense in foster care. Her allowance doesn't make it seem worthwhile, barely covering the realistic cost of bringing up a child in this day and age, with less and less for the occasional trip to the cinema or bowling, let alone a holiday. It amazes me how anyone does it, frankly. I also hear that so many foster carers are leaving because they just can't deal with the stress of the lack of support combined with the fear of allegations that might come their way, either from the foster children or the social workers. I must admit, every time I receive a referral, that I worry that I might be jeopardising mine and my family's safety and sanity.

And yet, I still do it, because I can't not.

Acknowledgements

I would like to thank Catherine Lloyd, Alexandra Plowman and Karen Furse-Cope for their insightful comments on early drafts of the manuscript, and to Annamarie Smith for her beady eagle eyes. Their help in shaping the finished text is invaluable. Thanks also go to Anna McEvoy, for her guidance and generous twin-wisdom.

Thank you to Theresa Gooda, who is always my companion with each story. We share eye-rolling, gasps and jokes as each account unravels.

My gratitude, as always, to Jane Graham Maw, my special agent who has my back; Beth Bishop, my editor; and the team at Welbeck Publishing for their work and faith in my stories.

Finally, thank you to my family, without whom none of this would be possible: Lloyd, Jackson, Vincent, nanny Margaret who lives next door, my foster children (who cannot be named for legal reasons), and Millie, Mitch and baby Maeve (who is now walking, and driving the handed-down racing car up and down the hall).